KARKHANAS

UNDER THE MUGHALS
From Akbar to Aurangzeb

A Study in Economic Development

To the memory of
My Beloved Father
SHRI S. R. SETHI

KARKHANAS
UNDER THE MUGHALS
From Akbar to Aurangzeb

A Study in Economic Development

Tripta Verma

PRAGATI PUBLICATIONS
DELHI
2026

PRAGATI PUBLICATIONS
43/82/4B, Ansari Road, Darya Ganj,
New Delhi-110002

First Published 1994
Reprinted with Corrections 2026

13 Digits ISBN 978-81-7307-022-8
10 Digits ISBN 81-7307-022-9

Published by VIKAS KAPOOR for Pragati Publications
43/82/4B, Ansari Road, Darya Ganj,
New Delhi-110002

Contents

Foreword

In this work Dr Tripta Verma has made an attempt, which deserves the attention of the scholars of medieval India, to state emphatically that the medieval institution of *karkhanas* was not imported from Persia, but was an indigenous one. She has successfully traced its origin and growth and discussed fully the organized form which the Mughals gave to it in the medieval period and whose example was emulated by many other contemporary Indian powers.

Dr Verma's main thrust is the nature, organization and functioning of the Mughal *karkhanas* but she has also discussed the functioning of this institution under the Delhi Sultanate with a view to providing a historical backdrop for a better understanding of the subject. The book is, however, essentially a study of economic development under the Mughals, promoted by the *karkhanas* which were supported by the state as well as organized by the private parties namely the princes and the nobles. Originally the institutions started on a modest scale to meet the requirements of the Royal household, but in course of time, they became a centre of major economic activity giving impetus both to the artisans as well as to the industrial development of the state.

It is heartening to note that Dr Verma has made good use of the contemporary original Persian source material while making out a case for the creation and development of the *karkhanas*. The main purpose of this institution was to encourage the skilled artisans for better and finer production of handicrafts in an era prior to the industrial revolution. But by and large, says the author, the condition of artisans, craftsmen and industrial workers as portrayed in the contemporary sources was bad during the sixteenth and seventeenth centuries. It seems, however, that no authentic data is available on the rate of wages paid to the workers in various industrial activities.

In this book which has grown out of her doctoral work, Dr Verma has made a valuable indepth study of an important institution, and I am sure that scholars in this field will appreciate this welcome contribution to the economic history of medieval India.

Pune
9 March 1994

A.R. Kulkarni
Professor Emeritus and Vice-Chancellor,
Tilak Maharashtra Vidyapeeth, Pune

Acknowledgements

I should first like to express my deep sense of gratitude to Professor H.C. Verma for not only suggesting the theme of the work but also for his invaluable guidance and constant advice.

I have several other debts to acknowledge. It is a great honour for me that Professor A.R. Kulkarni, Vice-Chancellor, Tilak Maharashtra Vidyapeeth, Pune has very kindly written a foreword to this book. I am also deeply thankful to Professor Iqtidar Hussain Siddiqui, Aligarh Muslim University and Dr Dilbagh Singh, Jawaharlal Nehru University for their valuable suggestions and keen interest in the progress of the work.

Besides, I am very thankful to Dr Tasneem Ahmad, Deputy Director, ICHR for his help in procuring Persian manuscripts for my work.

I must also thank the authorities and staff of the Centre of Advanced Study in History, Maulana Azad Library, Aligarh, ICHR Library, National Archives of India, Nehru Memorial Museum and Library, Central Library, University of Delhi, Ratan Tata Library, Delhi School of Economics, South Delhi University Campus Library, Archaeological Survey of India Library and Central Secretariat Library for providing me necessary facilities for this work.

I am deeply thankful to Mrs Suman Bala Verma for her generous hospitality and unfailing support in my work.

My thanks are also to Mr Vinod Kapoor of Pragati Publications for his help in bringing out this book in record time.

Finally, I am deeply indebted to my husband Lajpat Verma for his constant inspiration and encouragement and to my children Saurabh and Surabhi for their affectionate moral support.

TRIPTA VERMA

Preface

Among several institutions introduced by the Mughals, perhaps the most important was the karkhanas (workshops and store houses). It was far more successful than any other experiment. Not only did the workshop bring diverse craftsmen together under one roof by fostering better communication among them, but it also became a place where the craftsmen could experiment with new ideas and techniques. These experiments contributed significantly to the visual revolution of the Mughals. Although very little is known about individual craftsmen in Mughal India, there is considerable information about the techniques and methods adopted by them.

In medieval times most of the articles of luxury needed by the rulers to maintain the splendour and pageantry of the royal court and household could not be manufactured in the ordinary market. The rulers were, therefore, forced to establish state factories producing luxury articles for them. Though K.M. Ashraf thinks that the system of the royal karkhanas was probably borrowed from Persia, the fact is that the state factories were an ancient institution in India. The karkhanas had multiple functions in the political and social life of the rulers of medieval India.

The present work is an attempt to assess the working of karkhanas in the Mughal period. Unfortunately there is no single independent monograph on this subject. Scattered references are available in all the works dealing with the administration of Mughals. Thus to cater to the needs of the vast household, the rulers maintained various karkhanas or royal stores.

In the Sultanate period there were several types of karkhanas. A clear and detailed description of royal karkhanas of the sultans of Delhi before Firuz Shah Tughluq is not available in the contemporary Persian chronicles, but there is no doubt that such karkhanas had existed prior to Firuz's reign and were casually referred to by Barani. Muhammad bin Tughluq is credited with having a manufactory in which 400 silk weavers were employed and where the stuff of all kinds for the dresses of persons attached to the court, robes of honour and robes meant for presentation were manufactured. Firuz's reign witnessed an unprecedented expansion of palace workshops. Afif's *Tarikh-i-Firuzshahi* gives a detailed description of the management of these factories. The data available is not sufficient to warrant a comprehensive study of this period.

With the expansion of the empire under the Mughals the need for various types of equipment necessary for an efficient army was fulfilled by the emperors only. The army being the backbone of the empire, it obviously could not be left under the control of nobles, governors or the administrative wing of the central government. Therefore the state took up the entire responsibility of catering to the needs of army by supplying necessary material under the state-controlled apparatus, the karkhanas. These karkhanas were not confined to capital alone but were spread all over the empire. Every provincial headquarter was supposed to have a sizeable karkhana from where the governor could supply to the emperor such commodities as were specialities of the province.

In establishing a karkhana, the Mughal emperor was following the practice prevalent in the Persian court. Shah Ismail, the Persian emperor, had formed such a workshop consisting of copyists, painters, gilders, colour grinders, gold mixers and others and appointed the celebrated Bihzad to head this group. Akbar's karkhana at Fatehpur Sikri was composed in similar pattern as is known from Abul Fazl and Father Monserrate, the Jesuit who visited the capital in 1580-82. It is evident from Bernier's observation that the karkhanas continued to exist under Aurangzeb. Some nobles of the Mughal empire maintained their private palace workshops where skilled artisans manufactured articles of luxury not only for their own use but also for purposes of presentation to the emperor and fellow nobles as a matter of administrative practice or social etiquette. Sometimes the European companies, too, felt the need for centralized production and control and tried to organize karkhanas of their own. Their object was not to effect 'economies of scale' or use capital equipment of power but cater their own needs, viz., to guarantee regular supply of standard goods and to exclude or limit the competition of others. The karkhanas exercised considerable influence on urban life and on relations between the village and the town. These helped mobility of labour from village to town. Country artisans of proven technical ability were drawn either voluntarily to the karkhanas or forcibly. This occupational specialization helped the artisan to acquire status. Further, the karkhanas reinforced the organization of exclusive castes and guilds. On the basis of the material available to us a number of problems arise regarding the working of karkhanas, their organization, expansion and growth.

Closely linked with this issue is the nature of this organization. Did it cater to the needs of royal household and army alone or was it also comprehensive enough to cater to the requirements of nobles and other government officials, and sometimes even of the common people? This requires the study of raw materials, their zone of supply and the mechanism involved in the business transactions between the supplier and the state.

Further a closer study of persons employed in the karkhanas reveals their socio-economic status. Was the labour functioning as an organized sector or recruited in the karkhanas on individual basis? Were they employed on hired system, on daily wage basis or on monthly salary? Some of these questions have clearly been examined in the present study.

University of Delhi — TRIPTA VERMA
19 March 1994

Abbreviations

Ain	Ain-i-Akbari
Afif	Tarikh-i-Firuzshahi
AN	Akbarnama
Badauni	Muntakhab-ut-Tawarikh
Barbosa	An account of the countries bordering on the Indian Ocean and their inhabitants
BM	British Museum
BN	Babur Nama
CEHI	The Cambridge Economic History of India
CHI	The Comprehensive History of India, Vol. V, The Delhi Sultanate
ED	History of India as Told by its own Historians, Elliot and Dowson
EF	The English Factories in India
IC	Islamic Culture
IESHR	The Indian Economic and Social History Review
IHR	The Indian Historical Review
IO	India Office Library, London
JAS (Bengal)	Journal of the Asiatic Society (Bengal)
JAS (Bombay)	Journal of the Asiatic Society (Bombay)
JBORS	Journal of the Bihar and Orissa Research Society
JIH	Journal of Indian History
JRAS	Journal of the Royal Asiatic Society
MIQ	Medieval India Quarterly
PIHC	Proceedings of the Indian History Congress
Purchas	Purchas His Pilgrimes
TFS	Tarikh-i-Furuzshahi of Ziauddin Barani
The Rehla	The Rehla of Ibn Batuta
Tuzuk	Tuzuk-i-Jahangiri

1

Karkhanas: Nature and Organization

PERSIA

The karkhanas generally required to cater to the ruler's demand for its household and army in the form of articles of luxury goods and war auxiliaries. It emerged as an industry in Persia in the sixteenth-seventeenth centuries[1] although in a rudimentary form it was in existence under the later Ghaznavids in the twelfth century. In the time of Bahram Shah (1118-52) there were also royal workshops Karkhanas supervised by a 'Mihtar' and a 'Mushrif', where the rich embroidery of 'tiraz' was sewn to the robes. It is very probable that royal workshops existed under earlier sultans.[1a] It was linked with the captive and enslaved workers who were captured in thousands in wars waged by the Ilkhans (thirteenth and fourteenth centuries) and the Safavid rulers (sixteenth and seventeenth centuries). With such a vast labour force behind Persia witnessed considerable expansion of these karkhanas from the fourteenth century onwards. They were found in several cities in Persia which specialized in various types of industries such as tanning, pickling, preserving, soap manufacture, paper making and dyeing. The mints were also listed among these state karkhanas. The income from mint flowed constantly into the royal treasury.

These court workshops and court industries of the Safavids were located inside the royal palace grounds. Their function was chiefly the preparation of every imaginable product that the court might need. The *buyutat* comprised firstly of departments connected in any way whatever with the supply of victuals for the court. Near the court kitchen were the food warehouse, the bakery, store room for drinking water and fruit juices, the wine seller, slaughter house, the coffee kitchen, the pharmacy and the rest. Then there were store houses, rooms of various kinds for firewood torches and lamps, for table cloths, plates and crockery, for carpets and robes of honour. The royal treasury too must be listed here. In fact all the departments which employed manual labour for the provision of the needs of the court household were court workshops in the true sense. Thus the court controlled its own looms, its own tailoring, shoe making, fur and leather industry. Besides many other departments there was a goldsmith's workshop and a copper smithy which supplied the court with all kinds of tools and utensils. Lastly, there were the harness makers, workshop, the armoury, the ordinance foundry and the library in which manuscripts were not only collected but specially produced by a staff of artists. The stables and many other offices were also part of the *buyutat*.[2]

In support of his charge that the policies of Shah Abbas were devoid of any entrepreneurial spirit Amin Banani cites the case of the royal workshops (*buyutat-i-Khasa-yi-Sharifa*) of which there were 32 at the time of Chardin and 33 at the time of compilation of the *Tazkirat-i-Muluk*[3] about 1726. It is true that many of the royal workshops such as the kitchen, scullery, stables, kennels, etc., were simply what Minorsky called 'domestic departments', some, however, were 'run like real state owned manufactories'[4] and in general these workshops gave employment to some 5000 artisans and craftsmen and contributed to the overall prosperity of the economy. Some workshops as the dye works and silk factory had been abolished and replaced by a system under which linen to be dyed was sent into the town and silk and gold thread were issued for the making of all kinds of textiles, brocades and carpets.

Court administration was under the care of a supreme major domo or intendent general (*nazir-i-buyutat*) who also had the charge of court workshops. The administration of the royal household was carried on by a separate department headed by *nazir-i-buyutat* or superintendent of the royal workshops (*buyutat-Khasa-yi-Sharifa*) of which there were eventually about thirty-three.[5] The artisans in the royal workshops were organised in royal guilds which continued to provide some of the court needs. The royal workshops made large profits for the Safavid Shahs; they not only produced goods such as textiles and rugs for the court, but also sent expensive silks as textiles to Europe and India and paid the profits made in this way to the Shah. Each royal workshop was in charge of *shahib-jam* and a *mushrif* and the *nazir-i-buyutat* and had in addition many other subordinate officials who assisted him in the discharge of his multifarious duties. These included the preparation of an estimate of the expenditure of the royal household (which was then submitted to the central vizier for approval) agreeing on the price of and signing contracts for, foodstuffs and other goods supplied to the royal household and supervision of the day to day expenditure of the various royal workshops, the maintenance of all the buildings connected with the royal household and the general supervision of the management of the royal stables and the arsenal. The administration of the harem and the private quarters of the Shah did not come within the purview of *nazir-i-buyutat*, but constituted an entirely separate branch, the internal palace administration staffed mainly by eunuchs.

As a rule there was a director (*sahib-i-jam*) and a controller (*mushrif*) over each department. This rule was broken however where for operational reasons several departments worked closely together and were therefore from time to time put under a single *sahib-i-jam* or a single *mushrif*. In the late Safavid period the *buyutat* were entirely under the direction of *nazir-i-buyutat* (overseer of the court workshops). This had not always been so at the beginning of the seventeenth century; the *nazir-i-buyutat* had controlled only certain specific court industries and workshops. Later, however, he was de facto incharge of the whole royal household and was reckoned to be one of the most powerful and influential ministers of state.

Countless workmen and specialists with a variety of professional skills were employed in the court industries. In contrast to their colleagues in the bazars they enjoyed a number of privileges. Each employee was given a deed of appointment which indicated precisely the manner of his work and his rate of pay. The workmen in the royal workshops constituted a privileged class of artisans. In the late Safavid period the annual wage of a workman ranged from two *tumans* to the considerable sum of 55 *tumans*. This was paid in the form of *barat*—the assignment of certain tax returns. One of the employees was commissioned to cash these tax cheques on the spot, so that, in fact, most employees get a cash payment, although forfeiting in the process 5 to 10 per cent of the wage stated in their deed of appointment. Every third year an employee at a court workshop counts on receiving a wage increase. In addition to their wages, the amount of which was stated in the artisan's letter of appointment and which was raised every three years, each workman received *Jira*, or rations in the form of quarter plate, a half plate or a plate. A plate consisted of 'everything necessary for subsistence and could feed 6-7 persons.[6] If he wished, the workman could take cash in lieu of *Jira*. Its cash value was about 20 *tumans*. When this is compared with the wage scale which ranged from 2 *tumans* to 55 *tumans* a year, it is clear that the *Jira* constituted a very substantial benefit. In addition workmen who did particularly good work were given presents and in some cases workmen received a gift amounting to a whole year's salary in lieu of the technical wage increase. Workmen employed in the royal workshops had full job security. They were kept for life and never dismissed. In case of illness or diminished capacity for work their salary was not reduced and they received free treatment from the court doctors and chemists. Not only did they receive their pay whether they had received any commissions from the kin or not but there was no restriction on the amount of work they performed on the side for their private profit. The workmen who had to follow the court on its travels were given camels and horses but they easily obtained permission to stay at home or alternately were granted leave after 6-12 months absence. The children of the workmen were taken into service at the age of 12-15 years and after their father's death received their salaries.[7]

An appointment in the *buyutat* was normally for life. In case of illness or unfitness for work the salary continued to be paid. Moreover, it also happened that many of the workmen worked not only by royal commission but on their own account as well. All these facts show that a post in court industry at a court workshop was in many respects a privileged post and must have been much sought after.

Mention must be made of European workmen in the *buyutat*. Under Abbas I, Safi I, Abbas II a number of painters worked at the court at Isfahan. There are several reports of watchmakers, but it is not clear whether they were always attached to the *buyutat*. Several European specialists were employed in the ordinance foundry at court and it is possible that their number increased under Shah Sultan Hussain (1694-1722), for at this time the production of artillery was being stepped up.

The function of the royal workshops must not be overlooked. Rulers have understandably retained the powers of technology within their own grasp.[8] At Isfahan fine workmanship no doubt produced the exquisite astrolabes for which the Safavid monarchs are famed. According to *Tazkirat-ul-Muluk*, thirty-three such workshops were in active production in the reign of Shah Sultan Hussain. Employees in the *buyutat* received free drugs and attention, while in Tahmasp's reign a charitable dispensary was established.

The finest Persian carpets are considered to be those of the Safavid period. There are two possible reasons for this. Either this particular branch of the arts in Iran reached its zenith later than any other or else the judgement may be explained by the fact that none of the Timurid textiles have been preserved and that their evaluation is therefore based entirely on miniatures whereas Safavid carpets and fabrics attest their advanced stage of technical and aesthetic development.

No less difficult is the problem of origin, that is, the task of attributing to individual weaving centres the various groups which can be distinguished among Safavid carpets on the basis of their design and technical characteristics. Since the Safavid carpets must be the products of large establishments patronised by the court, it may be supposed that carpets were manufactured in the workshops of successive capitals. Early in the seventeenth century Florencio del Nino emphasized that Qazvini was an important trading centre where there was an abundance of silk and brocade carpets. In the case of Isfahan there is reliable evidence from various sources of the manufacture of carpets, brocades with gold and silver threads. Indeed Jean Baptiste Tavernier describes the exact location of the workshop in the Maiden quarter. But woollen carpets were also woven in Isfahan for Tavernier writes on another occasion, 'the Karkrone is the house of the royal manufactories where fine carpets of gold, silver, silk and wool together with gold and silver brocade, velvet, taffeta, and other such fabrics are made'.[9]

In one source of the seventeenth century, the royal workshop in Isfahan is mentioned as heading the list of most important textile factories and is described as follows: 'The royal weaving mill consists of various weaving shops in which silk as well as gold and silver brocades are manufactured. The director of the establishment is the superintendent of the traders who controls and supervises the selection of partners, the preparation of the raw materials and the storage of the completed articles. In addition he is head of all the workshops that supply the clothing needs of the royal household'. The superintendent of the traders who supervised the royal weavers, dyers, tailors and silk embroiderers was at the same time merchant and trading adviser to the king.[10]

Apart from what can be deduced from the biographical accounts nothing is known about the organization of the *Kitab Khana* until the last part of the period for which the *Tazkirat-i-Muluk* for about 1725 supplies some comparative statistics for the staff of all the royal workshops including the library. For the later Safavid period there is also some evidence from western travellers about the condition of painters and other artists and the way their work was organised.

Chardin gives the idea of the scale of employment in 32 royal workshops, mentioning for instance that in his time there were

72 painters on the strength of the establishment all enjoying, an annual salary, partly paid in free messing as compared with 180 tailors. He also describes the manner of recruitment to these establishments by scrutiny of the specimens of the work submitted by candidates first to the head of each specialist's workshop and then for confirmation by the *nazir* incharge.[11]

Sultans of Delhi

The sultans maintained very big household staff. Besides his harem, the slaves and other attendants and his courtiers, the sultan employed host of people to look after the protection of his person, his recreation and his domestic attendants in general. To cater to the needs of these vast household the sultan maintained various 'karkhanas' or royal stores. These karkhanas had multiple functions in the political and social life of the rulers of medieval India. K.M. Ashraf has aptly remarked that 'besides meeting the requirement of the household staff and other officials, the karkhanas maintained separate sections for the supply of royal standards (*alam khana*) and the care of the royal library (*kitabkhana*) and the gong and chronometer (*ghariyal khana*), the jewel house (*jawahar khana*) and the royal pastures. The karkhanas looked after the provisioning of the royal stables and the supervision of the royal buildings for which they maintained a whole army of masons and architects. Finally they undertook to supply the menial attendance and the domestic service for the palaces and other royal buildings. The enumeration, however, is by no means complete. The karkhanas were under the charge of a distinguished noble who was assisted by other subordinate superintendents (*mutasarrifs*) who were themselves nobles of rank and were appointed directly by the Sultan'.[12] All of them were paid very high salaries, and the charge of a store was considered quite as remunerative as the governorship of a big town like Multan.[13]

Although the literal meaning of karkhana is the place where a 'workshop' is generally located for public use, it had a very different connotation in medieval India. The medieval chroniclers used it to include workshops of manufacturers, the stores, the royal household, the royal court and the animal stables etc. As most of the articles of luxury needed by the rulers to maintain the splendour and pageantry of the royal court and household could not be manufactured in the ordinary market, the sultans were forced to establish state factories producing luxury articles for them. It became a major policy decision with the state of the Sultanate. It is generally believed that the system of royal karkhanas was probably borrowed from Persia;[14] though its much earlier existence in India could not be ruled out.[15]

A clear and detailed description of the royal karkhanas of the sultans of Delhi before Firuz Shah Tughluq is not available in the contemporary Persian account, but there is no doubt that such karkhanas existed prior to Firuz Shah's reign and were casually referred to by Barani.[16]

Muhammad Tughluq is credited with having a manufactory in which 400 silk weavers were employed and where the stuff of all kinds for the dresses of persons attached to the court, robes of honour and robes meant for presentation were manufactured. Likewise the Sultan kept in service 500 manufacturers of golden tissues who wove gold brocades worn by the wives of the Sultan, and given away as presents to the amirs and their wives.[17]

In Delhi the sultans had their own karkhanjats in which thousands of weavers engaged for the manufacture of silk cloths and other textiles for the royal robe. In these karkhanjats artistic work in gold and silver was also done. The private industries, not within the purview of the karkhanas, specialised in the manufacture of textiles, calico printing, liquors, arms, brass work paper, clay work, bricks, enamel work, embroidery, leather work and shoe-making.

The accounts of the contemporary chroniclers as well as foreign travellers show that private industries of considerable importance and magnitude were developed during this period. The biggest of them was the manufacture of textile of all kinds such as cotton cloth, woollen cloth and silks. The manufacture of cotton cloth attained classical perfection and became proverbial all over the world. Other important industries were wood work, stone work, metal work, leather work, embroidery, indigo and paper. The factories were known as karkhanas or workshops. These were supported by the state as well as enterprising businessmen. Almost all the sultans of Delhi maintained big karkhanas where vast stores of silk and fine muslin were manufactured for the use of Imperial Harem and Courtiers. The royal factories of Delhi sometimes employed as many as 4000 weavers of silk alone, besides, manufacture for other kinds of goods for the royal supply. It may be observed that if arts and industries flourished abundantly during the early Muslim period, it was mainly due to the patronage of the state. The karkhanas of the sultans of Delhi or at a later date of the rulers in various regional Muslim kingdoms were best equipped and most efficiently organized.

The royal factories catered to the demands of the sultans. Some idea of a royal demand may be gathered from the fact that Muhammad Tughluq used to distribute 200,000 complete robes of honour, twice every year, in the spring and the autumn, those of the spring consisted chiefly of goods manufactured at Alexandria, while those of the autumn were made of goods partly manufactured at Delhi and partly imported from China and Iraq. The Sultan employed no less than 4000 manufacturers of golden tissues for brocades (*zarkis*) used by ladies of the royal 'Harem' or given away in presents to nobles and their wives. Practically every article of royal use for instance caps, shoes, curtains, tapestery, waist bands, sashes, saddles, etc. was supplied by these karkhanas.

The karkhanas similarly manufactured vast stores of the muslins and other goods for gifts and presents to other rulers in return for similar gifts from them. Enumerating the presents sent by Muhammad Tughluq to the emperor of China, Ibn Batuta mentions, among other things, 100 pieces of 'bairami' cloth made of cotton in which beauty had no equal, 100 pieces of silk cloth called khazz, the silk of each of them being different from four to five different colours, 100 pieces of *shirinbaf*, 100 pieces of *shanbaf*, 500 pieces of Kashmir woollen materials of which 100 were black, 100 were white, 100 red, 100 blue, 100 pieces of green linen (besides) 100 pieces of wrapper, ten embroidered robes of honour of royal type and ten caps from those of the Sultan himself one of them being studded with pearls, ten quivers of gold brocade, one of them being set in with pearls, ten swords, the scabbard of one of which was set with pearls and gloves (*dastban*) studded with pearls.[18]

Under the Delhi Sultanate Firuz Shah alone had devoted his energies towards the state karkhanas and he had a large establishment and a separate department for them, but it is not clear from the account given by Afif whether the department only stored articles or manufactured them as well. All references suggest that it only kept stores and its importance consisted in large stocks[19] and regular supplies of fresh and uptodate articles of all kinds.

The department of the royal karkhanas does not represent anything new in the government of Firuz. The only remarkable feature noticeable in his reign was its vast expansion of palace workshops. The eulogist Afif writes that the Sultan attached great importance to his karkhanas and treated them on a par with 'Iqtas'. He used to say that the ownership of a karkhana is no less important than the governorship (*muqti*) of a region like Multan.[20] The Sultan maintained 36 karkhanas and tried his utmost to collect raw materials for them. Brocades and other goods required for the karkhanas were purchased at the market price on cash basis. A complete list of these karkhanas is not given at one place by Afif but the following are mentioned in various parts of his text:[21]

Peel Khana or Fil Khana (elephant stables), *Paigah* (horse stable), *Mutbak* (kitchen), *Sharab Khana* (wine cellar), *Shama Khana* (the departments of lights and candle sticks), *Shutur Khana* (camel stables), *Saq Khana* (dog kennels), *Abdar Khana* (water supply of the palace), *Jamdar Khana* (wardrobe), *Alam Khana*[22] (royal standard), *Farrash Khana* (furniture tents and carpets), *Rikab Khana* (saddlery and harness etc.), *Shakradar Khana* (hunting store), *Silah Khaṇa* (arms and arsenal), *Tashtdar Khana* (ewer bearers and baths), *Jawahar Khana* (jewellery), *Jandar Khana* (body guard department), *Naubat Khana* (kettle drum store), *Targhak Khana* (watch and ward), *Chawki Khana* (stools and small table stores), *Kitab Khana* (library), *Ghariyal Khana* (time keeping and gong), *Itardar Khana* (scents), *Chatar Dar Khana* (canopy store), *Pardhadar Khana* (curtain stores, probably concerned with the royal harem), *Yuzban Khana* (hunting, panther keeping departments), *Siyah Goshdar Khana* (lynux stable), *Satu bandan Khana* (quadruplet cattle stable), *Khasdar Khana* (betel box), *Daroodar Khana* (medicine stores), *Sangtarash Khana* (stone cutting department), *Saqqa Khana* (water bearers), and *Zarad Khana* (armour and war material department).

It is evident from the names of the various karkhanas listed above that all these cannot be called factories or workshops proper. Some of them were factories proper while others were stores and establishments connected with the Court, the Sultan's household and animal stables.

Afif[23] classifies the royal karkhanas into two categories namely, *Ratibi* and *Ghair Ratibi. Ratibi* were those which had fixed annual grants, such as *Peel Khana, Paigah, Matbak, Sharab Khana, Sag Khana, Abdar Khana* and *Itardar Khana.* One lakh sixty thousand tankas per month was the fixed grant of these *Ratibi Karkhanas*, besides the plant, furniture and the wages of their accountants and other officers which also amounted to one lakh and sixty thousand tankas. Among these *Ratibi Karkhanas, Paigah* was the most important. It was scattered in division and stationed at different places. The first and the biggest was at Saharwan Sultanpur, the second at Kibla, the third near the Court called *Paigah Mahal Khas* (palace stable), the fourth at *Shakar Khana-i-Khas* and the fifth and the last was that of selected slaves. The *Kar-*

khana Nafar (camel stable) had numerous camels. Most of these were sent to the *shiqs* of Doblahan[24] where the whole villages were appropriated to them and their keepers. The number of camels increased every year because the *muqtis* of various *iqtas* presented camels along with other presents.[25]

Ghair Ratibi karkhanas were those which did not have a fixed grant, such as *Jamdar Khana, Alam Khana, Farrash Khana, Rikab Khana, Zard Khana, Silah Khana* and *Tashtdar Khana* (hamams and baths).

Firuz Shah had thirty-six karkhanas divided into *Ratibi*, which provided daily food for men and animals and *Ghair Ratibi* which dealt with commodities produced by human labour. Afif says that his father and uncle were incharge of *Alam Khana* (concerning the insignia of royalty etc.), the *Rakab Khana* (dealing with the equipment for horses) and the elephant stables of the left wing and that he worked with them. In the *Ratibi Karkhana*, 1,60,000 tankas a month were spent on the provision of food alone; this amount did not include the salaries of officers and servants employed. The figures of expenditure given by Afif for other karkhanas are—*Jamdar Khana*, 6,00,000 tankas for the winter clothes alone, *Alam Khana*, 80,000 tankas a year (exclusive of salaries) and *Farrash Khana* (for carpets), 2,00,000 tankas.

The expenditure upon these karkhanas varied from year to year in accordance with the quality of new goods ordered to be made each year. In the winter season six lakhs were spent on *Jamdar Khana*, in addition to the expenditure incurred in summer and spring. Eighty thousand tankas were spent on *Alam Khana* on the purchase of articles, besides the salaries of accountants and wages of artisans. About 2 lakh tankas were spent in the *Farrash Khana* and so on.[26]

Each karkhana was placed under the charge of a khan or a malik of high rank and a general superintendent (*mutasarrif*) was appointed over them all. He had to maintain the accounts of his department separately and submit to the office of *Diwan-i-Wazarat* for annual audit. These appointments used to be made by the Sultan personally. Khwaja Abul Hasan was the chief *Mutasarrif* or director general of the karkhanas and all royal orders went to him in the first instance. Afif quotes Firuz Shah as saying: 'Just as lakhs of revenue are collected in the provinces, similarly lakhs are collected in the karkhanas. The turnover (*tasarruf*) of a karkhana of mine is not less than the turnover of the city of Multan'.[27]

The karkhanas had their separate *diwan*. The *wizarat* to which their accounts were submitted, was as lax in controlling the accounts of the karkhanas as it was in controlling the accounts of the *iqtas*. There was plenty of *hashiya* (marginal corruption and mal-expenditure) in every karkhana. Never during the thirty-eight years of Firuz's reign, Afif asserts repeatedly, were the accounts of the provinces or of karkhanas examined in accordance with the correct principles of accountancy. 'It is not that Firuz Shah was ignorant of the principles of accountancy', Afif remarks, 'he knew them only too well. But he saw everything and preferred to close his eyes, so the auditors (*ahl muhasibah*) also overlooked the acts of the officers incharge (*ummal*)'.[28]

The following persons were appointed to act as *mutasarrifs* in some of the departments. Malik Ali and Malik Ismail were incharge of *Jamdar Khana*, Malik Dilshad also called Dilshad Shannal Nafar, was incharge of *Karkhana-i-Shutur*, Malik Khiza Bahram was incharge of *Shakar Khana*, Malik Muhammad Haji was incharge of *Alam Khana, Paigah Khas* and *Rikab Khana*, Malik Mubarak Bala was incharge of *Tashtdar Khana* and Khwaja Jahan Sarwar-i-Sultani was incharge of *Jawahar Khana*. The *Mutasarrif* (superintendent) was appointed by the Sultan himself. Malik Kamaluddin Turti Khan was *Mutasarrif* of *Jamdar Khana*. Afif's father and uncles held the posts of *Mutasarrif* of *Alam Khana, Rikab Khana* and *Peel Khan-i-Maisra*.[29]

The general superintendent (*tasarruf*) of all the karkhanas was Khwaja Abdul Hasan. When the Sultan wanted anything to be made, the royal order was first of all sent to the general superintendent who in turn passed it on to the superintendent of the karkhana concerned where the order was quickly executed.[30]

Besides the superintendent, each karkhana had a number of accountants. For all the karkhanas a separate *Diwan-i-Majuma* of karkhana was set up where the accounts of the karkhanas were maintained. These accounts were audited by *Diwan-i-Vizarat* (finance department) like the accounts of *iqtas*. The *muharrirs* (clerks) of the karkhanas were called in and questioned every year. After the audit, the annual balance of cash and kind was struck.[31]

The absence of any reference to karkhanas during the reign of Sultan Firuz's successors in the contemporary sources is rather enigmatic. This may be due to the almost non-existence of Sultanate as an effective instrument of political expansion. As these karkhanas involved huge financial resources of the government which by all accounts had become extinct, there was thus no need to maintain it. Karkhanas were no longer a necessary limb of the state both politically and economically. Industries of considerable importance and proportions flourished in the provincial kingdom under the patronage of their independent rulers. Gujarat and Bengal are said to have led the whole of India in the manufactured export of textile goods. The harbour facilities that they enjoyed as well as their commercial relations with other countries enabled them to build a textile industry of a vast magnitude. Mahuan, Varthama and Barbosa are warm in their praises of textiles of Bengal, particularly cotton cloth, muslins, gold embroidered caps and silk handkerchiefs which were manufactured in large quantities to meet internal as well as external demand. Gujarat was famous for the manufacture of cotton and silk cloth. Barbosa[32] informs that Cambay (Khambayat) was an important centre of manufacture for all kinds of coarse and fine cloth. The varieties of velvets, thick carpets, silk muslins, saten taffetas and printed cloth were manufactured in other parts of Gujarat also. Barbosa was greatly impressed by the very fine work of the goldsmiths of Gujarat. Mahadevnagri and Deogir in Deccan were equally important centres of cloth manufacture. Cloth made there was of exceptional fineness and beauty. According to Amir Khusrau, it was so fine as to tempt a fairy.

References

1. A special form of industry emerged under the Safavids of Persia in the sixteenth and seventeenth centuries which goes by the name of *buyutat* (literally houses) or royal workshops and court industries. An important feature of this organization was that it was located inside the royal palace grounds. For details see Engelbert Kaempfer, *Amoenitatum*, Book I (tr. W. Hinz), *An Hofe des Persischen Grosskonigs 1684-85*, Leipzig, 1940, pp. 106ff; Jean Chardin, *Voyages en Perse, et'autres lieux de l'orient*, new edn L. Langles, pp. 330ff. An incomplete trans. by E. Lloyd titled *Sir Jean Chardin's Travels in Persia*, 2 Vols, London, 1720; Vladimir Minorsky, ed, *The Tazkirat-i-Muluk: A Manual of Safavid Administration*, London, 1943, p. 50. See Peter Jackson and Laurence Lock Hart, ed, *The Cambridge History of Iran: The Timurid and the Safavid Periods*, Vol. 6, p. 531.

1a. C.E. Bosworth, *The Ghaznavids*, p. 137.

2. Kaempfer, op. cit., pp. 106ff; Chardin, op. cit., Vol. II, pp. 33ff; Minorsky, op. cit., p. 50.
3. Minorsky, op. cit., p. 30.
4. Ibid., p. 29.
5. Keyvani Mehdi, *Artisans and Guild Life in Later Safavid Period*, Berlin, 1982, pp. 48-50.
6. Minorsky, op. cit., pp. 31, 153.

7. Ibid., p. 21.
8. Akbar was not alone in his knowledge of 'the Mechanick Arts' and his interest in the manufacture of weapons in his own palace.
9. Tavernier, *Travels in India* (tr. V. Ball), London, 1889, Vol. I, pp. 444, 654.
10. Kaempfer, op. cit., Tr. W. Hinz, op. cit., 2nd edn (incomplete), pp. 86, 120.
11. Chardin, op. cit., Vol. V, pp. 499-500; Vol. VII, p. 329 in Peter Jackson and Laurence Lock Hart, ed, op. cit., p. 888.
12. K.M. Ashraf, *Life and Conditions of the People of Hindustan*, p. 64.
13. Afif, *Tarikh-i-Firuzshahi*, pp. 271-72, 338-39.
14. Special mention may be made of the Ilkhan's *karkhanas*. Rashiduddin refers to them in Khabushan, Nishapur, Tus, Tubriz. (Alizade, ed, *Jami Al-Tawarikh*, pp. 30, 179, 414). Vassaf speaks of karkhanas and craftsmen belonging to individual Chingizids in Bukhara and Samarqand while Saif mentions a 'karkhana' in Herat. Boyle, *Cambridge History of Iran: The Saljuk and the Mongol Period*, Vol. V, pp. 511-13. For a reference under the Abbasids one is referred to P.K. Hitti, *History of the Arabs*, pp. 345-46. Also P.M. Holt, A.K.S. Lambton and Bernard Lewis, *The Cambridge History of Islam*, Vol. 2A, p. 31. In Fatimid Egypt a clear distinction was made between state and private enterprise which is indicative of the fact that the industry as a whole was not exclusively the state monopoly. Some of these state factories were run on gigantic scale and engaged in producing robes of different styles. The robes produced in these karkhanas were officially given away as presents in large quantities, the whole court received new garments twice a year. A large wardrobe was a form of investment not to be despised in a period when the hoarding of objects of value was a surer way of saving money than investing capital in industry. When the robes were finished in their places of manufacture they were sent to Cairo, where those meant for the Caliph were filled in one of the women's apartments of the palace where 30 girls worked under the supervision of a manageress.
15. The Iron Pillar of Mehrauli is a case in point which seems to have been made in the royal foundry which however was mainly concerned with the manufacture of arms and armour. See S.K. Maity, *Economic Life in Northern India*, pp. 135-36.
16. Barani, *Tarikh-i-Firuzshahi*, pp. 50, 109. Barani refers to these karkhanas in his account of Sultan Balban's reign (1266-87). Nobles posted in the provinces as governors also maintained karkhanas and efforts were made to employ master craftsmen to work there. These karkhanas contributed greatly to social mobility in urban centres. Many slaves trained in the karkhanas attained important positions. They took active part in the politics of Delhi Sultanate, emerging as a powerful group after the death of Sultan Firuz.
17. Shihab al Din al umari (d. 1348), *Masalik-al-Absar fi Mamalik al Amsar* (Elliot and Dowson, *History of India As Told by Its Historians*, Vol. III, p. 578). Also I.H. Siddiqui and Q.M. Ahmad, tr., *A 14th Century Arab Account of India*, p. 39.

18. Mahdi Hussain, tr., *The Rehla of Ibn Batuta (India, Maldive Islands and Ceylon)*, 2nd edn, Baroda, 1976, p. 151.
19. The Sultan often used to say that in a kingdom, there are two valuables, one includes *iqta* lands, parganas and the other karkhanas. As millions of money came from the *iqta*, goods worth millions are stored in these karkhanas. Accordingly the possession of Firuz's one karkhana is in no way less than the proceeds of the city of Multan (Afif, op. cit., p. 339). The Sultan had 36 karkhanas. He always made strenuous efforts to store goods in them and every karkhana was full of goods of variety and quality (Afif, op. cit., p. 356). Different karkhanas were under different amirs but the entire charge was under Khvaja Abul Hasan, who received royal orders and communicated them to the amirs concerned who carried them out immediately. Whenever goods of quality were available they were purchased for karkhanas and payments were made every day on the purchase (Afif, op. cit., p. 99).
20. Afif, op. cit., pp. 99, 337, 339.
21. Ibid., pp. 271-72, 337-40.
22. Jadunath Sarkar reads (*ilm khana*) and therefore equates it with schools. See his *Mughal Administration*, p. 132.
23. Afif, op. cit., pp. 337-38.
24. A mahal in the Sarkar of Delhi, *Ain*, Vol. II, p. 285.
25. Afif, op. cit., p. 340.
26. Ibid., p. 338.
27. Ibid., p. 339.
28. Ibid., pp. 295-96.
29. Ibid., pp. 338-39.
30. Ibid., p. 339.
31. Ibid., pp. 340-41.
32. Durate Barbosa, *The Book of Durate Barbosa* (tr. L.M. Dames), Vol. I, pp. 141-42; Vol. II, p. 154; Ludovic di Varthema of *Bologina, Travels in Egypt, Syria, Persia, India, Ethiopia (1502-8)*, p. 212; *Journal of the Royal Asiatic Society of Great Britain and Ireland*, London, 1895, p. 532; *Journal of the (Royal) Asiatic Society of Bengal*, Calcutta, 1935, p. 307.

2

State Karkhanas during the Mughal Period

Moreland has long ago pointed out there were two forms of industrial organizations during Mughal India, the artisan system in which the independent artisan supplied his own capital however small, his own material and his own labour in manufacture and the karkhana system in which the artisans worked to order in state controlled karkhanas[1] or workshops. While the former prevailed generally in the majority of towns and the karkhanas were established, e.g., Delhi, Agra about which descriptions have been left by Afif in the Sultanate period and Abul Fazl and Bernier during the hey day of the Mughals.[2]

Supplies came not only from private individual weavers and dealers but from private establishments of provincial governors or high officials. This would imply either that these high officials maintained private karkhanas where the artisans worked under directions with materials supplied by officials themselves or that they engaged in private trade themselves procuring manufactured articles by purchase in the market with the help of their agents or brokers. Moreland actually surmised the existence of private workshops similar to imperial karkhanas[3].

If the artisan system represented in a way independent single artisan labour, followed by decentralized cooperation karkhana system was characterized by compulsory labour, centralized control over numerous wage earning artisans of various crafts and controlled cooperation. The karkhana system differed from the artisan system in several ways. It not only marked a different stage of production but it also constituted an important and novel development, and it exercised a significant influence on economic life. In the first place, the karkhanas were examples of collective and large scale employment of artisans or craftsmen in different industries in a big manufacturing organization. The potentialities of future development were immense. The biggest was the imperial karkhanas. As regards imperial karkhanas, the emperor issued instructions to governors, officers and jagirdars in the provinces to induce the best master artisans and workers in various arts and crafts from all over India to join the karkhanas.[4] Even foreign workers were invited by Jahangir from Turkey, Persia, China and European countries to these.[5] Secondly, there was a certain amount of coercive regimentation of labour. After recruitment, it was like conscript labour. The workers had to work under the direction of a *malik* on a wage basis.[6] Thirdly, the raw materials for the workshop were not obtained through open purchases in the market by the artisans but these were supplied to them by means of monopoly purchases by the state. Fourthly, though the workmanship belonged to the artisans, the initiative for designs rested not with them but with the state officials guiding them according to imperial desires. Under Akbar, who took special interest in these karkhanas there were possibilities of improved designs and workmanship. Fifthly, the manufactured articles were not intended for sale in the market but for meeting the needs of the state in the court and the camp and for distribution among the nobles, constituting the elite, and among the foreign ambassadors for presentation to brother rulers. Lastly, the karkhanas in turn served as radiating centres of skill. Abul Fazl remarks that skilful masters and workmen settled here to teach the people an improved system. The workshops furnished all stuffs made in foreign countries.[7]

Like the Safavids of Persia as discussed earlier the term *buyutat*[8] was also generally used by the Mughals for karkhanas. The association of the *buyutat* with the household in the mind of Mughal administrators is thus quite obvious. The more ancient and popular karkhana, however, persisted. The karkhanas played an important role not only in the sphere of the Imperial Household but also in military and fiscal set-up of the empire. Besides they had considerable impact upon the industrial progress of the territories. For this reason the entire organization was under the general supervision of diwan.[9] Thus the karkhanas or *buyutat* as the department was called, included factories and stores maintained by the central government for purposes of state. The department can neither be placed under the category of the dargah nor of the household. It dealt with every article from pearls, precious stones and swords, scimitars to guns and heavy artillery. It maintained horses and elephants for the army, beasts of burden for baggage and other animals for the royal hunt.[10]

The Mughal emperors took special interest in the karkhanas and saw to it that state maintained karkhanas were set up not only in the capital but also in the provincial headquarters as well as in other important industrial towns. They wanted that the karkhanas should not only produce articles for meeting the general requirements of the state but also produce articles of choice and quality. The word karkhana, however, has been used in the sources in a very wide sense and includes animals in the state stables, articles of food and drink stored for the royal use, finished goods kept in government stores and work-shops where raw material was used and worked upon to produce finished commodities by employed labour either on daily wage basis or on monthly salary.

Further, in order to get clear idea of the economic activities of the state, it is necessary to distinguish between the two classes of things which our Persian authorities designated by the name of *karkhanas* and include in the same list, viz. (a) stores of animals, articles of food and drink and things in finished or usable condition, acquired by the government and kept in the palace which required no further working up and (b) factories proper where raw materials were worked up by salaried servants of the state into fully manufactured goods fit for use.[11]

In Mughal India the state was the largest manufacturer or rather the only manufacturer on a large scale in respect of several commodities. The modern practice of government buying readymade goods in the market or giving orders for large quantities to contractors would not have answered in those days of cottage industries when production on large scale by private entrepreneurs with a view to sale was unknown. The state was therefore forced to manufacture the commodities it needed. Its need was very large. Twice every year in the rainy season and the winter a robe (*khilat*) suitable for the season was presented by the emperor to every mansabdar whose number in 1690 is given as nearly 7500 and who were paid in cash. Besides, there were 7000 mansabdars who held jagirs.[12] For the higher nobles, one suit of the robe of honour consisted of several articles of apparel. In addition to these two seasonal gifts, the princes of the blood, the Hindu chieftains and many of the mansabdars and the court officials received robes of honour at the two birthdays of the emperor (according to lunar and the solar calculations), the lunar anniversary of his coronation, the two Ids and down to Aurangzeb's reign, on the old Persian New Year's Day (*Nauroz*) when the sun enters the Aries. As a matter of rule, *khilats* were also bestowed on most persons when they were presented at court or took leave, or were appointed to posts, and, for some time in Aurangzeb's reign, on converts to Islam.[13]

It is thus seen that the imperial government had to keep a vast stock of cloth and readymade robes for its need during the year. Their supply was assured by the state maintaining many karkhanas of its own in the principal cities of the empire, where skilled workmen were brought together, sometimes from distant provinces, and placed under the *darogha* (government superintendent), paid daily wages, and made to produce the handicrafts which were duly stocked in the stores.

The same thing was done with regard to various articles of consumption and luxury required by the emperor's household. It was the business of *Khan-i-Saman* or Lord High Steward to buy such goods as were available in the market and manufacture the others well in advance of the time when they would be required. A detailed study of the karkhanas will only give an idea of the immense field of state activity in the industrial sphere.

The Mughal government was forced to supply its own wants by becoming a producer of nearly everything it required, for in the sixteenth and seventeenth centuries, the modern private organization of production and transport were found wanting and the government itself took a somewhat patriarchal attitude in dealing with its servants and subjects. Such state factories were an ancient institution of the land, as throughout the middle ages they were necessitated by the circumstances of the times.

Undoubtedly the Mughal rulers encouraged manufacture of various items which also catered the need of the common public although the evidence on the latter is scanty. In these workshops there were produced arms and ammunition. Carriages and portable litters for the emperor, carpet mattresses, harness for the horses in the imperial stable, beds, tents, clothes, jewellery, gold and silver wares, perfumes, medicines, shawls, turbans and other metals. The articles were supplied to the various government departments at market rates. The profits were shown as the income from karkhanas.

The main function of the karkhanas was to keep the palace and some branches of government supplied with the commodities which they needed. These varied from the food served on the monarch's table to the pieces of artillery required by the imperial forces. The *buyutat* included the public treasury because the final trustee of the public funds was the monarch himself and he had unquestioned authority over the disposal of the resources of the government, the mint was included because the minting of the coins of the realm was an imperial responsibility, given up only when the emperors were no longer able to control the provincial governments. The artillery once again was attached to the household because it was considered imprudent to leave it in the hands of mansabdars. Parts of artillery were placed under their command but they did not have artillery as part of their routine equipment.

The emperor gave away thousands of robes of honour to his officers and others, and it was considered economical to get the cloth manufactured and the robes tailored directly in the imperial workshops. Precious stones were cut, pearls pierced, ornaments made in the karkhanas not only for the use of the monarch but also for presents; horses, elephants, camels and mules were bred and trained for various duties; animals and birds were tamed and taught to help the monarch in the hunt; in short all the needs of the monarch and court were met through these institutions. It is, therefore, not surprising that they should have multiplied with the growth of luxury in the court and the extent of the empire. Their close connections with the administration can also be seen from the nature of their functions. The treasury, the mint and the arsenal have an obvious relationship but even some of these related more closely to the person of the monarch played some direct or indirect part of the business of the state.[14]

The imperial household was a great miscellany of offices, factories, departments and institutions. It was a microcosm, a complete independent unit where the economic processes of production, consumption and exchange went full circle. The standard of the articles and services consumed at court were so high and the amounts required were so large that no private agency or set of agencies could be relied upon to meet the demand with a reasonable degree of satisfaction.

Some of these indeed were of a kind usually managed by state, such as mint or an arms factory. But it is proof of the fastidious taste of the aristocracy in general and the emperor in particular that everything consumed by the court was specially produced by various offices. These offices constituted the main spring of life at court like all main springs invisible to outside observers, but vitally necessary. To realize the significance of court life and ceremonial one should understand the inner workings of the machinery that was behind it. This machinery was to the imperial court what anatomy is to the art of animal sculprure—foundation of its being.[15]

About the number of karkhanas also the sources vary. In popular parlance there were 12 treasuries and 36 karkhanas. The Marathi histories namely the *Sabhasad Bakhar* (written in 1694), and the *Chitnis Bakhar* of Shivaji (written in 1810), mention only 18 karkhanas, though these two works do not agree with each other as to their names. The *Zawabit-i-Alamgiri*[16] gives a list of 69 karkhanas. The *Ain* separately describes 26 of the karkhanas and indirectly or briefly refers to 10 others making a total of 36.

Further, in the contemporary literature 36 *buyutat* or the karkhanas are mentioned. Abul Fazl mentions the following in the *Ain*: the treasuries, the mint, the *farrash khana*, illumination and lights, the *qurkhana*, the workshop for making the royal seals, the *abdar khana*, the kitchen, the fruitery, the perfumery, the wardrobe and the bedding and mattresses, the *pilkhana*, the stables for horses, the camel stables, the cow stables, the mule stables, buildings, the library, the arsenal, the workshops for the manufacture of shawls and textiles.[17] Other authorities mention many more. Jadunath Sarkar has collected more than seventy names from various sources. It seems more probable that the number thirty-six was traditional, having come down from the days of the Sultanate when it had some relevance.[18]

Under the Mughals the number of various factories, workshops and stables grew in view of new needs. Some of the older ones had to be split into independent organizations. It was not considered necessary to confine the number to the traditional thirty-six or to make out lists of a strictly logical nature. Every need which was felt had to be fulfilled and a store or a workshop was added to the existing establishments. The staff of every karkhana varied in accordance with the needs; for instance the *matbakh* or kitchen would have chefs and cooks whereas the library would employ calligraphists and painters.[19] At the head of every karkhana, however, there was a *darogha* or a superintendent, assisted by clerks and accountants.

Classified List of Karkhanas

The Mughal karkhanas as enumerated in the *Zawabit* can be classified into the following six groups:

A. Animals

Horse stables (*paga* or *astabal-khana*), elephant stables (*fil-khana*), cow-pens (*gao-khana*), camel stables (*shutar-khana*), mule stables (*ashtar-khana*), deer park (*ahu-khana*), menageries of tame hunting animals (*shikar-khana*), hunting leopards (*chita-khana*), aviary for falcons (*qush-khana*).

B. Stores

They were mere collections of things manufactured elsewhere. Royal insignia (*qur-khana*), arsenal (*silah-khana*), *palki-khana, chaudol-khana* or sedan chairs, *rath-khana* or carriages, portable throne or litter (*takht-i-rawan*), candle sticks and lamps (*shama and chiragh*), torches (*mashal*), library (*kitab-khana*), chinaware (*chini-khana*), *khilat-khana* or store of dresses of honour intended for distribution.

C. Factories and Stores

Carpets (*farrash-khana*), wardrobe or mattresses (*toshak-khana*), *jamdar khana* in Firuz's history, harness, saddles and bridles (*zin-khana*), bedding and advance tents for the emperor's journeys (*bistar-khana* and *pesh-khana*).

Kir-kiraqi Khana[20]

Apparel of children (*rakhwat*, wrong plural of *rakht*). The same of *khawases*. But elsewhere the *Zawabit* (14a) speaks of *rakhwat* or trappings for (a) leopards, (b) elephants, (c) the *Haveli* and (d) the *barish-khana* or monsoon-house, goldsmith's department (*zargar-khana*), blacksmithy (*ahangar-khana*), jewellery store (*jawahir-khana*), goldware (*tela-alat*), silver ware (*nugra-alat*), inlaid-ware (*murassa-alat*), copper ware and cauldrons, gold-embroidery (*zardoz-khana*), ivory work (*dandan-i-fil*), setting shells (*khatam bandi khana*), perfumery (*khushbuh khana*), rose water department (*gulab khana*), oil or ghee (*raughan*), mint (*dar-ul-zarb*), paintings (*naqqash khana* or *tasvir khana*), dispensary (*dawai khana* or *shafa khana*), shawls, scarf weaving (*chirabafi khana*), *huqabandi khana*, factory of silk cords and tapes. Cloth store (*kotha*, or *kuthi-i-parcha*). This was quite different from the mahal of *kathra-i-parcha* mentioned in the *Mirat-i-Ahmadi*,[21] as one of the sources of state income in Gujarat. It meant the custom duty on cloth, and this meaning comes out clearly from its popular title, *mahal-i-sada panj*, or the branch of 5 per cent because in Aurangzeb's reign the rate of duty on goods sold was 5 per cent for the Hindus, 3½ per cent for the Christians and at first 2½ per cent, then nothing for the Muslim traders.

D. Offices or Departments of Administration and Court Life

Band-room (*naqqar-khana*), artillery (*top-khana*), including all classes of fire arms and munitions. The Marathas had a separate store for gun powder, called *daru-khana*, buildings department (*imarat-khana*), records (*daftar-khana*), Emperor's chapel (*ja-namaz-khana* or *tasbih-khana*), store room for heirless property (*kotha-i-baitul mal*), purchase department (*ibtia-khana*). The Marathas had a *saudagari kosh* to designate this. Free food kitchen (*bulghur-khana* or usually *langar-khana*), school (*talim-khana*), in Firuz's time called *ilm khana*. A Marathi historian translates *talim khana* as the wrestling school. Department of hire and wages (*kiraya wa ajura*), games (*chaughan, chaupar*). In the seventeenth and eighteenth centuries there was a department called *bewa-khana* for the maintenance of widows of the Emperors, who lived in Sohagpura suburb of Delhi.[22]

E. The Emperor's Personal Service

Kitchen (*matbakh* or *bawarchi khana*), drink or butlery (*abdar khana*). Some Persian works read *sharbat khana*, some *sharabi khana*, but the latter term here means wine seller. The Marathi histories name *sharbat khana* and also *sharabi khana*. Fruits (*mewa khana*), *bhanda khana* (large earthen pots), *sahat khana* (conservancy or latrine), store of kauris or small shells to serve as the lowest small change, *khar muhra khana, charkhi khana*, store of fire wheels, *majuma khana* (miscellaneous).

The five (*maqa-khana, bhanda khana, sahat khana, kharmuhra khana* and *charkhi khana*) are given in the *Zawabit* which contains, in addition, nine illegible names of karkhanas. The Marathi histories add the following three:

Ambar khana or granary, *zarayat* or *jins khana* (this *jins khana* would correspond to the *ajnas* department in the Mughal empire, that is, the store of things from which the mansabdar were supplied as part payment in kind), theatre or *natak khana*, besides the *sahat khana* and *sharbat khana* already noticed under other heads. The printed Persian text of Afif's *Tarikh-i-Firuz Shahi* gives nothing new except *shakra kh na* and *zarad khana* (which has been corrected to *nugra* and *zardoz* respectively) and *rikab-khana* and *tashtdar khana* meaning the stores of trays and ewers, which are included by the *Zawabit* in the kitchen department. In the *Akhbarat-i-darbari-i-muala* there are found three other names, *shora khana, bulbali khana* (department of singing birds)[23] and what looks like *ilur khana* which may be a mistake for *yuz khana* (department of hunting leopards or dogs).[24]

The *karkhanajat*, says Abul Fazl, were more than a hundred in number and each was like a city, in fact, like a kingdom.[25]

The treasury stored valuables of all kinds, coins gold and silver, precious stones, and useful and ornamental things made of these, as well as articles of virtue prized for rarity or workmanship. Several departments were concerned with the royal table such as kitchen, *nanba khana* (bakery), *hawaij khana* (for pot herbs, seasonings, sweets etc.), *mewa khana* (fruitery), *abdar khana* (for water), *rikab khana* (pantry) and *aftabchi khana* (for ewers etc.). Nor far removed in function were *sharbat khana* and *tambul khana* (for betel leaves). Lighting up was in charge of *chiragh khana* (lamps) and *mashal khana* (torches), while *khusbu khana* (perfumery) supplied scents (*itr*, essences and oils).

A large number of well organized factories where articles were manufactured and stored in proper order also formed part of the household. These were karkhana factories properly so called. The mint stamped its seal on the current coin of the realm, and the *qur khana* produced arms and equipment of war. Another department engraved royal seals.

The following karkhanas were concerned with the weaving of textile fabrics and the needle work connected with them, *farrash khana* (for tents and carpets), *kurkyaraq khana*[26] and *tosh khana* (for dresses and stuffs of all kinds used for weaving apparel etc.), and the shawl department.

In other workshops skilled artists and artisans worked in metal, stone, ivory and other substances, and the upper reaches of art were approached in the work of goldsmiths and painters. Each department was conducted and supervised by master workers of established reputation.[27]

In the middle of the seventeenth century the French doctor Bernier saw these factories at work during his visit to the Mughal capital. Bernier has left an eyewitness elaborate account of these karkhanas which he saw them growing considerably during his stay in India. There is also available the list of karkhanas in the official manuals called *dastur-ul-amals* and certain other historical works composed at the end of the seventeenth century and later. State factories were also maintained in provinces at Burhanpur, Aurangabad and Kashmir. The state *karkhanajats* manufactured goods to meet the royal demands. State was thus the biggest entrepreneur. The Mughal emperors monopolized the best skilled workers.

The Muslim chronicles do not write much about industries and trade but lot of information is found in the pages of *Ain-i-Akbari* and the writings of European travellers though they cannot always be relied upon. Moreland who made a special study of the economic condition which prevailed under the Mughals writes that India was more advanced in matters of industry than Eastern Europe.[28] The state had karkhanas or royal workshops where silk was manufactured and other kinds of costly goods for the king and nobles. Abul Fazl writes that sometimes as many as 4000 weavers of silk alone worked in them.[29] The state supplied its own needs and became the principal producer and manufacturer, the chief patron and manufacturer of luxury goods, the principal banker and chief trader in the empire. From the account given by Bernier it appears that these karkhanas were large halls in which the artisans worked.

The system of palace workshops had expanded enormously under Akbar about the end of the sixteenth century. Abul Fazl mentions 'more than a hundred offices and workshops, each resembling a city or rather a little kingdom, and by unremitting attention of His Majesty, they are all conducted with regularity and are constantly increasing their improvement being accompanied by additional care and supervision on the part of His Majesty'.[30] The character of these karkhanas and the attitude of nobles towards the artisans employed in them is brought out by Bernier in a well known passage. He says: 'Workshops, occupied by skilful artisans would be vainly sought for in Delhi, which has very little to boast of in that respect. This is not owing to any inability in the people to cultivate the arts, for there are ingenious men in every part of Indies. Numerous are the instances of pieces of workmanship made by persons destitute of tools, and who can scarcely be said to have received instructions from a master. . . . The rich will have every article at cheap rate. Sometimes they imitate so perfectly articles of European manufacturer that the difference between the original and the copy can hardly be imagined. When an omrah or mansabdar required the services of an artisan he sends to the bazar for him, employing force, if necessary, to make the poor man work; and after the task is finished, the unfeeling lord pays, not according to the value of the labour, but to his own standards of fair remuneration, the artisan having reason to congratulate himself if the 'korah' (whip) has not been given in part payment. . . . The artists therefore who arrive at any eminence in their art are those only who are in the service of the king of some powerful omrah and who work exclusively for their patron'.[31]

Large halls are seen in many places called *karkhanays*. Bernier testifies their existence. He writes that within the fortress, 'Large halls are seen in many places called karkhanas or workshops for the artisans. In one hall the embroiders are busily employed, superintended by a master. In another you see goldsmiths, in a third painters, in a fourth varnishers in lacquer work, in a fifth, joiners, turners, tailors, and shoe makers; in a sixth, manufacturers of silk, brocade and those fine muslins of which are made turbans, girdles, with golden flowers, drawers worn by females, so delicately fine as frequently to wear out in one night. This article of dress which lasts only a few hours, may cost ten or twelve crowns, and even more, when beautifully embroidered with needle work. The artisans repair every morning to their respective kar-kanays, where they remain employed the whole day; and in the evening return to their homes. . . . The embroiderer brings up his son as an embroiderer, the son of a goldsmith becomes a goldsmith, and the physician of the city educates his son for a physician. No one marries but in his own trade or profession and this custom is observed almost as rigidly by the Muhammadans as by the Hindus'.[32]

The royal karkhanas were found all over the country. Big centres were found in Kashmir, Lahore, Agra, Ahmedabad, Fatehpur and Burhanpur. The workmanship of Kashmir was renowned. Its palkis, bedsheets, trunks, inkstands, boxes and spoons were used all over India. But its shawls were superb. 'Great pains have been taken to manufacture similar shawls in Patna, Agra and Lahore but notwithstanding every possible care they never have the delicate texture and softness of the Kashmir shawls'.

The subedars of various subahs could not have maintained state factories of their own (except on a very small scale) as they were liable to frequent transfer. But they patronized the local products as they had to supply the emperor all the same with choice specimens of these.[33] As Manucci writes: 'The king and the princes keep officials in every one of these provinces whose business it is to put in hand the best goods that can be fabricated in each place with this object in view they keep an eye certainly upon what is being done in that respect'.[34] The development of Indian art industries under state patronage is thus described by Abul Fazl, 'His Majesty pays much more attention in various stuffs, hence Irani, European and Mangolian articles of wear are in abundance. Skilful masters and workmen have settled in this country to teach people an improved system of manufacture. The imperial workshops, in the towns of Lahore, Agra, Fatehpur, Ahmedabad, Gujarat, turn out many masterpieces of workmanship; and the figures and patterns, knots, and variety of fashions which now prevail, astonish experienced travellers. His Majesty himself acquired in a short time a theoretical and practical knowledge of the whole trade; and on account of the care bestowed upon them the intelligent workmen of this country soon improved. All kinds of hair weaving and silk spinning were brought to perfection, and the imperial workshops furnish all those stuffs which are made in other countries. A taste for the fine material has since become general and the drapery used at feasts surpasses every description'.[35]

The state karkhanas worked on lines of large scale industries in which the raw material, the tools and implements, and the workshop was provided by the state. The worker who was the real producer was concerned only with the wages he received and had nothing to do with the consumption of the goods produced by him. They could not develop into real commercial factories. The karkhanas cared to produce the commodities more according to the taste of the Emperors which displayed the skill of the workmen. Though accounts of the costs involved in their production were properly maintained it was not a factor to decide production cost. The state had no dearth of finance and the emperors had no end to their fancy and refinement of taste. Under the circumstances these karkhanas could never develop into commercial industries, on the contrary their existence depended on the choice and taste of the emperor and the state requirements. As a result of this with the decline of the Mughal Empire these karkhanas also declined.

Karkhanas at Lahore

Numerous industries flourished at Lahore and skilled artisans in different kinds of crafts abounded. The carpet weaving karkhanas, produced[36] silken, woollen, cotton and mixed goods both plain and flowered. The bordered woollen carpets were specially famous or those were regarded superior in texture to the woollen material known as *saqarlat-i-firingi.*[37] The English factors occasionally invested in the Lahore carpets.

The state extended its patronage to manufacture and Lahore was a great centre of handicrafts where 'art or crafts was practised'.[38] Elaborate arrangements were made for importing raw materials. Cloth was also manufactured by private concerns as for instance shawls and carpets at Lahore. There were more than a thousand workshops of shawls in Lahore only. A kind of shawl called *mayan* is chiefly woven which consists of silk and wool mixed. As a matter of fact it was not a regular shawl at all because it was used for *chiras* (turbans) and *fotas* (loin bands) etc.[39] Coarse varieties of woollen goods were also produced and 20 kinds of Lahore woollen stuffs were on sale in the Agra market. The silk industry seems to have been in a flourishing state here as it turned out brocades and velvets which again were on sale in the Agra market. The cotton goods, ormesins, aljaks, embroidered goods and painted stuffs were specialities of Lahore. In addition bows, arrows, swords, saddles and shoes were produced here in large quantities.[40] Ships and boats too were built here.[41] Agra manufacturers too turned out a variety of goods. Amongst the textiles, carpets occupy the most important place though cotton goods too were produced. Silken stuffs and very fine cloth of gold and silver were woven for turban lace or other adornments for women.

Besides this, brocaded velvet,[42] silk, cotton cloth[43] and woollen stuffs[44] were also prepared. Sialkot, Bajwara and Sultanpur were also famous for embroidery. *Mansinghi* and silken paper of very fine texture, white, clean, and durable was produced at Sialkot. Many kinds of *bafta, chira, fotah, sozni, adsaka*, table cloth, tray covers, small tents with figures were also manufactured there.

Gujarat a city of the Punjab which had soon grown up into a great industrial town by the time of Aurangzeb became a great manufacturing centre famous for swords, Jandhars and embroidery. To create demand for the home industry Akbar had ordered that 'people of certain rank must purchase certain articles'. The value of these articles depend upon the cost-lines of the material as well as on the artistic skill spent upon them, so these crafts, could never become popular in spite of the active imperial patronage.

The manufacture of velvet, embroidered with gold or silver in the royal karkhana at Ahmedabad deserves special mention, because beautiful pavillions made of this rich material were sent from this city to the imperial court at Agra. In 1635, Sipahdar Khan who had been newly appointed as viceroy of Gujarat, forwarded to the emperor a magnificent present as *peshkash*, the details of which are thus given in the *Mirat-i-Ahmadi*:

'On the day of the Nauroz (New Year), Hizri 1044 (AD 1635) a velvet pavillion, woven with gold, prepared at the royal factory in Ahmedabad, on which the expert artisans of Gujarat had exhibited all their diversified skills which had pillars of gold and silver and which had cost one lakh of rupees, was erected in front of the royal palace. On the same Nauroz day, the emperor sat on *Takht-i-Taus* (the Peacock Throne) made at a cost of one crore of rupees'.[45] On the occasion of the inauguration ceremony of Delhi fort, gorgeous canopy (*aspak dal badal*) prepared in the royal factory at Ahmedabad, measuring 70 *gaz* by 45 *gaz*, and costing a lakh of rupees, was raised by 3000 active *farrashes.*[46]

Reference made by historian Ali Muhammad Khan in the *Mirat-i-Ahmadi* is indicative of the high reputation and primacy enjoyed by Gujarat throughout the Mughal period among all the Imperial Provinces not only because of the fertility of the soil but also by virtue of the excellence of its manufacturers of silk and brocades. In the province of Gujarat 'the beauty and ornament of India, all kinds of fine arts and crafts were flourishing and that the articles made in the royal karkhanas at Ahmedabad were rich, splendid and lustrous and of proper weight'.[47]

In the *Ain-i-Akbari* Abul Fazl speaks of the existence of various 'state workshops' in Akbar's palace at Agra at the end of the sixteenth century. He is particularly enthusiastic about the weavers' shops in which master craftsmen produced all sorts of textiles. The city of Agra was renowned for its wide range of economic activities which included commerce, in land and foreign made industries and handicrafts. Agra remained one of the biggest commercial centres under the Mughals. According to Sujan Rai, author of the *Khulasat-ut-Tawarikh*, 'articles of seven divisions of the globe are brought and sold here'.[48] Monserrate mentions that every necessity of human life could be obtained in the markets of Agra including articles which have to be imported from distant corners of Europe.[49] Bernier describes the markets being well supplied with all goods and separate market for every commodity.[50] Agra was also a principal centre for precious stones such as pearls and rubies, gold and silver were used in making exquisite jewellery by very skilled goldsmiths. Pelsaert describes a huge market where horses, camels, oxen, tents, cotton goods and many other things were sold in the morning.[51]

Agra was not merely a trading centre. Ample evidences point to its teeming with local industries and flourishing crafts. According to Abul Fazl, the masterpieces of workmanship of Agra astonished experienced travellers.[52] In his *Memoirs* Jahangir says: 'Inhabitants of Agra exert themselves greatly in the acquirements of crafts . . .'.[53] It was the textile industry on which the fame of Agra rested chiefly. Cotton, silken and woollen cloth of different types was manufactured in large amounts. Manucci mentions the manufacture of cloth of extreme fineness incorporating gold and silver threads used for turbans and laces and other adornments for women. In addition to textile the manufacture of carpets was an important industry. 'Carpets woven in moderate quantities and can be obtained to order, fine or coarse as required'.[54]

Another important industry was metallurgy. Besides articles of silver and gold, those of copper, iron and brass were manufactured in Imperial workshops for domestic use by talented artisans in Agra. Thevenot mentions child labour being used for metal industries.[55] The brass rings were manufactured in Agra and chemicals were used to dissolve the brass.

The conquest of southern states necessitated the establishment of centres at various cities like Burhanpur and presumably at Bijapur and Golconda.[56] The most remarkable form of large scale production in the medieval Deccan as in other parts of India was the number of karkhanas established by kings in their capital to manufacture and store arms, ammunition, robes, furniture, ornaments and so on as well as to construct the buildings which were all required by them and their nobles. As they were not meant for commodity production, they did not always represent the general industrial development of the country but they certainly indicated the technical skills and organizational sophistication of the age. In Golconda for instance Qutb-Shahi kings used to collect excellent workmen, who included a number of workers on precious stones and were kept too busy at the karkhanas to do any work for anybody else.[57] In Bijapur, the head of the royal household though technically incharge of private affairs of the sultan wielded considerable influence on the administration. The royal bodyguards and slaves functioned under his supervision. There were many karkhanas or workshops in Bijapur which manufactured articles required by the king, the army and other departments of the state.[58] High standard of skill at the karkhanas was symbolized by the famous canon called *Malik-i-Maidan* produced at Ahmadnagar, although the organization of such royal factories as well as the method of recruitment of workers is not at all clear for the seventeenth century. At the Golconda court guns, muskets, expensive arms and cloth etc. were produced.[59] These workshops were natural in the sense that they were concerned with the immediate consumption of the court, the nobles, the army and not connected with the market. The labour in such workshops might be compulsory to some extent. It seems that this form of production did not develop much in south India which may perhaps be explained with reference to the limited resources commanded by the south Indian rulers in comparison with the Mughal emperors. The Sultan of Golconda himself had to look after the affairs of the karkhanas. Desirous of going to the sea coast, the Sultan ordered Janab Asaf-dauran Mir Muhammad to collect and arrange for the goods of the karkhanas and all requisites of the journey and to settle the consequential administrative problems for reasons of safety. The Sultan ordered that several thousand excellent *banduqchis, naikwars* and *kotwals* should be kept ready that the heaps of food articles be prepared, that the *top khana* be rebuilt. Reaching Weyoor the Sultan ordered Mir Muhammad to go along with Chahur Khan, the Subedar of *farrash khana* and other karkhanas towards the port and set up the tents. Mir Muhammad offered lavish praises and thanks for the Sultan's favours. The Sultan accepted the *peshkash* and then visited a salt karkhana. He also met one Malik Alamas, an old *malik* and an important officer of the kingdom acting as *havaldar* of some karkhanas, viz. *sarkar-i-imarat* (government building), *zarrad khana* (armours shop), *zargar khana* (goldsmith's department) and *top khana* (artillery). The Golconda state like the Mughal Empire had its karkhanas for supplying its needs.[60]

Masulipatam, long in the Golconda kingdom, was the house of many artisans skilled in calico printing and there are letters in which Aurangzeb, then viceroy of the Deccan, requests that some of these artisans might be sent to work in the state factory at Delhi or Agra.

The establishment of the Kasim Bazar unit might be regarded as a development of some importance in the emergence of the large scale production in Mughal Bengal. This was not simply because of the size of the unit, though that certainly was an important element. Manufacturing production on this scale under one roof on a regular wage employment basis was rare in Mughal India.[61] The imperial and other karkhanas were not fully comparable to the Dutch Unit for two reasons. First, the goods manufactured in the karkhana were intended almost exclusively for use by the royalty, the nobility, rich merchants and others and for the army rather than for sale in the market. Second, at least some of the big karkhanas appear to have been operated on the basis of under paid drafted labour rather than with free contract labour.[62] Both these factors make the karkhanas quite different from the Dutch silk manufactory. Bernier also gives the reference of that at Kasim Bazar. The Dutch had employed seven or eight hundred workmen in their karkhana as was also done by the Englishmen and other merchants.[63]

It is quite clear from *Buddhi Vilas*[64] that Jaipur was not only a flourishing market place, it had also many industries and handicrafts. The book also mentions that there were 36 karkhanas in the city (it had been adopted from the Mughal pattern). Many of the karkhanas or departments were government factories which met the demand for arms, weapons, jewellery, cloths etc. of the palace. Others were stables for elephants, camels, horses, cows etc. Some of the karkhanas were meant for the supply of the daily victuals like food, *pan*, etc. or for the supply of medicines, perfumes, etc. Amber was another important centre where its rulers in the eighteenth century had made elaborate arrangement of the karkhanas organized largely on the Mughal pattern.[65]

Karkhanas of the Marathas

A karkhana, according to Dowson, is a royal establishment while to Jadu Nath Sarkar it is a factory. The Maratha historian Ram Chandra Pant classified even the *zenana* as a karkhana. Dowson's translation, however, seems to be quite appropriate. The eighteen karkhanas were:[66] *khajina* (cash), *jawahir khana* (jewel store), *ambari khana*[67] (elephant trappings), *sharbat khana* (medicines), *top khana* (artillery), *daftar khana* (record department), *jamdar khana* (public treasury containing all sorts of coins), *jirat khana* (agriculture), *mutbakh khana* (kitchen), *ashtar khana* (camels and their trappings), *naqar khana* (band), *talim khana* (gymnasium), *pil khana* (elephant sheds etc.), *farash khana* (carpets, tents and accessories), *abdar khana* (drink), *shikar khana* (game, aviary, chess and allied materials), *daru khana* (magazine), and *shahat khana* (conservancy department).

List of karkhanas as compiled from *Raj Vyavhar Kosh*:[68] *khajina* (treasury where the cash is kept), *pote* (treasury where from payment is made), *jawahir khana*, *mudbak khana*, the *mudbakhi* or cook and taster, *ruchigraha* (are mentioned in this connection), *abdar khana*, *jalasthana* (literally water department, not only drinks but intoxicants like tobacco and opium on the one hand and musk, otto, essence of flowers and scented oils on the other are mentioned in this department), *sharab khana* (wine store); the officer incharge was the *sharabdars,* (*tambul* or betel leaf and its accessories are mentioned in this connection), *Dawa khana* (dispensary), *shikar khana* (aviary), *farrash khana* (the department of carpets, tents etc.). The officer incharge was styled *havaldar, jirat khana* (armoury). No separate *top khana, daru khana* is mentioned but in the list of arms and armours given in connection with this department *top* (artillery) and *daru* (gun powder) are mentioned. *Talim khana, pil khana, mahavats* or elephant drivers, elephant trainers and elephant keepers are mentioned in this department. *Paga* (stables), *bahili* (chariots), *shutur khana* (camel stables), *alam khana* (band and music), *ambar khana* (granary). This department is mentioned under *durgavargah* or forts and herein probably lies the distinction between *kothi* and *ambar khana imarati*. This department is also mentioned under the forts. Karkhanas as compiled from Chitnis[69] were: *pil khana, ambar khana, naqar khana, top khana, sharbat khana, abdar khana, shutur khana, farrash khana, shikar khana, talim khana, jawahir khana, mudbakh khana, shile khana, sharab khana, gadi khana* (conveyance), *jinas khana* (stores), *daftar khana* (secretariat), *nat khana* (music etc.). Chitnis says that Shivaji had about 300 to 350 elephants, about 1000 to 1500 camels, 2000 to 4000 cows and 5000 buffaloes. A glance at the list mentioned here will show that the Maratha karkhanas and those of the Mughals were really speaking state departments and not state owned or state controlled factories. There were 18 karkhanas which Shivaji found it necessary to organize for administrative purposes. These were: *khajana, jawahir khana, ambar khana, sharbat khana, top khana, daphatas khana, jamdar khana,*[70] *jirat khana, kudbakh khana, ushtar khana, naqar khana, talim khana* (gymnasium),[71] *pil khana, farrash khana, abdar khana, shikar khana, daru khana, shahat khana.*

The terms of these eighteen karkhanas are of Persian extraction first organized in Shivaji's time and continued down to the close of the Peshwa period. Most of them in all probability copied from Muslim originals (Mrs Beveridge tells us that most of them had Persian synonyms). The treasury (*khajana*) of *Sabhasad*, the mint (*tanksal*), the harem (*darune sabhasad*), the *farrash khana*, the *abdar khana*, the imperial kitchen (*mudbakh khana*), the arsenal, the elephant stables (*pil khana*), the *gau khana* or cow sheds are mentioned in the *Ain* as forming different departments. A Mir Shikar[72] is mentioned and the mention of hunting leopards and falcons under the same *Ain* leaves but little doubt that here we find the origin of Shivaji's *shikar khana, Sabhasad*, unlike Abul Fazl, gives no detailed account of these departments. But so far as *shikar khana* is concerned the necessary information can be fortunately called from a much later work *Peshwa Bakhar*. In the *Shikar Khana* of the second Madhava Rao, there were 7 or 8 talking mynahs and talking green parrots. There were several *chaudols* (the pyramid crested wood lark), several ducks cormorants, several pairs of peacocks, and hundred or two hundred deer, hunting leopards, tigers and rabbits.[73] An adequate number of keepers were appointed to look after animals. This *Bakhar* also tells us that these leopards were used for hunting. Although this small menagerie offers but a poor comparison to the grand hunting department of Akbar consisting of 100 of animals and birds, yet there is no doubt that the Peshwa's *shikar khana* was an imitation of that of the Mughal Empire.

The chiefs were to collect *chauth* from the territories assigned to them; they could if they liked extend their activities further in their immediate neighbourhood. They were to make a stipulated contribution to the royal treasury and to meet the expenses of some of the karkhanas or royal establishments. During the eighteenth century many of the karkhanas of the Maratha government seem to have been worked by means of forced labour (*vethbegar*) of artisans of different kinds. For the construction of government buildings a certain number of carpenters, brick-makers, masons and brick-layers were requisitioned from the districts and sub-districts for the period of eight to fifteen days per annum. Similarly government stables acquired necessary labour through forced services of leather workers, rope makers, saddle makers and so on from various regions for fifteen days to two months a year. These forced workers were sometimes paid a small amount of cash or grain.[74]

References

1. The word karkhana was used in a very wide sense in contemporary sources, both Persian and Maratha such as animal stables, stores of articles of food and drink besides true manufactories or workshops where raw materials were converted into consumable articles.
2. W.H. Moreland, *India at the Death of Akbar*, pp. 172-74.
3. Ibid., pp. 186-87.
4. Tapan Raychaudhuri and Irfan Habib, ed., *The Cambridge Economic History of India*, Vol. I, pp. 286-87.
5. *Tuzuk-i-Jahangiri* (tr.), Vol. I, p. 215.

6. A.I. Chicherov, *India: Economic Development in the 16th-18th Centuries*, pp. 182-85.
7. *Ain-i-Akbari* (tr. Blochman, Delhi Reprint, 1977), Vol. I, pp. 93-94.
8. It is a double plural of the Arabic word *bait*, a house.
9. *Ain-i-Akbari* (text), i, p. 4.
10. Ibn Hasan, *Central Structure of the Mughal Empire*, p. 235.
11. Jadunath Sarkar, *Mughal Government*, pp. 122-23.
12. *Zawabit-i-Alamgiri*, Br. Museum Or. 1641, 15a.
13. Jadunath Sarkar, *Mughal Administration*, p. 7.
14. Bernier, *Travels of the Mogul Empire*, pp. 128, 292.
15. Abdul Aziz, *The Imperial Treasury of the Mughals*, pp. 1-2.
16. *Zawabit-i-Alamgiri*, MS (British Museum, now British Library, London), Or. 1641, f. 132b. For further details see Jadunath Sarkar, *Mughal Administration*, p. 125.
17. For the traditional number of 36, Shakir Khan, *Tarikh-i-Khani*, MS (British Museum, now British Library, London), Addl. 6585, f. 13b. *Farrash khana*—the store for carpets etc., *abdar khana*—water and drinks, *pil khana*—elephant stables. For further details see I.H. Qureshi, *The Administration of the Mughal Empire*, p. 59.
18. I.H. Qureshi, *The Administration of the Sultanate of Delhi*, pp. 69-70.
19. *Ain*, Vol. I, pp. 59-61, 102-15.
20. *Kir-kiraqi-Khanah.* At first explained by Blochman, *Ain*, Vol. I, tr. p. 93 as evidently meaning a wardrobe; but in his addenda (616) he derived it from the Turki words *kurk* and *yaraq*, meaning 'the fear of supplex', Beveridge (*Tuzuk*, i, 45n) accepts this meaning. In Shaikh Suleman Efendis 'Chagatai—Osmanli Worter buch (ed. by Kunos), *kirqu* is translated as sparrow-hawk. Forbes (Hindustani Dic., 544) explains *qirqira* as the damoiselle crane, ardea Virgo. But the author of *Mirat-i-Ahmadi* with his life long experience as a Mughal provincial *diwan* clearly explains *kirkiraq* as 'whatever is ordered by the emperor for his dress such as *chikan-dozi*, naqqashi (ii, 184). The last meaning therefore must be accepted.
21. *Mirat-i-Ahmadi*, Vol. II, p. 179.
22. *Dastur-ul-Amal-i-Aurangzeb*, MS (Br. Museum, now British Library, London), 6598, f. 55a. William Irvine, *Later Mughals*, i, 254n.
23. *Tashtdar*, a servant who pours water on the hands when washing an ewe-holder, is also called *aftabchi*. *Shora* is saltpetre for cooling drinks. The quarter of Delhi where the royal singing birds were kept and which contains the tomb of Sultana Raziya is still called *Bulbuli Khana*.
24. *Ain* (tr.), Vol. I, pp. 16, 50, 52, 55-57, 59, 68, 78, 93, 97, 113, 115, 123, 140, 151, 157, 168, 232, 292-96, 301, 306, 309-15.
25. Ibid., p. 12.
26. For its meaning and explanations see Abdul Aziz, *The Imperial Treasury of the Indian Mughals*, pp. 4-6.

27. As an example, by no means isolated, may be cited Behdal Khan, the *darogha* of goldsmith's workshop in Shahjahan's time, who was a celebrated lapidary, a great calligraphist and also an author of some respectable verse. See Muhammad Salih Kambo, *Amal-i-Salih* or *Shahjahan Nama* (Bib. Indica edn, Calcutta), Vol. II, pp. 89-90.
28. Moreland, op. cit., p. 172.
29. *Ain* (tr.), Vol. I, pp. 93-94.
30. Ibid., p. 12.
31. Bernier, op. cit., pp. 254-56.
32. Ibid., p. 259. Incidentally in the palace of Maharaja of Banaras, at Ramnagar, may still be seen excellent examples of such 'palace workshops' which have served not a little to maintain high standard of workmanship or many of the specialities of the district or workshops for the artisans.
33. Bernier, op. cit., pp. 128, 292.
34. Manucci, *Storia do Mogor*, Vol. II, p. 405.
35. *Ain*, Vol. I, pp. 93-94.
36. Ibid., p. 57; Manucci, op. cit., Vol. II, p. 399.
37. Anonymous, *Ajaib-i-Duniya*, I.O.L., Ethe, 720, 182b.
38. Father Monserrate, *The Commentary of his Journey to the Court of Akbar*, p. 160.
39. *Ain*, Vol. I, p. 98.
40. Manucci, op. cit., Vol. II, p. 399.
41. *Ain* (tr.), Vol. I, p. 290.
42. Ibid., p. 93.
43. Ibid., pp. 94-95.
44. Sujan Rai, *Khulasat-ut-Tawarikh* in Jadunath Sarkar, *India of Aurangzeb*, Calcutta, 1921, p. 95.
45. *Mirat-i-Ahmadi*, I, 209; Abdul Hamid Lahori, *Badshah Nama* (Text), I, pp. 78, 85-86.
46. *Delhi Fort, A Guide to the Buildings and Gardens* by G. Sandarson (Archaeological Survey of India), 1, 2. The original passage will be found in *Amal-i-Saleh* (Bib. 2nd), pt III, 6-7.
47. *Mirat-i-Ahmadi* (Text), I, p. 352.
48. Sujan Rai, op. cit., p. 23.
49. Monserrate, op. cit., p. 35.
50. Bernier, op. cit., pp. 292-93.
51. Pelsaert, *Jahangir's India* (tr.) Moreland and Geyl, Cambridge, 1925, p. 4.
52. *Ain*, I, p. 93.
53. *Tuzuk-i-Jahangiri* (tr.), p. 7.
54. Pelsaert, op. cit., p. 9.
55. S.N. Sen, ed., *Indian Travels of Thevenot and Careri*, New Delhi, 1949, p. 55.
56. Various services indicate that there was a karkhana at the court of Shah of Golconda in the seventeenth century.
57. S.N. Sen, ed., op. cit., p. 138.

58. Rafi-al-din, *Tadhkirat-al-muluk*, f. 93a; Muhammad Ibrahim Zubairi, *Basatin-al-Salatin*, pp. 131, 357; Tavernier, *Travels in India*, Vol. I, pp. 233-34.
59. Jagdish Narayan Sarkar, 'Some Aspects of the Qutb-Shahi Administration', *JBORS*, XXX, 1944, p. 194.
60. Jagdish Narayan Sarkar, *Life of Mir Jumla*, Calcutta, 1979, pp. 15, 25.
61. It is true that a large number of workers had to be assembled for constructing forts and other big buildings, as well as ocean-going vessels. But in these cases, as W.H. Moreland has pointed out, the organization brought into being did not survive the completion of the particular project for which it had been assembled. The royal mints in the various parts of the empire were undoubtedly fairly big units also. But it should be obvious that the implications of the production of coins by individuals employed on a salary basis by the government were somewhat different from those of the production of goods in a manufactory of the type of the Dutch silk-reeling unit at Kasim Bazar. (*India at the Death of Akbar*, pp. 173-74).
62. The English factors at Kasim Bazar, for example, reported the following in 1681: 'The tafftas at Maxudabad and Ameen Bazar have come in but very slowly these many days occasioned by the king's corconna–his forcing the weavers of all sorts to attend there to work in that manufactory because the Nawab wants a tent to be finished in time. We sent our Vakil to Bal Chand several times but he has been able to do nothing about it because he says that till the tent is finished he cannot release the weavers from working in the manufactory'. Diary kept at the Kasim Bazar factory at East India Company, Vol. 2, f. 1. There are similar references available in the records of the Dutch company. See particularly H.B. 11.1.1684 K.A. 1273, f. 427. At a later date, Abbe Raynal had this to say: 'It was a misfortune to them (the artisans) to appear too dexterous because they were then forced to work only for the government which paid them ill and kept them in a sort of captivity' (quoted in B.C. Allan, *District Gazetteer, Dacca*, Allahabad, 1912, p. 106). For details see Om Prakash, *The Dutch East India Company of Bengal (1630-1720)*, Delhi, 1988, p. 117.
63. Bernier, op. cit., p. 422.
64. Bakht Ram Saha, *Buddhi Vilas*. This work mainly deals with Jaina rituals. It was written in 1770 in Jaipuri dialect. It contains a description of contemporary Jaipur city. It also describes a conflict between Jainas and non-Jainas that took place at the time of writing of the book. It was published by the Rajasthan Oriental Research Institute, Jodhpur in 1964. *Buddhi Vilas*, a poetical work written in mixed Braja and Jaipuri languages gives one of the earliest descriptions of the foundation of Jaipur city and of its condition. It deals mainly with religious beliefs and rituals; it also contains the description of the rulers of Amber and Jaipur and what is more important, it describes the city of his time. Bakht Ram also mentions the fact that tax concession was one of the main incentives to many artisans and traders who were invited to come to the new city.

बहु विधि के कारीगर अनूप
परिवार सहित बुलवाय भूप
तिनको पुर में दीन्हो बसाय
हासिल सबका माफी कराय।।

Ashim Kumar Roy, History of Jaipur City, 1978, pp. 56-57

ऊँचे दरवाजे सुगम वाट।
कँचन सम जटित बने कपाट।।
लगते बनवाये चौक ईस।
तह रहे कारखाने छत्तीस।।
यह हुतो कारखाने तनीस।
पारसी नाम ता मध्य दोस।।
नृप कादि हिंदवी नाम कीन।
गृह संग्या यह ठानी नवीन।।

बुद्धि विलास, राजस्थान पुरातत्व मँदिर, जोधपुर १९६४ ई०

नँदकिशोर पारीक, जयपुर जोधा।
राजदरबार और रनिवास।।

जयपुर, १९८४, पीपी. ४५-४६

65. For Jaipur see Ashim Kumar Roy, *History of Jaipur City*, 1978, pp. 56-57; for Amber, Sumbul Halim Khan, 'Karkhanas of a Mughal Noble: Evidence from the Amber/Jaipur Records', *PIHC*, Delhi Session, 1991-92, pp. 432-38.
66. The eighteen karkhanas are referred to in K.N. Sane, ed., *Peshwanchi Bakhar*, p. 80, but the names given by Rao Bahadur Sane in the footnote are somewhat different.
67. In the text there is *ambar khana* which, according to Chitnis, means granary, but as *kothi* may also stand for a granary, it is *ambari khana* because the Muhammadans had something analogous. It should also be noted that Chitnis's division of these departments is somewhat different, for instance, *jamdar khana* is placed by him under the heading mahal. For his list see Malhar Rao Chitnis, *Bakhar*, pp. 75-76.
68. Raghunath Pandit, *Raj Vyavahar Kosh*. For details see S.N. Sen, *Administration of Marathas*, Calcutta, 1976, pp. 43-44.
69. S.N. Sen, *Administrative System of Marathas*, p. 45.
70. *Jamdar khana* was *vasangar* or royal wardrobe according to the *Raj Vyavahar Kosh*, p. 6.
71. Jadunath Sarkar translates *talim khana* as school (*Mughal Administration*, p. 194). Much has been relied on the *Raj Vyavahar Kosh*. Raghu Nath Pandit, the lexicographer, who had first-hand knowledge of these karkhanas translated *talim khana* as *mallashala* (p. 13), and the word is mentioned under the heading *shastra vargah*. The Marathi historian referred to by Jadunath Sarkar is therefore perfectly right when he calls it a wrestling school. The Marathas

did not blindly copy the Muslim institutions, though Shivaji was quite willing to borrow good institutions from all his neighbours. For instance, Shivaji's *daru khana* had no Muhammadan prototype (Jadunath Sarkar, *Mughal Administration*, p. 193) but the word is a literal translation of the Portuguese word *casadepolbora* into existence when in addition to *top khana* he decided to have a *daru khana* as well.

72. *Ain*, Vol. I, p. 282.
73. K.N. Sen, ed., op. cit., pp. 111-12.
74. H. Fukazawa, 'A note on the corvee system (*veth begar*) in the eighteenth century Maratha kingdom', Prof. D.D. Kosambi Commemoration Committee (pub.), *Science and Human Progress*, Bombay, 1974, p. 123.

3

Administration of the Karkhanas

The Mughal emperors maintained karkhanas or factories of their own for manufacture of articles of different kinds including cotton and silks. Within the wall of the fort was situated the office of karkhanas. The buildings round the courtyard were occupied by different imperial karkhanas. The Shah Mahal was furnished with carpets made in these karkhanas.

The Mughal period marked for advances in almost every department of human life. Babur had no time to devote to the industrial improvement of the newly conquered country. Yet it was he who founded the *Shuhrat-i-Am*[1] or public works department which later on played a very important part in the industrial development of the country. His son Humayun too had little leisure from his political preoccupation. Still he set the ball rolling by actively patronizing such artistic skill as was displayed in the construction of *qasr-i-rawan* (moving palace); *bagh-i-rawan* (moving garden) and *bazar-i-rawan* (moving bazars) which were built on boats and set in float on the river Jamuna.

The interest of the Mughal emperors in the workshops can be assessed from the following observations of Abul Fazl: 'His Majesty pays much attention to various stuffs . . . skilful masters and workmen have settled in this country to teach people an improved system of manufacture. The imperial workshops in the towns of Lahore, Agra, Fatehpur, Ahmedabad turn out many master-pieces of workmanship and the figures and patterns, knots and variety of fashions which now prevail astonish experienced travellers. His Majesty himself acquired in a short time a theoretical and practical knowledge of the whole trade, and on account of the care bestowed upon them the intelligent workmen of this country soon improved'.[1a]

Akbar patronized the public works department and personally inspected the karkhanas at times. He had a mechanical turn of mind and established workshops on a large scale within his palace enclosure.

During his reign fine textiles were manufactured at Agra and Fatehpur Sikri, good cotton cloth at Patan in Gujarat and at Brahmpur in Khandesh while Sonargaon was famous for its fine fabrics, the best and finest cloth made of cotton all over India. The furnished products produced under his patronage were such as are said to have done credit to the artisans of the twentieth century.

Abul Fazl refers to more than a hundred offices and workshops each resembling 'a city' or rather 'a little kingdom' all under the *diwan-i-buyutat*. Each workshop was concerned with the over-turn of a particular article and was supervised by one expert of the article concerned besides two officers and accountant and a *mushrif* and various other persons. Each was virtually animated by Akbar's personal interest, the range of which extended to different articles. Father Monserrate, an eyewitness and who was in Akbar's court (1580-82), writes that Akbar 'did not shrink from the craft of an ordinary artisan. Akbar, so devoted to building that he sometimes quarries stones himself, along with the other workmen. Nor does he shrink from watching and himself practising, for the sake of amusement the craft of any ordinary artisan. For this purpose he has built a workshop near the palace, where also are studios and workrooms for the finer and more reputable arts, such as painting, goldsmith work, tapestry making, carpet and curtain making and the manufacture of arms. He very frequently comes and relaxes his mind with watching at their work of those who practise these arts. In the karkhanas for cotton weaving, dyeing and printing, silk and shawl manufacture, Akbar is said to have introduced new designs or varieties but even acquired 'theoretical and practical knowledge' in some of the trades. In the arms workshop where many workmen were always engaged in the manufacture of muskets and swords Akbar introduced improvements in guns and matchlocks. In the mint constituting a distinct karkhana craftsmen belonging to trades exceeding twenty were engaged.[2]

The attention which Akbar paid to his karkhanas and to recruiting artisans from different countries and in training local men in every art, is recorded in the *Ain* under each industry and is noticed by Father Monserrate also.[3] For example, Abul Fazl says: 'formerly shawls were often brought from Kashmir, industry developed and received a new life. In Lahore alone more than one thousand karkhanas exist [prices varied from 150 gold mohars (Rs 1050) to Rs 6 per piece.]'[4]

During the reigns of Jahangir and Shahjahan the karkhanas flourished. There is abundant material scattered in the chronicles of the period to trace the gradual development of every industry under these three monarchs (Akbar, Jahangir and Shahjahan). In the seventeenth century Bernier observed many karkhanas in which several skilled workers were employed by the state. A sword, dagger and a knife were manufactured by Ustad Daud from a 160 tola meteorite stone by mixing it with common iron. The sword turned out to be very sharp, equal to the best tempered swords. Islam Khan, Mughal governor of Bengal, after transferring the capital from Rajmahal to Dacca, organized state wharves, warehouses and karkhanas with carpenters, blacksmiths and other artisans.[5]

Jahangir and Shahjahan continued the patronage. Under these two rulers arts and crafts, industries and commerce flourished in India as never before during the Muslim period. This is borne out by the cumulative testimony of native historians as well as foreign travellers who visited India during that period. Among others, Sir Thomas Roe has paid a well deserved tribute to the skill of Indian artisans of Jahangir's reign. Bernier who visited India during the reigns of Shahjahan and Aurangzeb was no less impressed by the affluence and efflorescence of fine arts and the industrial advance of the country. He dwells at length on the achievements of Kashmiris in arts and crafts, describes the manufacture of shawls in Kashmir, Agra, Patna and Lahore, of citizens in Masulipatam and gives a graphic description of the karkhanas where arts and crafts were learnt and plied.[6]

The chronicler of Shahjahan's reign says: 'The carpet industry of Kashmir and Lahore has developed to such an extent that woollen carpets are now prepared there at a cost of Rs 100 per yard[7] and the woollen carpets prepared in the karkhanas of the rulers of Iran are like a sack cloth before them. Now all the halls of the royal buildings are furnished with these woollen carpets'.

Shahjahan's attention to and patronage of home industry is incidentally revealed in a case of charities of his reign. Once, before his accession to the throne, and again during the illness of his favourite daughter Began Sahib (Jahanara Begum), he had taken a vow to send Rs 5,00,000 to Mecca. When he succeeded to the throne and similarly when his daughter recovered, he fulfilled the vow, but unlike Akbar and Jahangir he did not send the amount in cash but ordered that goods to the value of the said amount should be purchased at Ahmedabad and then sold in Hejaz and the amount received, together with the profit, should be distributed there in charity at the sacred shrine in accordance with the instructions given for the purpose. In this manner he served the double interest of industry and piety.[8]

Shahjahan presented a gorgeous amber candle stick within a gold mesh and inlaid with gems and diamonds prepared by royal artisans worth two and a half lakh rupees to the holy shrine at Mecca. Bernier in mid-seventeenth century has left a graphic eyewitness account of these karkhanas at Delhi, then in more developed form than before. 'Within the fortress large halls are seen in many places. . . . This article of dress which lasts only a few hours may cost 10 to 12 crores and even more, when beautifully embroidered with needle work'.[9]

During the reign of Aurangzeb, the number of these karkhanas decreased. It is suggested that he hated luxuries, although it cannot be proved conclusively. In fact the incessant wars greatly affected the state owned karkhanas as there was no peace and order in the country. There is also the information that Aurangzeb during his viceroyalty of the Deccan made continuous efforts to persuade the artisans of Masulipatam who were skilled in calico printing to migrate to Delhi or Agra and work there in the state karkhanas. Later on during the period of the later Mughals the position of the karkhanas did not improve.

Thus the system of maintaining the karkhanas by the central government not only fulfilled all the needs of the state at a low price, but gave an encouragement and impetus to different industries of the country and the improved works executed and articles manufactured in state factories must have served as models and furnished better designs to local artisans.

The Mughal emperors took interest in the proper maintenance of these karkhanas. The department of *khan-i-saman* was managed with the greatest care and regularity. He submitted the statement twice a year giving full description of the articles produced and the materials used and required in the production. At the behest of the emperor, the periodical exhibition of the manufactured articles was organized. Often the emperor rewarded the skilled workman whose article he liked most. Jahangir had a flair for copying anything which he saw manufactured in other countries from a painting to a dagger blade or handle.

The King's interference and vigilance reached still further, when the regulation required the valuable articles manufactured in the government workshops of the capital or provinces or purchased from outside to be exhibited in the darbar before the king. Weapons of war, articles of luxury or any useful thing, which either for its importance or workmanship, could interest the king, was produced before him. This procedure not only brought the skill and the workmanship of the country to the notice of the monarch, but the artisan also, who was produced before him. Thus the credit did not wholly go to the department and its high officers for every achievement but to the artisans as well, who were at times lavishly rewarded to original designs, superior skill and unusual workmanship. This completed the control and the supervision of the king over the department from its finances down to its inner working and output.

The most conspicuous case under Jahangir besides numerous other cases of a variety of articles appreciated and artisans rewarded, is that of a dagger, the hilt of which was made of *dandan-i-mahi* (fish's teeth) with black spots (*ablaq*). One of the quality products was sent by Shah Abbas to Jahangir for which he took a fancy and a search was made for fish's teeth of the same quality and shade throughout the country, and Jahangir says: 'I appointed several skilful men to go to Iran and Turan to look for them and to bring same from anywhere and any person, anyhow, and at any price'.[10] By chance one piece of great beauty and delicacy was found and purchased for a trifle in the city of Agra, and was entrusted to the artisan of the state karkhanas for making hilts. Jahangir has recorded his opinions about his artisans, their workmanship, and the reward he gave to them on this occasion. 'I ordered the Ustads (masters or experts) Puran and Kalyan, who had no rivals in the art of engraving (*khatim bandi*) to make dagger hilts of a shape that was approved at this time and has become known as the Jahangiri fashion. At the same time the blade and the sheath and fastenings were given to skilful men, each of whom was unique in his age in his art (*yaktayan-i-rozgar*). Truly, it was well carried out according to my wish. One hilt came out coloured in such a way as to create astonishment. It turned out of all the seven colours, and some of the flowers looked as if a skilful painter had depicted them in black lines round it with a wonder working pencil. In short, it was so delicate that I never wish it to be apart from me for a moment. Of all the gems of great price that are in treasury, I consider it the most precious . . .; the masters, who . . . had exercised great skill and taken great pains were rewarded. Ustad Puran with the gift of an elephant, a dress of honour, and a golden bracelet (*kara*) for the wrist and Kalyan with the title of *ajaib dast* (wondrous hand) and an increased mansab, a dress of honour, and a jewelled bracelet (*pahaunchi*), and in the same way, everyone according to his circumstances and skill received favours'.[11]

Mir-i-Saman

As regards the administration of the karkhanas, the whole of the household department was under the supervision of *Khan-i-Saman*. The term *Mir-i-Saman*[12] was not in use under Akbar. In the *Ain* his duties are not mentioned nor his powers defined. In the *Akbar Nama* Abul Fazl, however, made a reference to *Mir-i-Saman* but had not mentioned either his powers or duties.[13] However, under Jahangir the term *Mir-i-Saman* is maintained throughout the period of his reign and there is only one reference to the term *Khan-i-Saman* in the fifteenth year in the *Tuzuk* in connection with Mir Jumla's appointment to the post of *Khidmat-i-Samani*,[14] but when he was replaced by Afzal Khan in the 21st year the term *Mir-i-Saman* was again used.[15] Under Shahjahan the term *Mir-i-Saman* is used by all contemporary writers.

But so far as *Dastur-ul-Amals* are concerned, which were mostly drafted or copied in the reign of Aurangzeb, the term *Khan-i-Saman* predominates.[16]

Thus Ibn Hasan concludes that under Akbar this officer did not hold the rank and position which he did under his two successors, and the entire work associated with his office had not devolved upon him in that reign. In connection with the karkhanas, the *diwan-i-buyutat* is more conspicuous under Akbar, and it was later developments which placed him incharge of the whole department and settled his position in the administrative machinery, and in this capacity he came to be known as *Mir-i-Saman*.[17] In accounts of Jahangir's reign frequent mention is made of his duties, and everywhere he is referred to as *Mir-i-Saman* and not as *Khan-i-Saman*. Under Aurangzeb he again becomes *Khan-i-Saman* in the official regulations.

The supply department of the Mughals was intended not for purchase or store alone (as the karkhanas of Firuz Tughluq were) but to be the biggest manufacturing concern in the state. Under Akbar at first it was the *diwan-i-buyutat* who was more conspicuous in the department. But gradually he came to be incharge and commonly known as *Mir-i-Saman* under Jahangir and Shahjahan and as *Khan-i-Saman* under Aurangzeb and afterwards. As the chief executive officer of the supply department, the *Mir-i-Saman* was placed incharge of the internal working of the karkhanas or *buyutat*, including factories and stores, owned and managed by the state for its own purposes, not only in the capital but in every provincial capital as well as in different parts of the empire. He could appoint and dismiss the various officers (viz. superintendents, accountants, cashiers or any subordinate) of the karkhanas and palace departments.

Duties of the Khan-i-Saman

Being the second highest officer in the realm the *Khan-i-Saman* stood immediately below the *diwan*. He has been well described as 'really the *diwan* of expenditure'.[18] He is thus instructed about his work, 'Take over the cash balance and collected articles in the Household Department, which are kept under the seals of the late *Khan-i-Saman* at the time of his office and the seals of the mushrif and tahvildar; satisfy yourself that the stock agrees with the records, or else call upon them to make the deficit good.

'Keep with yourself one set of the records of expenditure per annum arranged under the heads of the different karkhanas (i.e. stores and state factories). Find out how many *khilats* (robes) are there in the *khilat-khana* and so on in every karkhanah. If the requisite stores are wanting, write out a statement of the expenditure (*saranjam*) necessary for supplying the want, apply to the proper authority, take from him a payment order on the *diwan* for the *saranjam* and make the things.

'In order that the *Khan-i-Saman* may be in a position to supply all articles that may be required, it is his business to buy them with government money or on credit from traders, and keep them ready, and deliver them to government at need at the market price. If he is a rich man himself, he ought to buy and stock the things, so that he may not have to beg to others at the time of need, but issue them after valuation at the market rate. Thus his master will have no occasion to be displeased at delay in supplying. If the *Khan-i-Saman* supplies his own things at the market rate, most probably government will make a saving by the transaction; but the clerks of the government will allege that he is selling things to the state at a profit; therefore, he ought to ask the emperor beforehand to advance him money to buy everything and stock it for supply when needed.

'Old and second hand stores should be sold to the army, after taking permission (of the emperor) and learning their current prices from a *muqim* (broker or appraiser). Keep the price-list signed by the *muqim* with yourself (for your defence).

'Buy beautiful things which are likely to prove agreeable (to the emperor) and keep them (for presentation on suitable occasions). On the two Ids and other festive occasions, keep the robes (of honour) and other customary official gifts ready (for issue) a month or two before the dates, so that you may not have to plead inability to supply when they are needed. Treat well and attach to yourself by the ties of gratitude artisans like goldsmiths, enamellers, die-carvers (for coins), net-weavers, plain workers in metal (*sadahkar*, a class of goldsmiths), etc., etc.'

The duties of a *Khan-i-Saman* are thus enumerated in the *Dastur*:

1. Attestation (of the salary-bills) of the workmen and menials from the monthly, yearly and daily rolls (of attendance) of those newly appointed as well as increment (in the salary) of the old ones.
2. First appointment, dismissal and posting of *daroghas, amins, mushrifs*, and *tahvildars* (of the various karkhanas).
3. Laying down rules for the work of the karkhanas and treasuries (of the household department).
4. (Writing) slips for hire and wages of labour.
5. Replying to the prayers of the managers of the karkhanas.
6. Issuing permits for the granting (of state houses) as reward and for allowing (nobles to lodge temporarily in) them.
7. Inspection of *nim-gosht* and *pao-gosht*.
8. Taking bond for money security from the menials and managers (of karkhanas).
9. Considering applications from the workshops and stores.
10. Taking care of the *nazar*, charity-fund, and presents.
11. Fixing the daily rations of cattle.
12. Permits for the loan of articles from the karkhanas.
13. Permits for the distribution of food (from the royal kitchen), its increase or decrease, and the letters of order (*akham*)—except the letters of the female apartments. These were to be signed first by the *Khan-i-Saman* and then by the *buyutat*.
14. Reply to the final presentation of accounts (*muhasibat*) concerning the recovery of state advances (*mutalibat*).
15. Escheat of property. If the order is to restore (to the officer under audit), then send a copy of the order to the office (of the *diwan*), so that his *tankha* may be paid according to it.

16. Things made to order (*farmaish*) of the emperor in the provinces.
17. Taking the income from the gardens and the rent from the shops and residential houses (belonging to the state).
18. Long sheets of letters from the karkhanas.
19. The *diaries* and *awarija* of the subahs as well as the *awarija* of the imperial camp are to be sealed without change.
20. Initial the petitions from the officers asking for advances and the granting of residences for alighting in, etc.
21. Attestation of the attendance of the *daroghas, amins, mushrifs* and *tahvildars* of karkhanas.
22. Appraising the different articles of *peshkash* (tribute and present) and *amual* (escheated personal property of dead mansabdars).
23. Attestation of the cash reward which appertains to the commanders of squadrons (*sahib-i-risalah*).
24. Distribution of porters among the different karkhanas.
25. Arrangements for the marriages of the princes.
26. The *tumars* (registers) of the cash realization of the amounts due on audit (*muhasibat*), should be sent by the auditors to the office of the *Khan-i-Saman*, and copies of them should be given to the office of the *buyutat*.
27. Plans of lodgings and buildings (belonging to the state).[19]

He was responsible not only for the production or manufacture, procurement or supply of every article required from luxury articles and jewels to weapons of war and artillery but also for their stock and inventory. He arranged for and listed points made by the emperor out of previous presents or out of the products of the karkhanas and also for supply to provincial government. He certified the delivery of an imperial reward, if not in cash. The marriage celebration of royal princes was supervised by him. He looked after royal food and tents and maintained animals of the army, transport and hunting.

In another sphere, the *Mir-i-Saman* also was considered subordinate to the *diwan*, but this was only a matter of precedence and formality. The *Mir-i-Saman* was dependent upon the wazir in financial matters only, he too had direct access to the monarch and, in all probability, represented the point of view of the *diwan's* office of the financial aspects of the administration or expansion of the *buyutat*. He was also responsible for the proper administration of the internal finances of the *buyutat*. He drew the salaries of the staff from the treasury and disbursed them. He also made out the estimates of the expenditure twice a year and obtained the sanction from the wazir and the monarch.[20]

Truly speaking the *Mir-i-Saman* was not only responsible for the efficient working of the *buyutat* but had other important duties as well. The menial staff of the palace and such household officers as were not on the state pay roll received their monthly or annual salaries on his certification. He appointed the superintendents, accountants, cashiers of the various karkhanas and the departments of the palace. He was responsible for seeing that the articles produced by the karkhanas were probably listed and stocked, the presents made to the emperor were represented by his office either from the stock of presents received previously or out of the produce of the karkhanas and needed by the provincial authorities, he had lists of precious articles in the treasuries. He further drew up statements about the income of royal gardens, shops and houses, he was also responsible for the realization of all dues from those who had leased such property. It was he who fixed the daily rations of the various animals in the royal menageries and aviaries. When the emperor ordered the award of a present, if it was not in cash, he certified its actual delivery, he was incharge of all celebrations of the weddings of the royal princes. When the property of an officer or dignitory was to be sequestered or taken into temporary custody, it was the duty of the *Mir-i-Saman* to do so. As many of these duties had their financial aspects, he had constant dealings with the *diwan* and was for this reason theoretically his subordinate.[21] *Mir-i-Saman* looked after the royal food and tents and maintained animals for the army, transport and hunting. Thus he was incharge of 'the whole expenditure of the household in both great and small things'. He depended on the wazir only in financial matters. But his subordination to the latter was formal for he could deal directly with the king in all matters.

Mir-i-Saman had to present to the king in the *Diwan-i-Am* or *Diwan-i-Khas* reports about karkhanas, the goods and the accounts, animals or royal stables, artisans of merit and get royal sanction for the half yearly budget. He disposed of state cases arising out of property of the department. His department registered the presents made to the king and supplied the goods manufactured in the karkhanas to the king for presents or to the provincial government.

The *Mir-i-Saman* enjoyed equal status with the *Diwan* and *Mir Bakshi* with whom he had close contact and put his seal besides their own farmans. Only influential and trustworthy persons could hold this important but delicate office. Successful *Khan-i-Saman* were often appointed wazirs as we find in the case of Afzal Khan, Sadullah Khan and Fazil Khan. The high position and heavy responsibilities of the post exposed him to the risk of imperial displeasure. So he was suitably advised by the manual of officers duties to be careful about taking charge of cash balance and stock of stores and keeping all articles likely to be required or to be presented ready for delivery to the government at market rates by taking advances or on credit from traders and keep the artisans well attached to him by good treatment (full details of his duties and instructions to him all to be found in the manual). He was assisted in the charge of his duties by a staff of officials. The respective duties of each of the officers can briefly be summarised thus: The Mir Saman as the head of the department dealt with its executive side, and exercised general supervision over the internal working of each branch. He had the power to take the initiative with regard to the appointment or dismissal of the *daroghas*, *mushsrifs*, and *tahvildars*, and the right to take disciplinary action against any of his subordinates whenever necessary. He dealt with all the affairs of the department and attended to the orders received in the karkhanas from the provinces. Important matters or big transactions were brought by him to the notice of the king, while he dealt himself with the rest.

The *Mir-i-Saman* and *diwan-i-buyutat* were jointly responsible for the management of karkhanas and the working of the department but in spite of the joint responsibility, the inner working and the details of procedure followed, reveal that the *Mir-i-Saman* had a somewhat higher position than the *diwan* of the department although the *diwan* cannot be considered his subordinate.

In the darbar both of them had a right to appear and put matters connected with their duties before the king, but the *Mir-i-Saman* had precedence and he had also a right to bring to His Majesty's notice whatever he thought necessary for his department, while it appears that the *diwan's* right was limited to placing the necessary papers before the king.[22]

Similarly the *Mir-i-Saman* occupied a higher status in putting his seal upon the farmans. He put his seal on the second fold together with the *diwan* (wazir) and the chief *bakshi*, while the seal of the *diwan-i-buyutat* was placed on the third fold.[23]

The division of functions and the work of the department also revealed the same difference of status. All important papers were required to be countersigned by the *Mir-i-Saman*. He was solely responsible for dealing with state cases connected with property under the control of the department. In cases of attachment of property, the *diwan* acted in cooperation with him.

As far as their status in accordance with their rank is concerned, there is very scanty material under Akbar, but both under Jahangir and Shahjahan the *Mir-i-Saman* decidedly occupied a higher status and enjoyed a much higher rank than the *diwan* of their department. The following list of the *Mir-i-Samans* of Shahjahan's reign shows the importance which the office had by that time acquired.

Name	Rank	
Allami Afzal Khan	4,000 *zat*	2,000 *horse*
Mir Jumla	4,000 "	2,500 "
Aqil Khan	2,000 "	500 "
Sadulla Khan	3,000 "	500 "
Aqil Khan (second time)	2,500 "	800 "
Mulla Ala ul Mulk	1,500 "	500 "
Later on Fazil Khan reached the rank of	3,000 "	800 "

But it is interesting to note that in spite of this difference in their official ranks, both of them reached the *vizarat* directly, and the *diwan* was at a disadvantage as compared with *Mir-i-Saman*.

Various Other Officers of Buyutat

The staff of every karkhana varied in accordance with the needs, for instance the *matbakh* or the kitchen would have chefs and cooks, whereas the library would employ calligraphists and painters.[24] At the head of every karkhana, however, there was a *darogha* or a superintendent, assisted by clerks and accountants.[25]

As regards the officers of the department besides *Mir-i-Saman* as the chief executive officer responsible for the successful working and the general supervision of the department there were various other officers who are briefly listed likewise:

Diwan-i-Buyutat

He was another officer of high rank, chiefly responsible for the financial side of the department. He was jointly responsible for the management of karkhanas and working of the department but not subordinate to the

Mir-i-Saman. The latter did not scrutinize the papers i.e. financial matters sent by the former. The former depended on the latter's decisions in non-financial matters. He was really subordinate to the wazir. Both could deal directly with *diwan* and the king. The characteristic Mughal system of balance of powers marked this department also. He was the registrar of the property of deceased persons for escheat and safeguarding it for the heirs. He allocated funds and distributed provisions to different karkhanas, fixed prices and prepared estimates of requirements.

Duties of Buyutat

Buyutat is the double plural of the Arabic word *bait*, meaning 'house'. In Mughal India *Diwan-i-Buyutat*, popularly always shortened into *buyutat*, was the title of an officer who registered the property of deceased persons in order to secure the payment of the dues of the state as well as to safeguard the property for the heirs of the deceased. In addition, he was in some respects an understudy of the *Khan-i-Saman*, as the following list of his duties[26] will show:

1. To allot money to the various funds or cash balances out of the treasury of general expenditure and of the karkhanas.
2. To escheat the property of deceased nobles in cooperation with the *Khan-i-Saman.*
3. To make provisions (*saranjam*) for the karkhanas.
4. (To fix) the prices of articles.
5. Estimating the (necessary) treasury of the karkhanas. Send the estimate of the monthly expenditure to the *Diwan's* office.
6. Daily accounts of the karkhanas accompanying the Emperor during his marches.
7. Endorsement of receipts (*qabuz*).
8. The *buyutat* should write the date on the descriptive rolls (*chihra*) of the menials.
9. On the report of branding of cattle, he should write 'Brought to the branding'.
10. (Rejection or sale of) old articles in karkhanas according to the suggestions received from the different karkhanas.
11. Fixing halting days for the cattle.
12. *Siaha* of *tankha* from the expenditure treasury. The advances to the menials (*bargandazes*) and cattle should be paid in the presence of the *buyutat* himself.

13. The slips (*chithi*) granting articles (*jins wa ajnas*) should be kept in the office of the *buyutat*.
14. The rooms of the karkhanas should be sealed with the *buyutat's* seal.
15. Grants (to) petty officials for food store (*zakhira*).
16. Ascertainment of the prices of the things in the purchase and other departments and their cash, under the seal of the *buyutat*.
17. The requisitions of the karkhanas to be signed first by the *buyutat* and then by the *Khan-i-Saman*.
18. The *siaha* of the expenditure and the summary grant (*sarasari tankha*) for food of the cattle should go to the *buyutat's* office, and thereafter be signed by the *Khan-i-Saman*.

Mushrif-i-Kul O Juz (literally accountant of the part and the head accountant of the department). He had a *mushrif* in each branch of the department. The *mushrif* of each branch kept the account in the form of daily entries of cash advanced, material supplied and work done. In the day to day working of the karkhanas regular log book type registers were maintained by the *mushrif* of the branch in which daily entries were made of cash advanced, materials supplied and the work done.

Darogha (Superintendent)

Each branch or karkhana had a *darogha* who dealt directly with the artisans of his branch, distributed to them their daily work and took charge of the material left in their possessions every day and handed over to *tahvildar*. Thus the *darogha* of every karkhana took the raw materials and the unfinished articles from the *tahvildar* and distributed them to the artisans. At the close of the day the *darogha* was to take back the articles in whatever stage they might be on that day and after noting the amount of work done deposit them with the *tahvildar*. The unfinished would be reissued the next day by the *darogha* and again handed over to the artisans. This process was repeated till the work on the piece was finished. On the basis of these regular entries after completion of the work calculations were made of the total expenditure in the shape of wages for total number of days taken for its completion and the expenditure on the raw materials on the basis of which the cost price of the article was fixed. The final reports indicated the cost of the article, the name of artisan and also the name of the *darogha* under whose supervision it had been executed.

Tahvildar (Cashier and Store Keeper)

Like the *darogha* each karkhana had a *tahvildar* who had charge of cash and material required for his branch. He kept the cash and stored the necessary stock of material for use. Thus *darogha* took money and material from the *tahvildar* and distributed them to the workmen under him. When a piece of work was completed, say a carpet or a jewellery, the cost of the material used and the wages paid to the artisan with reference to the time spent were calculated and noted as the cost price of the commodity by the *tahvildar*.

Mustaufi (Auditor)

He audited the accounts of the karkhanas, verified the expenditure with vouchers, prepared a statement, signed it himself, put it before the *diwan* of the department, and finally had the seal of the *Mir-i-Saman* put to it.

Darogha-i-Kacheri (Establishment Officer or Office Superintendent)

He was incharge of the general supervision of the establishment of the office. It was his duty to see that all papers and registers were taken from one officer to another properly. He was also to see that no one behaved rudely towards the clerks and the servants of the office. He locked the doors of the office with seal of the officer concerned and put his own seal on each. Papers from one officer to another passed through the officers. Thus he appears to have been the head of the clerical establishment of the entire department.

Nazir

The *nazir* does not seem to have had any specific powers and duties. He assisted the *diwan* of the department and helped him to revise and check the accounts before submitting them to the central audit office. He came in rank next to the *diwan* of the department. The post was created in the thirty-fifth year (AD 1591) of Akbar's reign and a very efficient man, Qazi Ali Baghdad, was appointed to it. He had served as a *naib sadr* in the early part of the reign and besides various other duties he had also acted for some time as a joint *diwan*. The reason for the creation of this post is given by Abul Fazl in the following words:

'Though Sadiq Khan was a skilful *Mir-i-Saman* and Khwaja Ghiyasuddin Beg was the *diwan*, yet, as in every department there was much income and expenditure, the more help there was the better for the work'.[27] Thus he was intended to be an assistant and a help to the *diwan*.[28] According to *Dastur*, the *nazir* should go through whatever work is done by the *diwan* of the department and put his seal on it. In this capacity he becomes a revising officer to guarantee greater efficiency and accuracy. As far as the actual working of the department was concerned, he was connected more with the financial side than with the executive. He was decidedly below the *diwan* in rank and status, and nowhere does he appear as his equal.

It is interesting to note that under both Jahangir and Shahjahan there are several references to the *daroghas* and the *tahvildars*, who had the opportunity to appear before the king and place before him the articles of their karkhanas, whenever so required, but the *nazir* of the department who was concerned with the official routine is nowhere mentioned. He was neither prominent by the nature of his duties like the *darogha* and the *tahvildar*, nor conspicuous by his position like the *Mir-i-Saman* and the *diwan*.

The respective duties of each of the officers can briefly be summarized thus. The *Mir-i-Saman* as the head of the department dealt with its executive side, and exercised general supervision over the internal working of each branch. He had the power to take the initiative with regard to the appointment and dismissal of the *daroghas, mushrifs*, and *tahvildars*, and the right to take disciplinary action against any of his subordinates whenever necessary. He dealt with all the affairs of the department and attended to the orders received in the karkhanas from the provinces. Important matters or big transactions were brought by him to the notice of the king, while he dealt himself with the rest.

The *diwan* looked to the financial side, and in this capacity he dealt with the *nazir, mustaufi* and the *mushrif*. In all other matters also, he attended to the needs of the karkhanas but first brought them to the notice of *Mir-i-Saman* and according to the rules, acted in consultation with him. As in financial matters the *Mir-i-Saman* simply put his seal on papers which reached him through the *diwan* and the *mustaufi*, and did not go into the details so in all other matters the *diwan* relied upon the decisions of the *Mir-i-Saman*. The dual character, a sense of joint responsibility, and the balancing of powers, so conspicuous in every branch of the Mughal system, was maintained here. Though the powers of both the chief officers of the department were clearly defined, no strong barriers were raised, and the intermingling of the two sides of the administration was maintained to the advantage of the department.

The *nazir* had no distinct powers and duties and he worked in co-ordination with the *diwan*. His presence simply facilitated the work of revision and the checking of accounts before their submission to the central auditing department.

The *mustaufi* demanded the necessary papers, particularly the daily entry book and the abstract of daily cash receipts and disbursements from the *tahvildar* and *mushrifs* of each branch verified the accounts item by item and got them signed by the *diwan*. If there was anything of which the *diwan* needed an explanation, he noted it with his own pen.

After the sanction of accounts, he prepared sheets for the demand of money, and taking the signatures of the *diwan* handed them over to *darogha* of the *kacheri* so that the amount might be realized.

It was the duty of the *diwan* to see that no hardship accrued to anyone of his departments in this connection. He was responsible for all such transactions and accounts which passed through him.[29]

The *mustaufi* also prepared a statement about the income and expenditure of the department under each *tahvildar* and a report on the general condition of the affairs and accounts of each karkhana.[30]

The duties of the *tahvildar* and the *darogha* can only be gathered from the forms given in *Dasturs*, for recording the daily work done in each branch and payments made for the same.

The *tahvildar* kept the necessary amount of money for meeting the requirements of his branch. He also kept in stock the material needed for the work done in that particular branch. The *darogha* took money or materials from him and distributed them to the artisans under him. Entries were made of such transactions everyday, and at the close of the day, the *darogha* noted the work done by every artisan. If the work in hand was, for example, a piece of jewellery or a piece of cloth, the *darogha* would note the piece finished at the close of the day, and return it to the *tahvildar* together with the remaining material. Thus as the work proceeded day by day the material supplied and the quantity used were entered by the *darogha* and the *tahvildar*, and when a particular piece was finished, the price of the material together with the wages of the artisan for the number of days taken by him to complete it fixed the cost price of the piece, and a final report was prepared that such and such an article was prepared at the cost by such an artisan under the supervision of such and such a *darogha*.

The same process was followed in every branch, whether it were the kitchen where provisions in grains were supplied, or the building department which noted the number of bricks, the size of stones and the quantity of other materials used in an area of some particular dimensions, everyday.

Thus the *tahvildar* and the *darogha* dealt directly with the artisans. The one kept the cash and stored the necessary stock of material used, while the other distributed it to the artisan and supervised his work. The *mushrif* of the same branch wrote the account day by day, in the form of daily entries of cash advanced, material supplied and work done. The accounts were submitted to the *mustaufi* and the *tahvildar*, the *darogha* and the *mushrif* were jointly responsible.

The *darogha* of the *kacheri* formed a connecting link between these and the other high officers, and was responsible for the dispatch of all necessary papers to their respective destinations at each stage.

The King and the Karkhanas

The relationship between the karkhanas and the Mughal emperors centred around three ways, which taken together covered each and every aspect. Firstly the department submitted its financial statement and needs twice every year to the government. These were ultimately placed before the king and sanction was issued in the form of a farman on which the royal seal was placed.[31]

Such farmans which were issued for financial grants only were called *barats*[32] as distinguished from other farmans of a general nature. These statements included all financial transactions of the department–sales, purchases, stocks stored and expenditure incurred on regular establishment, temporary hands, and workmen with daily wages. They gave the balances with each *tahvildar*, together with the demands of each branch of the department, as submitted by it through the *diwan* of the *buyutat*.[33]

The king's duty did not end with the sanction of grants and the inspection of the financial statement every sixth month but it formed a part of his daily routine. Secondly, the *Mir-i-Saman* and the *diwan* appeared in the darbar every day, like other heads of departments, and represented important cases connected with their duties.[34] It was on such occasions that the king placed his own orders with the karkhanas, looked into the orders of other departments, learnt of all big orders placed by other and approved the prices fixed by the department.[35] Thirdly, some of these manufactured or purchased articles were presented in the court before the king, including the artisan if his work was of genuine artistic value. They may be rewarded for their work irrespective of race, creed or community and patronized their merit.

Thus the state requirements were supplied at a low cost, the different industries were encouraged and new and better models and designs were invented.

This completed the control and supervision of the emperor over the department from its finances down to its inner working and output.

REFERENCES

1. See S.M. Jaffar, *Education in Muslim India*, pp. 77-78, 201, 207.

1a. *Ain* (tr.), Vol. I, pp. 93-94.

2. Monserrate in his *Commentary*, p. 201, refers to karkhana of chiselling of stones into shapes, studios and workrooms for the finer and more reputable arts, such as painting, goldsmith work, tapestry making, carpet and curtain making and the manufacture of arms. Also see *Ain*, Vol. I, pp. 18-27, 115-16, 272.

3. Pelsaert's, *Jahangir's India*, pp. 19, 26-28, describes the demand for varieties under Jahangir and speaks of carpets with gold and silk thread no scope left for Chinese silk. Monserrate's *Commentary*, pp. 36, 207 speaks of a large number of artisans, iron workers and goldsmiths and of Akbar's interest in karkhanas, personally visiting and sometimes himself working there.

4. *Ain* (tr.), Vol. I, p. 98.

5. *Tuzuk-i-Jahangiri* (tr.), Vol. II, p. 204.

6. Bernier, *Travels of the Mogul Empire*, pp. 258-59, 402-04.

7. Abdul Hamid Lahori, *Padshah Nama*, Vol. I, p. 448; Salih Muhammad Kamboh, 'Amal-i-Salih', p. 515 says Rs 90 a yard.

8. The amount on both occasions was sent in several instalments, but orders for purchasing the goods in Ahmedabad and Surat were given on every occasion; (1) Fourth year, Lahori, p. 407, (2) Tenth year, II, p. 281, (3) Sixteenth year, II, p. 310, (4) Eighteenth year, Salih, p. 406, (5) Twenty-first year, p. 331, (6) Twenty-fourth year, p. 443. The last two references show that on all previous occasions a profit of 50 per cent had accrued from the sale of these goods. During the reign of Shahjahan large sums were constantly remitted for the benefit of the shariff and people of Mecca and Madina. Muhammad Waris remarks that from his accession till 1651, Shahjahan remitted to Mecca about

one million of rupees (Waris, f. 81b). The curious method of sending the money was that whenever any leading office started on the holy pilgrimage he was entrusted with merchandise which when sold in Mecca brought cent per cent profits. The profit together with the capital was divided between the shariff and poor and the destitutes of Mecca and Madina. For further details see B.P. Saxena, *History of Shahjahan of Delhi* (Reprint 1968), p. 301.

9. Bernier, op. cit., pp. 258-59.
10. *Tizuk-i-Jahangiri* (tr.), Vol. II, p. 96.
11. Ibid., pp. 98-99.
12. The *Mir-i-Saman* together with the *diwan-i-buyutat* is placed under the *diwan* of the empire, and the term *Mir-i-Saman* is used for the office instead of *Khan-i-Saman. Ain* (Text), p. 4. Blochman has pointed out one example of its use in a biographical note on Khwaja Jalaluddin Mahmud of Khurasan, but there it is used as a title conferred upon him by Humayun which under the circumstances was an empty distinction. *Ain* (tr.), Vol. I, p. 417.
13. Abul Fazl, *Akbar Nama* (tr.), Vol. III, p. 877.
14. *Tuzuk-i-Jahangiri* (Text), p. 314.
15. Ibid., p. 412.
16. *Mir-i-Saman*, appears in one manuscript of the *Dastur* which was written in the early part of his reign while in other works including the *Tarikh-i-Shakir Khani* written in the reign of Muhammad Shah, the term *Khan-i-Saman* is retained. *Dastur-ul-Amal-i-Aurangzebe*, MS (British Museum, now British Library, London), Add. 6599, f. 58. For details see Ibn Hasan, *Central Structure of Mughal Empire*, p. 237; Shakir Khan, *Tarikh-i-Shakir Khani*, MS, Add. 6585; Ibn Hasan, op. cit., p. 237.
17. Ibn Hasan, op. cit., pp. 237-38.
18. *Manual of Officers' Duties*, a Persian MSS, 17-21. For details see Jadunath Sarkar, *Mughal Administration*, p. 32.
19. *Zawabit-i-Alamgiri*, Br.Mus. Or. 1641, 20a-21b. For details see Jadunath Sarkar, *Mughal Administration*, pp. 34-35; *Dastur-ul-Amal*, IOL MS, Pers. 370, 83a-84a.
20. *Ain*, ii, Ain 1; *Zawabit-i-Alamgiri*, ff. 22b, 23a. For details see I.H. Qureshi, *Administration of the Mughal Empire*, p. 76.
21. *Zawabit-i-Alamgiri*, ff. 21-22a. For details see I.H. Qureshi, op. cit., p. 76.
22. Lahori, *Padshah Nama* (Text), Vol. I, p. 245.
23. *Ain*, p. 272.
24. *Ain*, Vol. I, pp. 59-61, 102-15.
25. *Dastur-ul-Amal-i-Agahi*, f. 36a, etc.
26. *Zawabit-i-Alamgiri*, 21b. For details see Jadunath Sarkar, *Mughal Administration*, pp. 35-36; *Dastur-ul-Amal*, 84a.
27. *Akbar Nama* (Text), Vol. III, p. 597; (tr.), Vol. III, p. 877.
28. *Dastur-ul-Amal-i-Aurangzebe*, Add. 6599, f. 37b.
29. Ibid., Add. 6599, f. 58; Add. 6526, f. 33a. For further details see Ibn Hasan, op. cit., p. 241.

30. *Dastur-ul-Amal-i-Aurangzebe*, Add. 6598, ff. 53b, 54 and 56-104. These contain the specimen papers of accounts and the method of recording the details of every karkhana as required by the regulations. The above procedure is framed after detailed study of these papers together with their comparison with scattered historical facts connected with these officers' duties. For further details see Ibn Hasan, op. cit., p. 241.
31. *Ain* (Text), p. 194.
32. A *barat* corresponded somewhat to the modern cheque. It was a statement of account which contained details of the service or work for which it was issued a pay order. It had to pass through many hands for 'counter-signature' before being actually cashed. The receipts and expenditure of the imperial workshops, the deposits and payments of salaries to the workmen of whom some draw their pay on military descriptive rolls, and others according to the services performed by them, and the men engaged in the imperial elephant and horse stables, and in the wagon department are all made by *barats* (*Ain*, Vol. I, p. 272).

    Emperor Akbar who organized in a very thorough manner all the various departments of state, being desirous of avoiding delay, 'and from motives of kindness' ordered that certain classes of state papers, among others *barat*, then all included in the term *sanad* need not be placed before him personally. This practice appears, from Bernier's statement, to have been continued by succeeding emperors, but apparently without satisfactory results.

    At the present day the word *barat* is applied to certain documents of state in Turkey, and in *The Standard*, London, October 1890, we read with reference to the doings of Mansignor Senessi the Bulgarian Archbishop, in Macedonia, that .... 'There can be little doubt however, that, by the terms of his *Barat*, he is strictly within his right in visiting all villages where the Exarchist population is in marked majority, and in consecrating churches for them. Furthermore, besides the written authority, which might count for very little, he seems to enjoy if not the countenance, at least the tolerance of the Turkish authorities. Bernier, op. cit., p. 216.
33. *Ms. Or. 164*, ff. 20 and 21b, clauses 1, 5 and 6. Procedure in preparing such statements: The accountant of each workshop or stable writes out annually two *barats*, one for the six months from Farfardin to Shahrivar (February to July) and the other from Mihr to Isfandarmuz (August to January) (*Ain* (tr.), p. 272). The English months entered in it are wrong. They do not agree with the Persian months of the text. He writes down the allowances on account of grain, grass etc. both in cash and stores, and the salaries of the staff, and signs the statement. The *diwan-i-buyutat* inspects them, approves the cash statement after inquiring into the increase and decrease if any, and writes on the margin *az tahvil-i-falan-i-barat-navisand*. Let a *barat* be made showing the amount to be deposited with such and such'. The word *mushrif* added in the translation is incorrect as the amount was not deposited with the *mushrif*, who was concerned with accounts only (ibid., p. 273). The *mushrif* of the karkhanas

carries out the order, writes out a receipt (or voucher), also signs and seals it. In a cheque for cash payments, one-fourth of the amount is deducted and a separate *sanad* is given for it. The *diwan-i-buyutat* then gives the order to have it entered in the office register. After this, the *barat* and the receipt are sealed and signed by the *mushrif* of the department. The *barat* thus prepared by the karkhana concerned and approved by the *diwan-i-buyutat* passes out of the department. It reaches the military accountant (because some of the employees of the department hold mansabs and draw their salaries on that list), *mustaufi, nazir, diwan-i-buyutat* (again to him lest there should be some need for alteration after being checked by the *mustaufi*), *diwan-i-kul, Khan-i-Saman* (or *Mir-i-Saman*, mushrif of the *diwan* (ala) and the *vakil* and is signed and sealed by each of them. In every case the estimate is sent along with it so that there may be no mistake. When it has been laid before His Majesty, the *mushrif* writes out the receipt which, in the same manner, is entered into several daftars. The mode of payment is also detailed on the back of it, i.e., one-fourth is to be paid in gold (*ashrafis*), one half in silver (rupees), one part in copper (*dams*) according to the fixed value of coins. A statement of accounts of the transaction is appended at the bottom of each *barat*. (All transactions of the department, deposits and payments of salaries of the establishment of everykind of workshops or stables, are made by *barat*). For further details, see Ibn Hasan, op. cit., pp. 245-46.

34. The regulation definitely provided for referring important cases to the king. *Dastur-ul-Amal-i-Aurangzebe*, Add. 6598, f. 33, clause 1.
35. The fixing of prices formed an important function. Expert advice was necessary, and it was sought and sometimes arranged by the king himself, yet he was officially responsible for it. *Zawabit-i-Alamgiri*, f. 20b. The importance of this duty can be seen from the prices entered in the *Ain* for such articles. See *Ain* (tr.), Vol. I, pp. 93-96 for cloth industry, tailoring department and king's wardrobe. See also ibid., pp. 97-102 for woollen shawls of all prices manufactured by the state; pp. 115-23 for weapons of all prices manufactured by the state, and pp. 232-39 for building materials.

4

Types of Karkhanas

Of the various items produced in the state karkhanas mention may be made of *khilat* which was a robe of honour distributed by the emperor on such occasions as the coronation anniversary, the two Ids, the Lunar and the Solar weighments and any other occasion of special function. Robe of honour (*khilat*)[1] was not peculiar to the military department. These robes of honour were given to everyone present at the court. Distinction was however made according to the position of the receiver. There were five degrees of *khilat*, those of three, five, six or seven pieces, or they might as a special mark of favour consist of clothes that the emperor had actually worn (*malbus-i-khas*). A three piece (*khilat*) given from the general wardrobe (*khilat-khana*) consisted of a turban (*dastar*), a long coat with full skirts (*jamah*) and a scarf for the waist (*kamarband*). A five piece robe came from the *toshak-khana* (store house for presents), the extra piece being a turban ornament called a *sarpech* and a band for tying across the turban (*balaband*). For the next grade a tight fitting jacket with short sleeves, called a half sleeve (*nimah astin*) was added. Tavernier also gives the details of the seven piece *khilat*, the cap, the cabaye or grand robe, i.e. royal robe (long gown), the arcalou (Turkish *arqaliq*, a coat with sleeves, a surtout, like the *qaba*, but having buttons, instead of strings, at the neck, breast, and waist), or cassock, two pairs of drawers, two shirts, and two girdles, with a scarf to be worn round the neck and upon the head for protection against the heat of the sun.[2] Abul Fazl mentions of *chakman* and *shawls* as two other items in which Akbar took special interest. According to Abul Fazl *chakman* 'is made of broad cloth or woollen stuff or wax cloth. His Majesty has it made of *Darai* wax cloth which is very light and pretty. The rain cannot go through it.[3] The karkhanas also prepared dresses for the royal wardrobe, ornaments, works of fine carvings involving specialized skill, various kinds of arms and heavy guns. One may thus say that the major portion of the articles of imperial consumption were produced in the various state karkhanas.

The harem clothes, garments, ornaments, shoes and hundred other items of requirements of inmates of the harem with specifications of size and shape were manufactured in the royal karkhanas and the workers knew that was being prepared and also perhaps for whom stitching and embroidery of course were meant for the artisans and workers of karkhanas. Clothes, embroideries, carpets, shoes, variety boxes, items of furniture and scores of other nick-nack were prepared in the royal karkhanas and imported from abroad. European ambassadors, traders and visitors were happy to provide large and small looking glasses, gold and silver laces, fine scarlet and green broad clothes and several articles of Chinese and Japanese workmanship.[4]

Thus valuable articles prepared in these karkhanas catered to the needs of the emperors in matters of luxuries and necessaries of life. These articles were fine specimens of workmanship.

Karkhanas of Paintings

Even in the most difficult times (August-September 1542 at Amarkot) Humayun had painters in his retinue. Further *tasvir khana* (atelier) was an integral part of the library. Bayazid Biyat's account of painting and painters of Humayun's court furnishes ample evidence of the later years of his life at Kabul and Delhi. Amongst the officials who accompanied him from Kabul to Delhi in 1555 Hashim Haini *darogha-i-kitab khana* or superintendent of royal library is noticed.

The organization of the imperial atelier received its particular stamp under Humayun's son Akbar. The Mughal art of painting may well be understood in the light of Abul Fazl's definition: 'Drawing the likeness of anything is called *tasvir*. His Majesty, from his earliest youth, has shown a great predilection for this art, and gives it every encouragement, as he looks upon it as a means, both of study and amusement. Hence the art flourishes and many painters have obtained great reputation'.[5] Monserrate (1580-82) refers to the imperial workshops for painters in the following words: 'For this purpose he has built a workshop near the palace, where also are studios and workrooms for the finer and more reputable arts such as painting, goldsmith work, tapestry making, carpet and curtain making and the manufacturing of arms. Hither he very frequently comes and relaxes his mind with watching at their work of those who practise these arts'.[6]

One of the premier projects of this workshop in the early part of Akbar's reign was the *Hamza Nama*. It is thus described by Arif Qandhari, who was writing about the same time as Monserrate.

'One of the curious events is that His Majesty ordered that the story of Amir Hamza, consisting of 360 tales, should be illustrated, inclusive of the 'assemblies' (*majlis*) so that a hundred unique painters, gilders, decorators and binders work in the making of that book. The size of that book is one and a half *qaz-i-shari*, the paper is coloured and the margin gold sprinkled (*jalkari*), and between every two sheets of paper muslin (*chautar*) cloth is inserted for better strength. All the pages contain pictures and guilding. It was ordered that writers of excellent style should read the tales and put them in suitable and proper prose, which should then be transcribed by skilled scribes. Despite this (effort), a volume takes one year to prepare and on each volume about two lakh copper *tankas* (Rs 10,000) are spent'.[7]

Akbar was the founder of karkhana system for painters in India. It is established on the basis of the description of the karkhana in the *Ain* wherein the Herat painters were asked to train pupils.[8] The karkhana might have been on the model of those formerly existing in the capital cities of the sultans of Hirat or the Safavid Shah. In the absence of the contemporary and near contemporary sources, it is difficult to make assumptions about the organization of this great body of the painters, whether it followed the movements of the court or remained stationary at one place. There was, however, an atelier at Fatehpur as is evident from a copy of *Gulistan*, in the library of the Royal Asiatic Society which was completed by the copyist Kashmiri at Fatehpur in AD 1582 and the borders of its pages were decorated by Manohar with a number of illustrations of birds. This must have been the atelier referred to by Father Anthony Monserrate who visited Fatehpur Sikri between AD 1580 and 1582. He tells us that 'Akbar had built an atelier (atrium) near this palace for the work rooms of the more honourable art, such as painting, gold work, weaving and manufacture of arms'.[9] We may have an idea of the working of Akbar's atelier from Shah Ismail's system. The Shah appointed Bihzad, the director of the Imperial Library and the establishment of painters was attached to the library. Brown dismisses the importance of the karkhana by saying that, 'the system of karkhana was a passing phase and Akbar encouraged it, thinking that in doing so he was giving an impetus to the art of painting',[10] which is wrong. Akbar's theory of *sulah kul* demanded that the high, low Muslim and Hindu artists come together.

The working of the karkhana becomes evident from the illustrated pages of manuscripts. The work done in karkhana was known as *ghan ki tasvir*. Generally, the composition (*tarah*) was done by an artist of established reputation and the work of colouring, correct outlining and finishing was entrusted to his co-workers. This system facilitated the production of illustrated manuscripts and big albums which, if entrusted to a single artist, could not have been finished within his life time.

Moti Chandra in his book, *Technique of Mughal Paintings* presents some idea regarding the functioning of the karkhana which throws some light on it. According to him, 'the painters assembled in a big hall under a head artist who entrusted each of them with the execution of that part of the picture with which he was well acquainted. Thus, Chihranami, the face of the august personage—the king, was entrusted to a competent artist who had the privilege to study his figure, the head artist sketched the composition, a second applied the colours, third finished the animals and scenery and a fourth gave finishing touch to the picture'. In this way the painting moved from hand to hand till it was finished. Finally, it was handed over to the *Wasilgar* decorator, gilders, and pagers. In turn the calligraphist wrote the inscriptions on a separate paper which was beautifully decorated with floral and other designs and then fixed it on the reverse of the painting. After it, the painting was handed over to the binder who bound it in an album (*muraqqa*) along with other paintings. 'The works of all painters are weekly laid before His Majesty by the *daroghas* and the clerks, he then confers rewards according to excellence of workmanship, or increases the monthly salaries. Much progress was made in the commodities required by painters and the correct prices of such articles are carefully ascertained. The mixture of colours had specially been improved. The pictures thus received a hitherto unknown finish. Most excellent painters are now to be found and masterpieces, worthy of a Bihzad, may be placed at the side of the wonderful works of the European painters who have attained world wide fame. The minuteness in detail, the general finish, the boldness of execution, etc., now observed in pictures, are incomparable, even inanimate objects as if they had life. More than a hundred painters have become famous masters of the art, whilst the number of those who approach perfection or of those who are middling, is very large'. The *darogha* and clerks, who were appointed there, laid all the works of the painters before His Majesty and then rewards were conferred, according to the excellence of workmanship, or increased their salaries.[11]

The most illuminating and bright aspect of Akbar's doctrine, which appeals tremendously, is his recruitment of the painters for the karkhana where, for the first time in the history of India, the artists were taken irrespective of their caste, colour, creed, birth, region and religion. This revolutionary step taken by Akbar helped the poor artists, most of them belonging to the oppressed sections of society and came forward to hold a respectable position in the society. The security of career, which Akbar provided to his painters in the shape of salary, mansab, jagir and rewards, helped him in building a large karkhana of master painters, among whom Khwaja Abdus Samad, Mir Sayid Ali of Tabriz, Daswanth and Basawan,[12] etc. were celebrities.

A brief sketch of the lives of some of the painters would help to understand how Akbar translated his policy of *sulah kul* there. Extolling the painters for their attainment, Abul Fazl says that 'Mir Syed Ali Tabrizi[13] learned the art from his father. From the time of his introduction at court, the ray of royal presence has showered upon him. He has made himself famous in his art and has met with much success.[14] Khwaja Abdus Samad style *shirinqalam* or sweet pen comes from Shiraz. Though he learnt the art before he was made a grandee[15] of the court, his perfection was mainly due to the wonderful effect of a look of His Majesty which caused him to turn from that which is spirit, 'from the instructions, they received, the Khwaja's pupils become masters'[16] says Abul Fazl. Daswanth and Basawan who established their reputation in portraiture, were disciples of Khwaja Abdus Samad. Praising the quality of Daswanth's work Abul Fazl says, 'He is the son of a palkee bearer (Kahar). He devoted his whole life for the art and used from love of his profession to draw and paint figures even on walls. One day the eye of His Majesty fell on him, his talent was discovered and he himself handed him over to the Khwaja. In a short time, he surpassed all painters, and became the first master of the age. Unfortunately light of his talents was dimmed by the shadow of madness; he committed suicide. He has left many masterpieces.[17] Basawan distinguished himself in backgrounding, drawing of features, distribution of colours, portrait painting and several other branches. His excellence was so great that many critics prefer him to Daswanth'.[18] Besides the artists mentioned so far, more than a hundred painters became famous, while the number of those who approached perfection was very large. The emperor's patronage to the art which led to the patronage of the painters, did not only provide social and economic security to them but also provided them with respectable position in the society. The execution of the paintings in the karkhanas brought the artists irrespective of their caste and religious differences closer and closer and fostered a feeling of brotherhood.[19]

Thus there were several leading artists viz. Basawan, Lal, Madhu,

Kesh, Mohesh, Mushkin, Khemkaran, Kanha, Sanwala, Jagan Farrukh Beg, Mukund and Shankar who have contributed their masterpieces. Anwar (Varanasi), Basawan, Lal and Mushkin are the main artists who contributed most of the miniatures to these memorable works of art. Their works hardly leave any doubt as to their excellent craftsmanship, accuracy of line, form etc. represented in the miniatures and in accepting them as the celebrated production of royal karkhana.

Several artists were employed at the court to paint the great treasure of Mughal miniatures. Abul Fazl has given a brief list of only seventeen artists possibly owing to want of space.[20] Hundreds of painters worked at the imperial karkhana. After a survey of the Mughal miniatures under the limited means 225 names of artists have been noted. There might have been more. The artists belonged to different places. Among the artists the Hindus were in a greater number. People from the lower castes, Kahar, etc. were also raised to the status of royal artist. It was the keen eye of the emperor which saw the potential talent in Daswanth, the son of a palki bearer. He was handed over to Khwaja Abdus Samad. Soon Daswanth surpassed his contemporaries. Besides, the painters, design artists, gilders, line-drawers and pagers were also employed in the karkhana.[21]

The karkhana was completely organized with *daroghas* and clerks. The former laid the work of painters before Akbar who conferred awards upon them according to the excellence of their workmanship. Further, to develop the art of painting he made the materials of painting easily available by ordering them to be sold at reasonable rates. Artists were paid monthly salaries. Abul Fazl has mentioned that many mansabdars, ahadis and other soldiers were appointed in this department.[22] It seems that under Akbar, no distinction was made between civil and military employees and the civil servants were paid according to military ranks bestowed upon them. Consequently, the painters were given the rank of mansabdars and ahadis and were paid accordingly. The pagers, line drawers etc. held the status of an ordinary soldier. *Ain* refers to the salary paid to a foot soldier. It varied from 1200 to 600 *dams*, which may be taken to be the lowest pay of a worker in the karkhana for painting.[23]

Abul Fazl has specially praised the work of the Hindu artists. He says, 'Their pictures surpass our conception of things. Few indeed in the whole world are found equal to them. The Hindu painters laid much emphasis on the representation of human character.[24] Basawan was a rival of Daswanth and has been referred to in the *Ain* just after him.

Abul Fazl mentions that a few critics preferred Basawan. He excelled in the art of painting of backgrounds, the drawing of features, the distribution of colours and portraiture.[25]

As Jahangir had a mania for precious stones which has been noted by every European traveller to his court, so he had a taste for painting. The skill he had acquired in judging the work of his artists is thus recorded in his own words. 'Abul Hasan, the painter who has been honoured with the title of *Nadiru-z-zaman*, drew the picture of my accession as the frontispiece to the *Jahangir Nama* and brought it to me. As it was worthy of all praise, he received endless favours. His work was perfect and his picture is one of the chefs d'oeuvre. At the present time he has no rival or equal. If at this day the masters Abdul Hayy and Bihzad were alive, they would have done him justice. His father Aqa Rizai of Herat, at the time when I was prince, joined my service. He (Abul Hasan) was a *khanzad* of my court. There is however no comparison between his work and that of his father (i.e. he is far better than his father). One cannot put them into the same category. My connection was based on my having reared him. From his earliest years up to the present time I have always looked after him, till his art has arrived at this rank. Truly he has become *Nadira-i-zaman* (the wonder of the age). Also Ustad Mansur has become such a master in painting that he has the title of *Nadir-ul-asr* and in the art of drawing is unique in his generation. In the time of my father's reign and my own these two have had no third. As regards myself, my linking for painting and my practice in judging it have arrived at such a point that when any work is brought before me, either of deceased artists or of those of the present day, without the names being told me, I say on the spur of the moment that it is the work of such and such a man. And if there be a picture containing many portraits, and each face be the work of a different master, I can discover which face is the work of each of them. If any other person has put in the eye and eyebrow of a face I can perceive whose work the original face is, and who has painted the eye and eyebrows.[26]

Shawl Karkhanas

The shawl karkhanas in Kashmir are of considerable antiquity. Sultan Zain-ul-Abidin (1420-70) introduced the twill tapestry technique, the bush and a new type of loom in the manufacture of Kashmir shawls. The introduction of the new loom revolutionized the industry. The woollen rug called *pattu* was exported to Persia[27] and Kashmir producion monopolized the market.[28] It was during this period that variagated plants and flowers were woven on the new type of loom,[29] but the needle work embroidery was the development of the Mughal empire.[30] Thus the view of Walter Lawrence that the shawl weaving technique was introduced by Babur in India and thence made its entry in Kashmir[31] is not supported by facts.

Under the Mughals it had become a craze with every noble to have a fine Kashmiri shawl, which was considered a symbol of prestige.[32] The state was the chief customer of the stuff. The Mughal emperors purchased Kashmiri shawls offered by subedars.[33] The shawls were bestowed upon nobles on festive occasions and were sent as presents to foreign rulers.[34]

During the time of Sultan Zain-ul-Abdin in the art of textile weaving in Kashmir, specially the manufacture of silk, had received great impetus and that a large number of artisans in order to show their art came to Kashmir to seek the patronage of the ruler. It is also significant to note that certain woollen goods which came formerly from different lands were, in the time of Zain-ul-Abdin, being manufactured in Kashmir. Herein possibly lies the origin of tradition that Zain-ul-Abidin had invited Turkish weavers and thus laid the foundation of shawl manufacturing industry in Kashmir. The tradition is further supported by Srivara's assertion that artisans came from distant lands to seek the patronage of the king. Turkistan is not specially mentioned, but the possibility that it was one of the countries from which artisans came to Kashmir could not be ruled out.

Considerable light on the shawl manufacture of Kashmir in the sixteenth century is thrown by the *Ain-i-Akbari* of Abul Fazl who has given exhaustive list of all kinds of textiles. In the *Ain* 31, Abul Fazl points out the great interest which Akbar took in various stuffs and that was the reason why Iranian, European and Mongolian articles of wear were available in plenty in the country. Besides this, his interest in textiles had attracted a large number of foreign craftsmen and workers who taught the people improved style in textile manufacture. The imperial karkhanas at Lahore, Agra, Fatehpur and Ahmedabad were noted for their excellent products whose patterns, knots and varieties of fashions astonished the travellers. Akbar himself had acquired a practical knowledge of the whole trade, and the encouragement he gave to the indigenous workers brought all round improvement. All kinds of hair weaving and silk spinning improved so that the imperial workshops could manufacture all the stuff in other countries. There was a constant demand for fine materials and at first time gave occasion for grand display of draperies.

All textile pieces bought, woven to order or received as tributes or presents, were carefully preserved and were inspected from time to time. Clothes were made for them or they were given away as presents. Articles were arranged according to their prices. Experienced people continually inquired about the prices of articles used formerly and in Akbar's time, as the knowledge of the exact prices was conducive to the increase of stock.[35]

In keeping with his interest in textiles Akbar showed great interest in the shawl manufacture of Kashmir. We are informed in the *Ain* 31 that to the generic term *sal* Akbar gave his own Hindi designation *param naram* (very soft), and he changed the name of *kapur-dhur* (camphor dust), a Tibetan stuff to *kapurnur* (camphor light). The *Ain* 32[36] gives a fairly good account of Kashmir shawls. The garments stored in the imperial wardrobe are arranged according to the days, months and years of their entries, and according to their colour, price and weight. Such an arrangement is now-a-days called *misl*, a set. And their variety is noted on cloth labels sewn to one of the corners of the shawls. In the Irani months of Azar and Farwardin they are brought to karkhanas and sorted out in accordance with their prices, varieties, colours and weights.

'The following is the order of colours: grey (*tus*), white (*safid*), striped (*alcah*), scarlet (*lal*), golden (*zarrin*), brass coloured (*brinji*), carmene (*qirmizi*), deep blackish green (*kahi*), almand colour, light yellow (*gul-pumbah*), sandalwood colour (*badami*), *sandali*, deep red (*arghwani*), mauve (*unabi*), majenta (*majithi*), colour of Kasni flower, apple green (*sikki*), grass green (*alfi*), pistachio (*pistaki*), purgul, orange (*narangi*), leaf green (*paran*), pink (*gulab*), blue (*asman*), birch bark (*zamurradi*), chinese blue (*cini*), a kind of purple (*banafsai*), flesh coloured (*cihrai*), mango green (*ambohai*), musk (*musqin*), grey (*fakhtai*) and *galghai*.[37]

'In former times', Abul Fazl further writes 'shawls were often brought from Kashmir, people folded them in four folds, and wore them for a very long time. Now-a-days they are generally worn without folds, and merely thrown over the shoulder. His Majesty has commenced to wear them double, which looks very well.

'His Majesty encourages in every possible way, the manufacture of shawls in Kashmir. In Lahore also there are more than a thousand work-shops. A kind of shawl, called *mayan* is chiefly woven there; it consists of silk and wool mixed. Both are used for *chiras* (turbans), *fotas* (loin bands) etc.'.[38]

From the above account of shawls many points are clear. Firstly, *tus* shawl was made from the hair of *tus* goat.[39] Secondly, the corded and patterned shawls (*tarah* shawls) were made of either white, black or mixed wool. The white kind was formerly dyed in three or four colours but in Akbar's time the number of colours was increased. Thirdly, attention was paid to the manufacture of the following varieties of shawls:

1. *Zardozi*–Apparently this shawl was embroidered with gold wire and sequins. Prince of Wales Musuem has already good examples of this kind of shawl.
2. *Kalabatun*–The design seems to have been brocaded with gold wire.
3. *Qasidah*–In this variety the pattern was embroidered and not woven.
4. *Qalghai*–This type was made either of silk or gold wire or bore pine cone patterns.
5. *Bandhnun* shawls had tye-dyed pattern.
6. *Chint* shawls were apparently painted or decorated with floral patterns in the manner of calico-prints. According to Moorcroft[40] even in the early nineteenth century some shawls with green flowers tied in small hard knots to protect them from the action of the dye were made. When united each flower was surrounded by a small white field to which small eyes of spots of yellow, red were added by the embroiderers.
7. *Alcah* was a white banded stuff.
8. *Purzdar* is described by Jarrett as all sorts of stuff of which the outside is plush-like.[41] There is little doubt that by *purzdar* that kind of shawl is meant in which the size is obtained by joining together several strips–the *khandasamghatya* of ancient times. Fourthly, it seems that the shawls before Akbar's period were narrow. By Akbar's order, however, shawls of a suit length were being made. Fifthly, Lahore, with more than a thousand karkhanas became a centre of shawl weaving and produced a stuff called *mayan* used for turban and waist bands. Undoubtedly the shawls were used by the royalty and aristocracy as a luxury. The nobles lived in urban centres and so the chief centres of production and marketing developed in the cities. Srinagar was the provincial

> capital and became the natural centre of shawl weaving industry. Since shawl weaving was a lucrative profession as compared to agriculture, a large number of village weavers migrated to it. The wool required for the manufacture of shawls known as *pashm* was produced in the Chinese provinces of Turfan, Chahthan and Tibet. In Kashmir it was imported from western and central Tibet and even beyond, from Kashgar and central Turkistan. The Kashmiri wool merchants monopolized the wool trade throughout western Tibet.

The entire wool trade was in the hands of the Kashmiri merchants who had their agents throughout the wool raising areas. The chief merchants advanced loans in cash and kind to wool producers and collected wool according to their choice. One of the manuscripts gives an additional provision which stipulates that the Kashmiri merchants be forbidden to raise such objections as that the wool was wet or that it contained dust particles and the like while collecting the wool.

The merchants known as *bakal* had their own store houses. Soon after the arrival of the merchandise, the local merchants called *pashm farosh* and *bakal* were invited and transactions were carried on through a broker. After a thorough discussion prices were fixed, and some nominal amount advanced to the merchant. The broker was also given some amount in lieu of his services.[42] The *pashm farosh* engaged a large number of women in order to spin wool into yarn. The yarn was purchased by the *karkhandar* from *pashm farosh*. The *karkhandar* was the proprietor of the weaving shop. The number of looms varied from three hundred to more.[43] Srinagar contained more than 24,000 looms on which shawls were woven.

The weavers were mostly poor because of exploitation of the *karkhandars*.[44] They were meagrely paid.[45] The rates paid during the period of the later Mughals were 14 annas per *gazi Akbari* and for embroidered Bengal Motif rupees one and a half.[46] The *karkhandars* employed artisans and paid them in cash. The artisans trained their children and the art went down from father to son.[47]

The factors sold the texture to the shawl merchants. The latter had their warehouses all over central Tibet, Nepal, Bhutan and Bengal. Payments from these places were mostly made by *hundis*.[48] The merchants organized daily trade fairs to display their goods.[49] The customers mostly demanded the shawls according to design of their choice. The shawl patterns were also suggested by them.[50] The Imperial Court was the main customer of shawls, and transactions worth lakhs of rupees were carried on at the Imperial Camp.[51] During the first half of the eighteenth century new techniques[52] were developed and embroidery was improved. Merchants from Persia, Russia and Turkistan came to Kashmir to purchase the shawls.

Manufacturing Process

Wool was obtained from the hair of goats, yaks and dogs of Central Asia through various agencies. The wool in its raw state was a mixture of external particles like dust, grass blades, thorns, coarse hair and fleece. Woman workers first disentangled the bails and then separated the fleece from the external particles. This fleece was turned into elastic pads. After spinning wool the *pashm farosh* sold the wefts to the *karkhandar*. This process of cleaning and spinning provided jobs to thousands of women and children.[53]

There were two methods of shawl weaving–*amlikar* and *kani* shawl (twill tapestry). The former was introduced by Sultan Zain-ul-Abidin, and the latter by Akbar. The famous designs textured were known as *pashming kani, jora kani, qasaba kani, romai, shah passand, tamvar* and *hashiya*. The *amlikar* shawls were made in the form of *qasaba*, handkerchiefs, scarves, *patka, du* shawl, *qaba*, angrakh, *kamar band* and *langoota*.

The twill tapestry method was complicated. It required the greatest concentration and skill. With the help of small sticks called *tuj bobins*, square pieces of various sizes with designs were prepared and then joined together. The *amlikar* method was comparatively easy. The cloth was woven on the traditional looms of different measurements.[54] The innovations of Akbar were not only in respect of the dye, but various new qualities were introduced as well. The use of silk and *kalabatun* in order to prepare the brocades were used along with the shawl wool. Gold thread and cotton was also used in some styles. Embroidery was introduced in the sixteenth century but as a matter of fact, it was already existing in Persia during Saljuq period (AD 1037-1557) under strong Chinese influence.[55] Persian influence affected the Kashmir style also. It seems that embroidery was introduced in the latter half of the sixteenth century and received impetus from Akbar. Some of the famous varieties were classified as *param naram, tharma, darma, qasaba, dushwal, jamvar, patha, jigha* and *goshpech*. *Tharma* and *param naram* were prepared from the wool of *tus*, an animal of Tibet and Central Asia. The red coloured shawls were called *shah pasand* or *shah tus*. The prices varied. An ordinary shawl such as *goshpech* cost one rupee while a full length shawl would be sold at a price ranging from rupees 20 to 1800 and even more. But at the same time an ordinary shawl was sold at Rs 150 with ornamented borders woven on the loom of a width of one foot.[56] *Jamvar* was a brocaded cloth made of cotton thread, silk and wool. This kind of shawl was of an ordinary value, costing not more than ninety rupees.[57] Costly shawls were also manufactured and disposed of at fabulous prices beyond the capacity even if the wealthy and so they were the exclusive privilege of the emperors. Such shawls fetched thousands of rupees per piece.[58]

There are several notices of shawl industry of Kashmir in the seventeenth century. Jahangir in his *Memoirs* makes the following remarks about the shawl industry of Kashmir: 'The shawls of Kashmir to which my father gave the name of *param naram* are very famous; there is no need to praise them. Another kind is *taharma* (*naharma* in the printed versions); it is thicker than a shawl and soft. Another is called *darma*. It is like a *jul-i-khirsak* (*jul* is a coverlet, and *khirsak* means a little bear, but is applied to a rough woollen coverlet a drugget. *Darma* is a name in Bengal for a reed mat put over carpets. With the exception of shawl they make other woollen material better in Tibet. Though they bring wool for the shawls from Tibet they do not make them there. Wool for shawls comes from a goat which is peculiar to Tibet. In Kashmir they weave the *pattu* shawl from wool, and sewing into shawls together they smoothen them into a kind of *sagarlat* (broad cloth) which is not bad for a raincoat.[59] From the above account of shawl it is clear that the shawl industry of Kashmir in Jahangir's time was in a flourishing state. The Hindi name *param naram* coined by Akbar for shawls continued and it seems to have formed a regular article for presentation to the nobles.[60] The *naharma* is translated by the editor (of *Tuzuk-i-Jahangiri*) in a footnote as 'like a river', for the shawl had waves (*maujdar*). Apparently this kind was decorated with a wavy pattern. The *darm* is explained as a little bear coverlet or drugget and was possibly something like modern *pattu* stuff generally used as a rough wear. Besides, the stuff mentioned there is tit bit information available about shawls in the *Memoirs*. Thus we are told that Jahangir once presented to Mirza Raja Bhao Singh a special Kashmir *phup* shawl.[61] *Phup* here is certainly meant for Hindi *pushpa* derived from the Sanskrit *pushpa* flower. Apparently it was a flowered shawl. At another place[62] it is said that *tus* shawl was a special prerogative of the king. It could only be worn when ordered by the king.[63]

With the expansion of the empire, new vistas were opened for the shawl trade. Shahjahan sent a large number of Kashmir shawls to the rulers of Golconda and Bijapur.[64] It was during this period that Kashmir shawls were sent to the Ottoman Empire (Rum), Persia and Egypt. In the late eighteenth century those were used as table cloth in France, and in the nineteenth century France was its chief European importer.

Lahore,[65] Ahmedabad,[66] Agra,[67] Gujarat[68] and subsequently southern India[69] emerged as main marketing centres of Kashmiri shawls[70] within India. Nepal, Lhasa and Kathmandu also imported Kashmiri shawls. Bernier rightly observed in 1662 that Kashmir derived much of its wealth from this industry.[71]

Bernier on his visit to Kashmir in 1665 has left the following account of shawls manufactured there. 'What may be considered peculiar to (Kachemire), and the staple commodity, that which particularly promotes the trade of the country and fill it with wealth, is the prodigious quantity of shawls which they manufacture, and which gives occupation even to the little children. These shawls are about an ell and a half long (ell = 45″) and an ell broad, ornamented at both ends with a sort of embroidery, made in the loom, a foot in width. The Mogols and Indian women as well as men, wear them in winter round their heads, passing them over the left shoulder as a mantle. There are two sorts manufactured: one kind with the wool of the country, finer and more delicate than that of Spain, the other kind with the wool or rather hair (called *touz*[72]) found on the breast of a species of wild goat which inhabits Great Tibet. The *touz* shawls are much more esteemed than those made with the native wool. I have seen some made purposely for the omrahs which cost one hundred and fifty roupies, but I cannot learn that the others have ever sold for more than fifty. They are very apt, however, to be worm-eaten, unless frequently unfolded and aired. The fur of the beaver is not so soft and fine as the hair from these goats. Great pains have been taken to manufacture similar shawls in Patna, Agra and Lahore, but notwithstanding every possible care, they never have the delicate texture and softness of the 'Kachemire' shawls, whose unrivalled excellence may be owing to certain properties in the water of that country.[73]

It is clear from the above account that in the time of Aurangzeb there was great demand for Kashmir shawls. It seems that the use of *tus* shawls was not a royal monopoly as in the period of Jahangir. This might have been due to the increase in production which is not conducive to the monopoly of any kind. Further, besides Lahore, shawls were being manufactured at Agra and Patna as well.

The *Kalpadrukosa* of Kesava, a seventeenth century Sanskrit lexicon, gives some interesting names for shawls. According to it,[74] *Ratnakambola, Kashmiri, mahorna, pravari, Pamari, Yaksika* and *Bhota* were different names for shawls. As the names *Kashmiri* and *Bhota* indicate their sources were Kashmir and Tibet respectively. *Ratnakambola* must have been a costly shawl; *Pravari*, a *cadar* and *Pamari* a foot-spread.

The *Khulasat-ut-Tawarikh* (AD 1695) speaks of woollen stuffs specially the shawls of Kashmir exported all over the world. Soft and beautiful broad cloths of wool were also manufactured. *Pattu* sheets in two pieces, as in the period of Jahangir were available.

From the above statement it is clear that by the end of the seventeenth century the shawls of Kashmir were being exported to other countries. The shawls imported by the East India Company in 1685 and 1704,[75] according to Irwin, were almost certainly intended for use as table cloths or counterpanes.

Forster in his travel to Kashmir in 1783 has made interesting observations on the shawl industry of Kashmir. As a matter of fact he travelled in the guise of a Turkish shawl merchant proceeding to purchase shawls in Kashmir.[76] At Bilaspur he met a Tumboo (Tambu) shawl caravan on its way to Delhi and Lucknow. It was through the help of their agents that he could clear himself from the Bilaspur customs.[77] According to Forster shawls exported from Kashmir were packed in oblong bales, whose outward coverings were made of buffalo or ox hide, strongly sewn with leather thongs. They were opened only in the destined markets.[78] The shawl wool was brought from Tibet. Originally of the dark grey colour, it was bleached with rice colour. The yarn was dyed as desired. The shawls were also washed after fabrication. Richly patterned borders were attached to the shawls so neatly as to allow no joints. The price of an ordinary shawl varied from 8 to 40 rupees but the value of a flowered shawl was considerably greater. A portion of the revenue of Kashmir was returned to Afghan capital in shawl goods. The shawls were in three sizes, the long and the square ones were in common use in India, the other long and very narrow ones with black preponderating in their colour scheme were worn as girdles by 'the Northern Asiatics'.[79]

Thus the Mughal period is remarkable for the organizational and technical development of this karkhana. The skilful artisans in various techniques, designs and artistic embellishment, the mode of production, the system of monopolization of resources and markets and concentration of surplus profits in the hands of the mercantile community points to the emergence and growth of a system under which the artisans manufactured the exquisite shawls neither for artistic display nor for profit sharing.

The Qur Khana (Arms and Armoury)

It was customary for men to wear arms and therefore there was a thriving industry for manufacturing swords, daggers, shields, armours, arrows, bows, spears and matchlocks. Indian knowledge of metallurgy[80] made swords manufactured in the country famous in the world. All this industry was sustained through manual work and needed a large number of workers.

The imperial department which manufactured arms and ammunition for the army and for the personal use of the emperor was known as *qur khana*. Here the weapons were manufactured, tested and stored as 'the order of the household, the efficiency of the army and the welfare of the country' was 'intimately connected' with it. Monserrate tells us that Akbar 'keeps many workmen always engaged in the manufacture of muskets and swords for the army'. He paid great attention to the working of the department. He now and then scrutinized the efficiency of the workshop. He also laid stress on the study of the new methods and the improvement in appliances of war, in offence and defence. Akbar carried out many experiments in cleaning of matchlocks.

'The order of the household, the efficiency of the army, and the welfare of the country, are intimately connected with the state of this department; hence His Majesty gives it every attention, and looks scrutinizingly into its working order. He introduces all sorts of new methods, and studies their applicability to practical purposes. Thus a plated armour was brought before His Majesty, and set up as a target, but no bullet was so powerful as to make an impression on it. A sufficient number of such armours has been made so as to supply whole armies. His Majesty also looks into the prices of such as are sold in the bazars. All weapons for the use of His Majesty have names, and a proper rank is assigned to them'.[81]

Thus weapons for the personal use of the emperor were known as *qur*. All weapons used by the emperors were assigned names. Besides the gun, sword was the most cherished weapon of the Mughal emperors. The fact that Akbar was keenly interested in and devoted serious attention to artillery is clearly attested by Abul Fazl's remarks about it in the *Ain*.

'Guns are wonderful locks for protecting the august edifice of the state; and befitting keys for the door of conquest. With the exception of Turkey, there is perhaps no country which in its guns has more means of securing the government than this. There are now-a-days guns made of such a size that the ball weighs 12 *mans*, several elephants and a thousand cattle are required to transport one. His Majesty looks upon the care bestowed on the efficiency of this branch as one of the higher objects of a king, and therefore devotes to it much of his time. *Daroghas* and even clerks are appointed to keep the whole in proper working order. His Majesty has made several inventions which have astonished the whole world. He made a gun which, on marches, can easily be taken to pieces, and properly put together again when required. His Majesty joins seventeen guns in such a manner as to be able to fire them simultaneously with one match. Again, he made another kind of gun which can easily be carried by a single elephant; such guns have the name *gajnals*. The guns which a single man may carry are called *narnals*. The imperial guns are carefully distributed over the whole kingdom and each suba has that kind which is fit for it. For the seize of fortresses and for naval engagements, His Majesty has separate guns made, which accompany his victorious armies on their marches. It is impossible to count every gun, besides clever workmen make continually new ones, especially *gajnals* and *narnals*'.[82]

Under Jahangir there were two thousand swords of German blades with 'hilt and scabbard set with jewels'. The swords of Mughal emperors contained gold or silver inlaid hilts, cross guards and circular pommels. Couplets or names of the emperor were inscribed upon the blade.

Aurangzeb's *khasah* armoury contained many swords each named separately. They were greatly valued and jealously kept. These were inspected and were never given out as presents. Those that were bestowed were either made 'to order' in the 'imperial karkhanas' or were bought for the purpose.[83] Some of the names mentioned by him are *dushman, kush, arpa, bijli, bikhata, dushmanistan, abdar, fateh lashkar, kafir kush, kamarzib, Alamgir, yar-i-wafadar, zalim kush, fateh-i-alam.*

Other *khasah* weapons out of which a selected number used by the emperor included forty *jamadars*, forty *khapwahs*, eight *khasah* knives (*kara*), twenty weapons, spears (*nizzahas*) and twenty lances (*barchah*). Among the *khas* weapons could also be counted eighty *mashnadi* bows, eighty *bhadayan* bows and the other bows manufactured elsewhere'.

(Four of each kind of bows used per month).[84] Matchlocks (*banduq*) was Babur's contribution to the science of warfare, in India whether he used heavy artillery in his campaigns or only small arms is a controversial point. But by the time of Akbar, both these arms, the heavy and the light were fully developed. Light arms (matchlock or *banduq*) was the cherished weapons of the Mughal emperors besides the sword. Regarding the *khasah* guns,[85] its different type was manufactured in imperial karkhanas or purchased. They were used by the emperor in many ways in campaign, in the *shikar* and for target practice.

'Matchlocks are in particular favour with His Majesty who stands unrivalled in their manufacture, and as a worksman. Matchlocks are now made so strong that they do not burst, though let off when filled to the top.'[86]

Broad Division of Matchlocks

Broadly speaking the imperial arsenal contained three types of guns (manufactured, purchased and presented). They are (1) *sakhtah*, manufactured in the imperial karkhanas, (2) *kharidah*, purchased, and (3) *pish-kash*, presented to the emperor. Each was further divided into two categories: *daraz* (long) whose barrel was 2 *gaz* in length and *kotah* or *damanak* (short) whose barrel was about 1½ quarter yard long. Those manufactured in the imperial arsenal (i.e. the *sakhtah*) were further divided into three classes: *sadah* (plain), *rangin* (coloured) and *koftkar* (hammered). All the guns for use of the emperor were properly ranked.[87]

Guns sent into the Harem

Every month one hundred and one guns are continually kept in the harem *khasah* guns and *kushk*. Out of many thousands of guns for the state armoury, 105 guns were selected as the *khasah* i.e. for his special use.[88] Jahangir and Shahjahan were very fond of *shikar*, specially the big game in which they used the gun and so did Aurangzeb in the first half of his reign.

The Farrash Khana

In medieval times the emperor was not expected to stay at one place. He took part in campaigns; he went on hunting expeditions. A large establishment was required to protect him from the inclemencies of the weather. During the Mughal period officers and men employed in the *farrash khana* looked after the tents of the emperors, their transport and their arrangement in the camp or the field thus providing the king 'an excellent dwelling place and shelter in summer, winter and rainy season. His Majesty considers this as the ornament of royalty. His Majesty looks upon its efficiency as one of the insignia of a ruler and therefore considers the care bestowed upon it as a part of Divine Worship. The department has been much improved, both in the quality and the quantity of the stores, and also by the introduction of new fashions.[89]

The whole establishment on the march was divided into 'two separate bodies of tents' each complete in its requirement. They were known as *pishkhaimah*. Bulky things were carried by elephants, smaller tents by camels, the baggage and the kitchen utensils by mules and the 'delicate' things upon the heads of porters. There is no specific mention of the department under Humayun, there is evidence to presume that a separate establishment of *farrashes* looked after his tents. Like his government divisions he also had separate tents made for his conferences with the three sections of the people such as *khargah-i-sadat* and *khargah-i-murad* for the assemblies held with the people of respective categories, while the *khargah-i-dawazadah burj* and *khargah-i-dawlat* served the purpose of emperor's quarters.

During the time of Akbar a large number of tents were kept in the *farrash khana*. They were of various designs, used at different occasions for diverse purposes. On feast days, some of them were pitched outside the public audience hall and on the march they protected the royalty from sun and rain. Most of them were dyed red or scarlet which was a prerogative of the emperor. Abul Fazl enumerates a number of them. It accompanied him on his military campaigns when he marched with his army or followed him on his distant expeditions. Such as his trips to Kashmir (or any other part of the country). It was usually 'elevated above all other imperial tents but ornamented with large and varied stripes. 'Coarse and strong cloth' was used in its making. About a thousand *farrashes* took a week's time to erect it with the help of machines. Those of plain variety (a *bargah* tent) without brocade and velvet were manufactured for Rs 10,000 and upwards each, while the prices of the ornamented were much higher.[90] The *chubin riwati* is raised on ten pillars. They go a little into the ground, and are of equal height, with the exception of two, which are a little higher as the cross beam rests upon them. The walls and the roofs consist of mats. The inside is ornamented with brocade and velvet and the outside with scarlet sack cloth, tied to the walls with silk tape. The *do ashiyana manzil* or house of two storeys is raised upon eighteen pillars six yards in height, which support a wooden platform. The inside and outside are ornamented. The *zamindoz* is a tent made of various forms, sometimes with one, sometimes with two door poles; screens are also hung up within, so as to form divisions. The *ajaibi* consists of nine awnings on four pillars. The *mandal* is composed of five awnings joined together and is supported by four poles. The *ath khamba* consists of seventeen awnings, sometimes separate, sometimes joined together, supported by eight poles. The *khargah* is a folding tent made in various ways, some with one and others with two doors. The *shamyana* awning is made of various sizes but never more than of twelve yards lighter material, is spread over it, which affords protection against rain and the sun; and round about it are fifty awnings, of twelve yards each. The *saraparda* was made in former times of coarse canvas but His Majesty has now caused it to be made of carpeting, and thereby improved its appearance and usefulness. The *gulabar* is a wooden screen, its parts being fastened together like the walls of *khargah* with leather straps, so that it can be folded together when the camp breaks up. The *gulabar* is covered with the red cloth, tied with tape.[91]

Shahjahan ordered his *dal badal* tent to be prepared in the imperial karkhanas at Ahmedabad costing a lakh of rupees. It was made out of velvet brocade (*mukhmal-i-zarbaft*). It could be erected by 3,000 *farrashes* in the period of a month with the help of cranes (*jari thaqil*). This tent was kept at the capital and was used on ceremonial occasions alone.[92]

On the expedition to far off places, the karkhana establishments went along with the arms to keep up a regular supply of arms and ammunition. In 1653 after the failure of Aurangzeb to capture Qandhar, Shahjahan put Prince Dara Shikoh in charge of the expeditions and established his own camp at Lahore to personally supervise the supply of equipment and provisions to the army beseizing Qandhar. As a result he was able to complete the arrangement of the supplies for this expedition within three months which, according to the contemporary writer Inayat Khan otherwise would have taken at least a year to accomplish.[93]

The war equipment was supplied to the centrally maintained troops from the imperial karkhanas. *Ain* mentions that Akbar used to pay a lot of attention to these karkhanas as the efficiency of an important segment of the army largely depended on the equipment produced there.[94]

Each soldier seems to have had the shelter of a tent, even if it consisted only of a cotton cloth raised on two stitches. The kinds of tents were numerous. The emperor and the great nobles were provided with tents in duplicate, one set being sent on to the next camping ground while the other set was in use.[95] The tents thus sent were known as the *pesh khana* (literally 'advance house'). The laying out of the emperor's camp, a plan continued to the last, is described in the *Ain*(i) 47. In the centre was the imperial enclosure of canvas screens. It was divided across in its length into four courts. Over the entrance, which faced in the direction of the next march, was the drum house (*naqar-khana*), in the second court was the audience tent, in the third a more private hall, and in the fourth the sleeping tents. Behind was a place for Akbar's mother, while outside and still more to the rear were the women's apartments, surrounded on all sides by guards. Along the outside of the enclosure were ranged on each side the karkhanas or departments of the household and arsenal, about ten tents on each side. Still further away and towards each corner, the tents of the guards were erected.

Gifts other than money were naturally of considerable variety. There is the following list from Danishmand Khan's history of the first two years of Bahadur Shah's reign (AD 1708-10).[96] Jewelled ornaments, weapons, principally swords and daggers with jewelled hilts, palkis with fringes of gold lace and pearls, horses with gold mounted and jewelled trappings and elephants. The order in which the above are given indicates roughly both the frequency with which these presents were granted and the relative value set upon them, beginning with those most frequently given least esteemed.

The generic name for arms and armour was *silah*, plural *aslah*.[97] Weapons and armour of all kinds were much prized in India, much taste and ingenuity being expanded on their adornment. Every great man possessed a choice collection. The arms consist of matchlocks, fuzees, rifles, fowling pieces, sabres, pistols, scimitars, spears, syefs (long straight swords), daggers, poniards, battle axes. The armour is of two kinds–either of helmets and plates of steel to secure the head, back, breast and arms of steel network put on like a shirt, to which is attached a netted hood of the same metal to protect the head, neck and face. Under the network are worn linen garments quilted thick enough to resist a sword on the crown of the helmet are stars or other small device, with a sheath to receive a plume of feathers. The steel plates are handsomely decorated with gold wreaths and borders and the network fancifully braided.[98] Armour was worn by all horsemen who could afford it, nay, officers of a certain rank were required to produce it at the time of inspection, subject to a fine if it were not forthcoming. Its use was never discontinued, it was even worn by men of European descent when they entered the native service. James Skinner says, 'as I was exercising my horse in full armour',[99] and again 'I was only saved by my armour'.[100] George Thomas, the Irish adventurer, also wore armour.[101] Nor is the use of armour entirely discontinued even to this day, as those can testify who saw the troops of the Bundel Khand paraded before the then Prince of Wales at Agra in January 1876.[102]

Swords

As to the mode of carrying the sword[103] Fitzclarence describing some irregular horse in the company's service (1817) says 'they have a sort of foppery with respect to their sword belts, which are in general very broad and handsomely embroidered, and, though on horse back, they wear them over the shoulder'. But the sword was not always carried in a belt hung from the shoulder. The generic name of a sword was *tegh* (Arabic), *shamsheer* (Persian) or *talwar* (Hindi). The Arabic word *saif* was also used occasionally.

Samsheer

This word when used with a more specific meaning, was applied to the curved weapon familiar as oriental sword of as it is frequently called the *scimitar*. It is purely a cutting weapon as its shape and the small size of the grip sufficiently demonstrate.

Dhup

There was a straight sword adopted from the Dakhin, of which the name was *dhup*. It had a broad blade four feet long and a cross hilt. This kind of sword was conferred as a distinction upon successful soldiers, great nobles or court favourites.

Khanda[104]

This weapon would seem to be identical with the *dhup*.

Sirohi

The *Maasir-ul-Umara*[105] tells us that these blades obtained then good repute from the work done with it 'whoever was struck on the head by these Indian blades was cleft to the waist, or if the cut were on the body, he was divided into two parts'. This sword had a 'slightly curved blade shape like that of Damascus'.

Patta

This is a narrow-bladed, straight rapier.

Gupti

It is a straight sword having a walking stick as 'its sheath, the name being from *gupt* (concealed)'.[106]

Shields

Along with the sword naturally comes the shield, the two being almost as closely connected as the arrow and the bow. A shield was insepa-rable from the sword as part of the swordsman's equipment.

The Mace

This formidable weapon, the mace (*qurz*),[107] usually formed part of the panoply of the Mughal warrior, at any rate if he were of considerable rank. The battle axe (*tabar*), spears (*sinan*), lance Neza were different types of weapons. Daggers and knives were of different types.

Bows

The Mughal horsemen were considered to be especially expert with their weapon, as Bernier says, 'a horseman shooting six times before a musketeer can fire twice'.[108]

Matchlock

This was the *tufanq*[109] or *banduq*. Great credit is claimed for Akbar in the *Ain*[110] for the improvements introduced by him in the manufacture of the matchlock–'these are in particular favour with His Majesty, who stands unrivalled in their manufacture, and as a marksman. Matchlocks are now made so strong that they do not burst, though let off when filled to the top. . . . His Majesty had invented an excellent method of construction. . . . From the practical knowledge of His Majesty, guns are now made in such a manner that they can be fired off, without a match by a slight movement of the cock. Bullets are also made so as to cut like a sword. Through the assistance of the incentive genius of His Majesty there are now many masters to be found among gun makers, e.g. Ustad Kabir and Husayn . . .'.[111] In spite of these, that weapon up to the middle of the eighteenth century was looked upon with less favour than the bow and arrow, which still held the ground. The matchlock was left chiefly to the infantry, who occupied much inferior position to that of the cavalry in the opinion of Mughal commanders. It was not until the middle of the eighteenth century when the way had been shown by the French and the English, that efforts were made to improve the arms and discipline of the foot soldier. The barrels of Akbar's matchlocks were of two lengths, 66 inches and 41 inches. They were made of rolled stripes of steel with the two edges welded together. Both the barrels (*nal*),[112] literally piple, tube, and the stocks *qundaq* were profusely decorated with the surface ornament for which India like the rest of the East, is so justly celebrated. The larger of the two weapons could only have been used by a man on foot. Part of the matchlock-man's equipment was a *prang* or tripod, called *shakh-i-tufang* on which the gun was placed when about to be fired.[113] According to Bernier the *prangs* were of wood.

Guns of European make (*tufang-i-farang*) were much prized, but were only found in the possession of the greatest nobles. To the end of the Mughal period the fire arm in ordinary use was the matchlock. The matchlock barrels were covered with elaborate damascened (*koft-gari*) work, and the stocks adorned wit embossed metal work or with various designs either in lacquer or painting or inlaying of different materials. The stocks were at times adorned with embossed and engraved mounts in gold or the butt had an ivory or ebony cap. The barrel was generally attached to the stock by broad bands of metal or by wire of steel, brass, silver or gold.

Pistols

This weapon was the *tamanchah,*[114] a sharp blow, a pistol.

Artillery Heavy Guns

The general name for this branch was *top khana* (*top*=cannon, *khana*= house, division). Every department connected with the artillery was included under one name, it comprised (1) manufacturing department, (2) a magazine or ordnance department, in both of which the imperial *Khan-i-Saman* (or Lord Steward) had the superior control over the *darogha* or *Mir Atash*, (3) the field artillery in actual use and (4) the guns in use in the fortresses. In these two last sub-divisions the *Mir Atash* seems to have been entirely independent of the *Khan-i-Saman*. There are some large guns of the Moghul period at Lahore.

The *top khana* was classed as one of the workshops or *karkhanjat* belonging to the imperial household, which were in charge of the imperial *Khan-i-Saman* and as *darogha* of *top khana*, used in this sense, the *Mir Atash* must have been a subordinate of the *Khan-i-Saman*. But in course of time as the artillery branch developed, the office of *Mir Atash* grew in importance, until he was the equal or more than the equal of his nominal superior, the *Khan-i-Saman* and as commander of the artillery in use he must have been wholly independent of the official.

Whereas there is no evidence of any restrictions being imposed on private persons to manufacture the guns and cannon, requirements of army were met entirely by ordnance factories attached to the royal karkhanas. The royal arsenal (*khasa*) contained also a large number of quality guns presented or sold out by foreign emissaries and travellers. The East India Company was selling guns at Rs 8 and Rs 9 per maund in the year 1673.[115] Before the advent of the Mughals cannon had been cast in Ahmadnagar where under the rule of Bahmani king, Burhan Nizam Shah, the great *Malik-i-Maidan* was cast in 1548.

In the north the first karkhana was established at Agra where by order of emperor Babur, the first cannon was made in 1526.[116]

Boats

India being a subcontinent contains many big rivers which are navigable. The Mughals used them for comfortable travels. There are innumerable references in the chronicles, describing their boat journey from Delhi to Agra and from Agra down the Jamuna to the East.[117] Emperors adopted the boat for the pleasure trips either in the Jamuna or the Ravi or as a means of transportation to the houses of nobles where they were invited at feast. When they moved on an expedition, the whole court moved with them and also the bazar on the boats.[118] Imperial boats were mostly constructed in the imperial karkhanas. They were usually fitted with luxuries linings and beautiful awnings. The barges constructed for Humayun were quite novel in execution among whom the *chahar taq* was the most fantastic invention of his mind. Four large barges, each containing 'a two storeyed square apartment', were manufactured. When they were joined together, 'the four apartments faced each other, and thus between each two of the four barges another apartment was produced. Consequently an octagonal courtyard appeared between them. He also got, other barges made on which gardens were planted.[119]

'In every part of His Majesty's (Akbar's) empire ships are numerous but in Bengal, Kashmir and Thatah (Sind) they are the pivot of all commerce. His Majesty had the sterns of boats made in shape of wonderful animals, and thus combines terror with amusement. . . . Large ships are also built at Allahabad and Lahore and are then sent to the coast. In Kashmir, a model of ship was made which was much admired.[120] They were placed under the supervision of the Mir Bahri who had a whole department under him. Akbar continued his father's practice of laying out gardens on boats and to construct floating shops. Jahangir carried boats on his *shikar*.[121] Shahjahan had a variety of them at his disposal whose description is given in Peter Mundy's *Travels*.[122]

The incidence of several large tracts of forest was of great value in the progress of the general but more so the urban economy of the empire. The timber yield from these forests was employed in building ships, boats and carts for conveyance overland and sea routes. While carts or carriages seem to have been built locally and everywhere, the ship and boat building industry was located in places which, on the one hand, were within easy reach of the forest tracts and on the other hand an easily accessible water course in order to ensure the conveyance of turned out vessels to the place of requirement. Thus Kashmir, Lahore, the Western Coast, Allahabad and Bengal had developed as the principal centres of this karkhana. In Kashmir, Thattah and Bengal this was the chief mode of transport. In Bengal bomboos were largely employed to fit out smaller vessels for movement within the subah. As a matter of fact numerous varieties of boats were produced here such as *Ulak, bajra*, a pleasure boat, *purgoobhar*–a floaty light boat patella, flat bottomed boat of exceeding strength and burden, are some as mentioned by Bowery.[123] There were others such as *ghurrab*[124] and *sabnak*.[125] The imperial *nawara* in Bengal was composed of one thousand *ghurrabs* which were the commonly employed boats of the Great Mughals. *Sabnak* was a small delicate boat used for accompanying large vessels. As a matter of fact India is said to have had the monopoly of ship building trade as far as the lands washed by the Indian ocean were concerned. Indian built ships reached the ports of Europe.[126] Though wooden palaces, except in Kashmir were no more thought of, the use of timber occurred on several occasions in the structures of the medieval period in India. Roofing, door and windows were commonly made of timber and wood. Abul Fazl has appended a list of the varieties of timber along with the prices in the *Ain-i-Akbari*[127] which were available in the Agra market. Thus ship building was an important industry. The forests of India provided the cheapest material for ship building. The Arabs used ships built in India for their trade in the Indian ocean.[128] Ship building continued to be a thriving industry throughout the Muslim period. In the fourteenth century Friar Oderic crossed the Indian Ocean in an Indian ship manned by Indian seamen. In 1670 East India Company's factor at Balasore wrote to the court of Directors at London: 'Many English merchants and others have their ships and vessels yearly built. Here is the best and well grown timber in sufficient plenty, the best iron upon the coast. Any sort of iron work is here ingeniously performed by the natives, as spikes, bolts, anchors and the like. Very expert master builders there are several here, they build very well and launch with as much discretion as in any part of the world. They have an excellent way of working shrounds, stays and any other rigging for the ships.[129] Shipping remained an important industry up to the end of eighteenth century.

Karkhanas of Carpet

Evidence exists to the effect that since about the beginning of the thirteenth-century carpets of all shapes, sizes, textures and grades had acquired an indispensable position in the life style in the Sultanate of Delhi. Fakhruddin Isami writing in the reign of Sultan Muhamad Tughluq (AD 1325-51) relates in the *Futuh-us-Salatin* that in the early decades of thirteenth century multitudes of skilled craftsmen including painters from Khurasan and China had converged on 'the developing city of Delhi'. It may be assumed that these craftsmen had imparted their skill to the indigenous artisans who were adept at acquiring new arts. Indeed, the employees in the carpet weaving establishment of Sultan Firuz Shah used to make *tanka* 200,000 worth of carpets to order every year. But a living proof of the period is manifested in a specimen carpet in fragments in the museum of Lourve Detroit, Washington,

St Louis and in private collections is traced to its Indian origin. Viewed together it displays on a wine red ground ungainly animal forms of every sort in a peculiar style a characteristically Indian motif. Similar motifs of Indian symbolism are depicted in another delicate piece in the Museum de Arts Decoratifs with animal head of vines whose matching fragment is preserved in Bostan. Mughal Emperor Humayun (1530-56) early in his reign, had a large sized royal rich *bisat-o-nishat* carpet prepared at Agra without any reference to imported craftsmen. Further, Arif Qandhari writing about matters prior to the second battle of Panipat (1556) attests to the production of *qali and zalochq-i-abreshmi* (luxurious silken carpets) excelling in workmanship and finesse to that of Iraq and Farangistan.[130]

Kashmir, Fatehpur and Jaunpur carpets were famous woollen carpets. The carpets display on beautiful variety of decorative designs. Some of the Akbari carpets preserved in the museum[131] display a remarkable degree of originality. Unlike the originals, the carpets painted in the miniatures are extremely repetitive and indicate a singular lack of imagination. It is worth noting that with Akbar's fondness of ingenuity the royal karkhanas produced such fine varieties that the carpets of 'Iran and Turan were no more thought of'. According to Abul Fazl, 'His Majesty has caused carpets to be made of wonderful varieties and charming texture, he has appointed experienced workmen, who have produced many masterpieces. The *qilims* of Iran and Turan are no more thought of, although merchants still import carpets from Goshkan (a town half way between Kashan and Isfahan), Khuzistan Kirman, and Sabzwar. All kinds of carpet weavers have settled here, and drive a flourishing trade. These are found in every town especially in Agra, Fatehpur and Lahore. In the imperial workshops single *qilims* are made 20 gaz 7 *tassujes* long and 6 gaz 11½ *tassujes* broad at a cost of rupees 1810, which those who are skilled in the business have valued at rupees 2715. *Takya-namads* or woollen coverlets are brought from Kabul and Persia but are also made in this country. There were *jajams, shatrinjis, baluchis*, and the fine mats which look as if woven silk.[132]

Cotton carpets were originally introduced by Emperor Akbar and karkhanas for their manufacture were set up at Agra, Lahore and Fatehpur Sikri. *Ain* makes a reference to silken carpets and brocades being extensively encouraged by state patronage.

Highly priced carpets costing Rs 1800 were manufactured besides large varieties of *jajams, shatranjies, baluchis* and silk mats. One of the

Lahore factory carpets was presented to the Girdlers Company of London by their masters. Abul Fazl, however, admits that the Persian carpets were heavy and in spite of state patronage the industry did not flourish.

Building Department (Mir-i-Imarat)

Babur was a shrewd critic of the art of building in this country as his *memoirs* repeatedly indicate. Although he praises the remarkable dexterity of masons, especially the stone masons, he complains of the slipshod manner in which they designed their structure without regularity or symmetry, faults which would readily offend the taste of the Mughals for strict formality and balance. In spite of this he embarked on several building projects of a fairly ambitious order as he states 'six hundred and eighty men worked daily on my buildings at Agra, Sikri, Bayana, Dholpur, Gwalior and Kuil. . . .[133] Humayun found no time for building though he laid the foundation of Delhi.[134]

In the building industry, bricks, stone mortar, lime and mud were specially used. The upper classes lived in tents and palaces. In Agra, Delhi and other provincial headquarters, the state engaged a large number of masons, and the architecture and their efficiency is visible from the high artistic building and monuments of the period.

It was not until Akbar had occupied the throne for eight years that the country became sufficiently settled to enable any large building operations to be completed. In his time the encouragement to building art began in right earnest. Labour was even imported from foreign countries. The bridge along the Gomti at Jaunpur constructed in AD 1564 was designed and carried out by workmen imported from Hazara. Agra and Lahore forts were the first notable effort executed under the supervision of Qasim Khan, the governor of buildings and ships.[135] Speaking about the regulations for buildings, Abul Fazl naturally takes building construction to be an urban phenomenon. They are required for the comfort of the army and are a source of splendour for the government. He says: 'People that are attached to the world will collect in towns, without which there would be no progress. Hence His Majesty plans splendid edifices and dresses the work of his mind and heart in the garment of stone and clay. Thus, mighty fortresses have been raised which protect the timid, frighten the rebellious and please the obedient. Delightful villas and imposing towers have also been built. . . . Everywhere also sarais have been built, which are the comfort of travellers and the asylum of poor strangers. . . . His Majesty has inquired into every detail connected with this department, which is so difficult to be managed and requires such large sums. He has passed new regulations, kindled the lamp of honesty, and put a stock of practical knowledge into the hands of simple an inexperienced men'.[136]

But Abul Fazl totally ignores the role of the Mughal nobility in erecting buildings. The *Khan-i-Saman* or *Mir-i-Saman* was the highest officer of the *buyutat* and one of his duties was to oversee the plans of the expenditure on lodgings and buildings belonging to the state.[137] The royal buildings department came under the general supervision of the *buyutat* whose officers noted the number of bricks, the size of stones and the quantity of other material used in an area of some particular dimensions every day.[138] It is learnt from the *Kalimat Taiyabat* that Aurangzeb once issued orders that the builders (*memaran*) at Aurangabad should remove mud (*qil* or *tai*), etc. from a large tank and fill it with clean water; he also specified that expenses should be paid out of *buyutat* account.[139] Thus the appointment of Mukarramat Khan as the superintendent of construction of the Red Fort was quite in order, as he held the post of *Mir-i-Saman*. As for Sadullah Khan, he had served as the *Mir-i-Saman*[140] in the 7th regnal year of Shahjahan. Fazil Khan was the *Khan-i-Saman* when he supervised the construction of the Jama Masjid in Shahjahan's 21st regnal year.[141] Iradat Khan, the jagirdar of pargana Jahangirabad (Kashmir), was once entrusted with the supervision of construction works there (*sarbarah imarat*) by Jahangir.[142] He was appointed to the post of *Mir-i-Saman* in the 10th regnal year, which he relinquished five years later to take up the governorship of Kashmir.[143] However, Ghairat Khan and Allahwardi Khan fall in a different category, the construction of the Red Fort was initially put under them successively, perhaps out of consideration for the fact that both were governors of the region.

The picture that emerges is that the *Mir Imarat* was an officer of the *buyutat* serving under the *Mir-i-Saman*, but at the same time was also the head of the royal building department attached to the *buyutat*. And it is in the latter capacity that he was assisted by other subordinate officials in his department.

Arif Qandhari mentions the term *darogha* with reference to construction work at Agra under Qasim Khan.[144] The *darogha* was an ubiquitous officer in every imperial department. Mir Abdul Karim was appointed *darogha imarat* in the 6th regnal year of Shahjahan at the centre.[145] Earlier he held the office of *Mir Imarat* at Lahore. He was replaced by a certain *mutallib* in the 9th regnal year[146] but very soon the latter, too, was replaced by Ghazi Beg.[147] Haider Malik Kashmiri was the *darogha imarat* at Virnag in Kashmir.[148]

Havell observes that Akbar's interest was mostly shown in a careful control of the expenditure.[149] At best he thinks, Akbar 'like any other ruler of his stamp, consulted his master builders and gave general directions for the arrangement and accommodation he required . . .'. Havell thus concludes that Akbar did not concern himself intimately with the art of building.[150] But there are references which depict Akbar's visit to a construction site accompanied by officials and attendants, which shows the sovereign's 'intimate' concern in the art of building. Monserrate also comments that 'Zelaldinus' (Akbar) is so devoted to building that he sometimes quarries stone himself along with other workmen. Nor does he shrink from watching and even himself practising, for the sake of amusement, the craft of an ordinary artisan.[151]

Apart from the *Mir Imarat* and the *darogha* there was also an accountant for royal building (*mushrif imarat-i-Padshahi*) describing the career of Rai Govardhan Surajdhwaj, the famous diwan of Asaf Khan. A contemporary source reveals that since Rai Govardhan came from a poor family, he once worked as a scribe under Hari Rai, the *mushrif* (auditor, treasurer) of the royal buildings, on a monthly salary of six rupees. As a scribe, Govardhan maintained the muster roll or register (*siyaha*) of labourers.[152] Besides scribes, site overseers or supervisors were appointed for overseeing workers and artisans. Site overseers exercised the powers and strict control was inevitable at the construction site to coordinate operations and avoid idle moments.

REFERENCES

1. *Khilat* was the general term for the robe of honour. William Irvine, *Army of the Indian Mughals*, p. 29; Tavernier, *Travels in India*, Vol. I, p. 18.
2. Tavernier, op. cit., p. 132.
3. *Ain* (tr.), Vol. I, p. 96.
4. Bernier, *Travels of the Mogol Empire*, pp. 128, 292.
5. *Ain*, Vol. I, p. 113.
6. Father A. Monserrate, *The Commentory of Father Monserrate*, p. 20.
7. Muhammad Arif Qandhari, *Tarikh-i-Akbari* (ed. text), p. 45. For details see S.P. Verma, 'Mughal Atelier', *PIHC*, 47th Session, 1986, Srinagar.
8. *Ain*, Vol. I, pp. 113-14.
9. Monserrate, op. cit., p. 20.
10. Percy Brown, *Indian Paintings under the Mughals*, pp. 63-68. Bernier stands

testimony to the fact that the karkhanas existed during the time of Shahjahan and Aurangzeb, though they had fallen on evil days due to the apathy of the rulers. For details see Bernier, op. cit., pp. 128, 228.

11. Motichandra, *Technique of the Mughal Paintings*, pp. 76-78. See also *Ain*, Vol. I, pp. 113-14.
12. The *Ain* (p. 114) contains a long list of painters. Some of them were Kesu, Lal, Mukund, Mushkin, Farrukh the Qalmaq, Madhu, Jagan, Mohesh, Khem Karan, Tara, Sawla, Haribas, Ram.
13. Better known as a poet under the name of *Judai* vide poetical extracts of the second book, *Ain*, Vol. I, p. 114.
14. *Ain*, Vol. I, p. 114.
15. He was a *Chaharsadi* vide the list of grandees in the second book, No. 266, *Ain*, Vol. I, p. 114.
16. *Ain* (tr.), Vol. I, p. 114.
17. Ibid.
18. Ibid.
19. Mounstuart Elphinstone, *History of India*, 2nd edn, p. 174. He remarks that 'the pictures executed by the non-Muslims surpassed court's conception of painting. Few indeed in the whole world are found equal to them, speaks the traditional colonial attitude which envisages to divide the Indians, among Hindus, Muslims, high and low for the narrow design while the real situation was completely different.
20. *Air* (tr.), Vol. I, p. 114.
21. Ibid., pp. 114-15.
22. Ibid., p. 113.
23. S.P. Verma, *Art and Material Culture in the Painting of Akbar's Court*, Delhi, 1978, p. xxvi.
24. Binyon and T.W. Arnold, *Court Painters of Grand Mughals*, Oxford, 1921, Vol. I, p. 45.
25. *Ain*, Vol. I, p. 114.
26. *Tuzuk-i-Jahangiri* (Text), p. 235; (tr.), Vol. II, pp. 20-21.
27. T.T. Modi, *Journal of Royal Asiatic Society*, Vol. 19, p. 241. For details see Abdul Majid Mattoo, 'Shawl Industry in Kashmir in the Mughal Period', *PIHC*, 1975, 36th Session.
28. Elphinstone, *Kingdom of Kabul*, II, pp. 382-83.
29. Shrivara, *Jaina Raja Tarangini* (tr.), p. 151.
30. Abdul Hamid Lahori, *Padshah Nama*, II, p. 404.
31. Walter Lawrence, *Valley of Kashmir*, p. 375.
32. Bernier, op. cit., pp. 402-03.
33. Amin Qazvini, *Badshahnama*, MS (British Museum, now British Library, London), Or. 173 (AMU).
34. *Tuzuk-i-Jahangiri* (tr.), p. 146.
35. *Ain*, Vol. I, p. 94.

36. At times the trade names given by *Ain* are obscene, but some light could be thrown on them with the help of mid-seventeenth century MS of the *Ain* in the Prince of Wales Museum, Bombay. It bears the marginal notes which either give the correct spellings of the words or offer short explanations. The translation of the text on shawls differs at places from Jarrett's translation in the light of new manuscript and it is as follows: 'His Majesty improved this department in four ways. The improvement is visible, first in the *Tus* shawls, which are made of the wool of an animal of that name, its natural colours are black, white and red, but chiefly black. Sometimes the colour is a pure white. This kind of shawl is unrivalled for its lightness, warmth and softness. People generally wear it without altering its natural colour. His Majesty had it dyed. It is curious that it will not take a red dye. Secondly, in the *Safid Alchas* also called *Tarhdars*, in their natural colours, the wool is either white, black or mixed. The first or white kind was formerly dyed in three ways. His Majesty has given the order to dye it in various ways. Thirdly, in stuffs as *Zardozi, Kalabatun, Kashida, Qalghai, Bandhnun, Chhint, Alcha*, and *Purzdar* to which His Majesty pays much attention. Fourthly, an improvement was made in the width of all stuff; His Majesty had the pieces made large enough to yield the making of full dress'. *Ain*, Vol. I, p. 97.
37. *Ain*, Vol. I, pp. 97-98.
38. Ibid., p. 98.
39. In the nineteenth century when Moorcraft visited Kashmir there were two kinds of goat wool *pasm sal* obtained from the wool of domestic goats and *asli tus* obtained from the hair of wild goats and sheep. It was chiefly black, white or reddish. Motichandra, *Costumes, Textiles, Cosmetics & Coiffure in Ancient & Medieval India*, 1973, p. 239.
40. Moorcraft, op. cit., Vol. II, pp. 191-92.
41. But according to the Prince of Wales Museum manuscript, it was however known in Turkish as *kark* and in Hindi *rusa*. The note further explains that it was a big piece made of various strips joined together or it had marbled (*abri*) design or its nomenclature was due to its good quality.
42. A.I. Chicherov, *India: Economic Development in 16th and 18th Century*, pp. 167-68.
43. Hasan b. Ali Kashmiri, *Tarikh-i-Kashmir* (MS, Department of History, AMU, Aligarh).
44. Muhammad Azam, *Waqiat-i-Kashmir*, p. 7 (Asiatic Society of Bengal).
45. Nath Pandith, *Gulshan-i-Dastur*, f. 53b.
46. Ibid.
47. Hasan b. Ali Kashmiri, op. cit., ff. 132-36b.
48. Ruqqt. ACC No. 2776 (Research Library, Srinagar). For details see Abdul Majid Mattoo, op. cit.
49. Fillipo De Filippi, *The Travels of Ippolito Desideri of Pistoia 1712-27*, London, 1937, pp. 132-33.

50. *Dastur-ul-Amal-i-Alamgiri*, MS Add. 6599 Rieu, ff. 70-71.
51. Hasan b. Ali Kashmiri, op. cit., f. 106a.
52. Ibid., I, f. 132b.
53. Bernier, op. cit., pp. 402-03.
54. Ibid.
55. Wulf E. Hans, *The Traditional Crafts of Persia*, p. 217. The embroidery work was made with needles but during the reign of Zain-ul-Abidin various designs of flowers and bales were woven on the loom.
56. Bernier, op. cit., p. 403.
57. *Ain* (tr.), Vol. I, pp. 97-98; *Dastur-ul-Amal-i-Alamgiri*, MS Br. Museum, Add. 6599, ff. 70-71.
58. Fillipo De Fillippi, op. cit., pp. 73-74; Hasan b. Ali Kashmiri, op. cit., Vol. I, f. 132a.
59. *Tuzuk-i-Jahangiri* (tr.), Vol. II, pp. 147-48.
60. Ibid. (tr.), Vol. I, p. 390; II, pp. 24, 26.
61. Ibid., Vol. I, p. 297.
62. Ibid., p. 384.
63. Ibid.
64. Waris, *Badshah Nama*, Aligarh transcript, I, f. 307.
65. Pelsaert, op. cit., p. 19.
66. Manucci, II, p. 328; *Factories in India*, Vol. 6, p. 135.
67. Pelsaert, op. cit., p. 19.
68. Ibid.
69. Sadiq Khan, *Tarikh-i-Shahjahani-wa-Alamgiri*, f. 206b.
70. Desideri, *travels* (tr.), pp. 73, 132-33, 317; Hasan b. Ali Kashmiri, op. cit., I, ff. 131b. 133a.
71. Bernier, op. cit., p. 403.
72. 'Tus' the 'shawl goat', by Article X of the Treaty of the 16 March 1846 by which the British Government made over for ever, as an independent possession, the Kashmir territory to Maharaja Golab Singh of Jummoo, he bound himself and his heirs for ever to acknowledge the supermacy of the British Government and in token of such supermacy of the British to present annually to the British Government 'one horse, twelve perfect shawl goats of approved breed' (six males, and six females) and three pairs of Cashmere shawls'. Editor's note in *Travels in the Mogul Empire*, p. 403, note 1.
73. The Mughals were very anxious to introduce shawl-weaving into Hindustan, while not neglecting to encourage the indigenous industry in Kashmir. The *Ain* contains some very valuable information on the subject of shawls, from which the following is an extract:

    His Majesty improved this department (i.e. of the shawls, stuffs etc.) in four ways. First in the Tus shawls, which are made of the wool of an animal of that name, its natural colours are black. . . . In Lahore also there are more than a thousand workshops (details given earlier on supra), pp. 114-15.

74. R. Sharma, ed., *Kalpadrukosa*, pp. 280-82.
75. Birdwood, *Report on Old Records*, p. 27.
76. G. Forster, *A Journey from Bengal to England*, I. For details see Motichandra, op. cit., p. 241.
77. Ibid., I, p. 211.
78. Ibid., pp. 247-48.
79. Ibid., pp. 18-19. The best account of shawl manufacture in early nineteenth century has been given by Moorcraft. During the course of his journey he found out that Amritsar had become an important centre of shawl manufacture owing to the migration of a large number of Kashmir craftsmen from their country to escape the Afghan tyranny. Before Moorcraft's time, shawl yarn to Amritsar came from Kashmir, but its export was banned to discourage the foreign manufacture of shawls. However, when he visited Amritsar the wool came from Tibet and Bokhara. The Amritsar shawls with double warp and weft were fairly thick and soft. The meagre wages of nearly two annas daily left the weavers miserably poor. Moorcraft has left an interesting account of shawl manufacture in Kashmir. The 'pasm' wool employed for shawl manufacture was obtained from domestic and wild goats and was brought from Tibet. Moorcraft and Trebnech, *Travels in Himalayan Provinces (1819-25)*, London, 1841, pp. 110-13.
80. A good example of Indian knowledge of metallurgy is provided by the iron pillar near Delhi which is the purest iron in existence and it does not rust because of its purity. I.H. Qureshi, *The Administration of the Mughal Empire*, p. 257.
81. *Ain* (tr.), Vol. I, pp. 115-16.
82. Ibid., p. 119.
83. Manucci, op. cit., Vol. II, p. 358.
84. *Ain*, Vol. I, p. 116.
85. For more descriptions and gradations, see *Ain*, Vol. I, p. 120.
86. *Ain*, Vol. I, pp. 120-21.
87. Ibid., p. 122.
88. Ibid., pp. 122-23.
89. Ibid., p. 55.
90. Ibid., p. 56.
91. Ibid., pp. 56-57.
92. Fazil Khan, *Shahjahan Namah*, MS, No. 235, Asifyah Library, 53b. He furnished some more details. 'Its length is 70 Shahjahani *dhara* and width 45 *dhara*. It rests upon four pillars each having a circumference of 2 and $1^1/_2$ *gaz* and the height 24 *gaz*. It covers a plot of 3,200 *gaz* (of measurement). Ten thousand people could stand under it'. For details see M.A. Ansari, *Social Life of the Mughal Emperors*, p. 131.
93. Inayat Khan, *Shahjahan Namah* (tr.), E&D, Vol. VII, p. 101.
94. *Ain*, Vol. I, p. 118.

95. Bernier, op. cit., p. 359.
96. William Irvine, *The Army of the Indian Mughals*, p. 8.
97. F. Steingass, *Persian-English Dictionary*, p. 693.
98. *Asiatic Miscellany*, i, 393, Calcutta, 1795.
99. J.B. Fraser, *Military Memoirs of Lieut. Col. James Skinner*, C.B., i, 125.
100. Ibid., p. 127.
101. Ibid., p. 229.
102. William Irvine, op. cit., p. 63.
103. Fitzclarence, *Journal of a Route across India, 1817-8, 1819*, 69.
104. *Ain*, Vol. I, p. 117 (number two of the list).
105. Shah Nawaz Khan and Abdul Hayy, *The Maasir-ul-Umara*, Vol. III, p. 152.
106. *Ain*, Vol. I, p. 117 (number three of the list).
107. Ibid., p. 117 (number 25 of the list).
108. Bernier, op. cit., p. 48.
109. Steingass, op. cit., p. 314.
110. *Ain*, Vol. I, p. 120.
111. Ibid.
112. Steingass, op. cit., p. 1378.
113. Anand Ram Mukhlis, *Mirat-al-Istilah*, MS, British Library, London, Or. 1813, f. 178a.
114. Steingass, op. cit., p. 819.
115. S. Chaudhuri, *Trade and Commercial Organization in Bengal*, 1650-1720, Calcutta, 1975, pp. 66-67.
116. *Babur Namah* (tr.), p. 326.
117. *Ain*, Vol. I, p. 45.
118. *AN* (Text), i, 116 (Trans.), i, 468, *Qanun-i-Humayuni* (Text), p. 63 (trans.), p. 44.
119. *Qanun-i-Humayuni*, p. 63 (tr.), p. 44.
120. *Ain* (tr.), Vol. I, p. 290.
121. *Tuzuk-i-Jahangiri*, p. 342.
122. Richard Carnac Temple, ed., *The Travels of Peter Mundy*, Vol. II, p. 224. Illustration, 152, 230.
123. Thomas Bowery, *A Geographical Account of Countries Round the Bay of Bengal*, pp. 227-29. For Bajra or pleasure boat also see P. Mundy, II, pp. 157-58.
124. *Badshahnama*, I, 486; *Tarikh-i-Tahiri* in Elliot & Dowson, I, 277.
125. Anand Ram Mukhlis, *Mirat-ul-Istiliah*, B.M. Or. 1813, 322.
126. I.H. Qureshi, op. cit., p. 175.
127. *Ain* (tr.), I, pp. 237-39 mentions seventy-two kinds of wood.
128. Barbosa, II, pp. 76, 93, 107.
129. Radha Kumud Mookerjee, *History of Indian Shipping*, Bombay, 1957, p. 333.
130. Hamida Khatoon Naqvi, *Agriculture, Industrial and Urban Dynamism under the Sultans of Delhi (1206-1555)*, p. 58.
131. S.P. Verma, *Arts & Material Culture in the Paintings of Akbar's Court*, pp. 40-41.

132. *Ain* (tr.), Vol. I, p. 57.
133. *Babur Namah*, p. 520.
134. Khondamir, *Humayun Nama* (Text), p. 78, (tr.), p. 53; E&D, Vol. V, pp. 124-26.
135. Abul Fazl, *Akbar Nama* (Text), pt II, pp. 246-47.
136. *Ain* (tr.), Vol. I, p. 232.
137. Jadunath Sarkar, *Mughal Administration*, p. 44.
138. Cf. Ibn Hasan, *The Central Structure of the Mughal Empire* (reprint), Delhi, 1970, p. 242.
139. Inayatullah Khan, ed., *Kalimat-i-Taiyabat*, Aligarh Collection, farsiya (39), no. 278, f. 22b.
140. Lahori, op. cit., Vol. II, p. 347.
141. Salih Kambu, *Amal-i-Salih*, ii, p. 52. Also Muhammad Kazim, *Alamgir Nama*, pp. 395, 452.
142. *Tuzuk-i-Jahangiri*, pp. 317-18.
143. Khwaja Kamgar Hussaini, *Maasir-i-Jahangiri*, pp. 205, 309.
144. Arif Qandhari, *Tarikh-i-Qandhari*, p. 148.
145. Cf. Kewal Ram, *Tazkirat-al-Umara*, Habib Gang Collection, AMU, farsiya no. 32/57, f. 194b. For details see A.J. Qaisar, *Building Construction in Mughal India*, p. 10.
146. Lahori, op. cit., Vol. II, p. 491.
147. Ibid., p. 509.
148. Salih Kambu, op. cit., Vol. II, p. 44.
149. E.B. Havell, *Indian Architecture*, London, 1910, p. 163.
150. Ibid., p. 161.
151. Monserrate, op. cit., p. 201.
152. Shaikh Farid Bhakkari, *Zakhirat-ul-Khwanin*, ed., Syed Moin ul Haq, Karachi, 1961, Vol. II, p. 403.

5

Karkhanas of Princes, Nobles and the European Companies

Princes and the greater nobles had a similar set of *karkhanjat* attached to their household of course on a descending scale of magnitude, according to the position and wealth of its owner. The biographical material contained in the histories produced under the patronage of the Mughal nobles provide the information of the contribution made by them in the progress of handicrafts. For instance, *Maasir-i-Rahimi*[1] gives the information about the interest taken by Abdur Rahim Khan Khanan in arts, literature and handicrafts. In his karkhanas, skilled craftsmen worked and frequently rewarded for excellence in their products. One of his servants, Muhammed Suleh Beg from Iran was an expert in manufacturing guns better than those imported from Europe. He could manufacture the like of any gun brought from abroad. The craftsmen in his service are reported to have been prosperous people due to his philanthropic qualities. Nihavandi[1a] says that everyone of his servants whether they worked in the karkhana or in some other capacity was found wearing fine clothes. Apart from the nobles, the princes and princesses also maintained karkhanas for providing their own needs. For instance we read in a letter from Aurangzeb to Shahjahan that owing to the scarcity of skilled hands the output of the imperial karkhanas and the karkhanas of princess Jahanara had been meagre. The work of the artisans employed in Aurangzeb's own karkhanas was not admired by the emperor.[1b]

In another latter addressed to Jahanara Begum, Aurangzeb assures that the management of the karkhanas would not be changed and the articles required by her would continue to be manufactured.[2] The desire for luxuries and for obtaining articles made according to their own tastes and specifications led the nobility in general to have their own karkhanas. Usually the scholars of today associate the term karkhana with the workshops maintained exclusively by the emperor, princes and nobles. But it must be added that the karkhanas were also maintained by foreign trading companies in the seventeenth century.[3] It may be assumed that the individual traders also maintained karkhanas or workshops for manufacturing robes, utensils, arms, furniture etc. which sometimes employed quite a large number of artisans.[4] Certain big nobles are said to have maintained their own karkhanas where chosen artisans were kept for making a number of things. Detailed information about the karkhanas maintained by the nobles is not generally available. One Bakhtawar Khan is said to have established a number of karkhanas in various towns.[5] Shujjat Khan also had a number of karkhanas. The cups, plates, vessels, etc. manufactured in the karkhanas of the nobles were much admired by Aurangzeb. Shujjat Khan sent these articles as presents to the emperor and other nobles.[6]

Undoubtedly some nobles of the Mughal Empire maintained their private palace karkhanas where skilled artisans manufactured articles of luxury not only for their own use but also for purposes of presentation to the emperor and fellow nobles as a matter of administrative practice or social etiquette. This corroborates Moreland's suggestion that private workshops existed in some handicrafts.[7] Local rulers, for example, the Maharaja of Banaras at Ramnagar also had his palace workshops.[8]

The idea of nobles concerning industry never went beyond karkhanas or establishments employing artisans at low rates for satisfying their needs for luxuries. The men may accordingly be hazarded that by and large their 'investments' were not of a nature likely to lead to an improvement in the techniques of mass production however large the patronage extended by them to skilled artisans was.

Ali Mardan Khan is found to have been maintaining some karkhanas in Lahore and Kashmir where goods such as carpets and shawls were manufactured. In the 30th year of the reign of Shahjahan (1657) on the occasion of the emperor's lunar weighing ceremony Ali Mardan Khan sent fine merchandise including woollen carpets and shawls to the emperor produced in his karkhanas.[9] Shahjahan confiscated the karkhanas of Fazil Khan, the diwan of Deccan and imprisoned him.[10]

During Farrukhsyar's reign, Mir Jumla, the Amir ul-Umara, had full control over the exchequer and without his permission not even a single *dam* could be had. He was busy arranging for the marriage of the emperor with Ajit Singh's daughter. Abdullah Khan controlled the affairs of *diwani, bakshigiri* and karkhana etc., but due to the presence of Mir Jumla he did not attend court. This work was therefore held up.[11]

A Baroda, Surat letter (14 November 1622) seems to indicate the existence of private karkhanas in Gujarat cotton manufactories. Thus the information is gathered about the suppliers of cotton goods coming from the princes' *sarkar* or Ishaq Beg's *sarkar* meaning evidently the private establishments of Prince Khurram, then Mughal subedar of Gujarat and of Ishaq Beg spoken in records as governor or military commander of Surat. Private workshops of nobles however did exist and continued also in the eighteenth century. But the inference about the private karkhanas maintained by Prince Khurram and Ishaq Beg is rendered doubtful by the Baroda, Surat letter of 19 November 1622. It tells us that Ishaq Beg's broker at Baroda declared that he could not fulfil his engagement to supply 24,000 *mahmudis* worth of *baftas* and *bucker* but would try his best to make up the deficiency with other piece goods.[12] This strongly suggests that Ishaq Beg, the governor of Surat, must have his own private trade, having brokers to collect cotton manufacturers of the locality from the weavers and settle them at a profit. Private workshops of nobles however, did exist and continued even to the eighteenth century. This inference about private trade of high Mughal officials is supported by references in English factory records to the various forms of administrative interference in the cotton trade of Gujarat.

In the seventeenth century there existed also private karkhanas. According to F. Manrique the nobility appointed the labour of skilled craftsmen in their private workshops for the production of luxury articles for themselves and to be given to the Shah and other lords which was a vital part of the feudal hierarchical ceremonial.

Of interest is also the information of private workshops given in the chronicle of Ali Muhammad Khan, *The Mirat-i-Ahmadi*, describing the organization of a karkhana founded by Raja Jai Singh in the village of Jai Nagar. He settled artisans in the village who produced cloth which he wanted to be superior to the famed Ahmadnagar textiles. To achieve this he ordered that the tools for the karkhana be made of special kinds of wood.

In the eighteenth century special establishments were organized on the nawab's orders for the manufacture of quality muslins for the Delhi court in Dacca, Shargaon, Junglebaree and Basetpoore, the largest centres of cotton cloth production in Bengal. They were included in the *nuzzur*, the yearly offering of the Nawab of Bengal to the ruler of the Mughal Empire. The cloth was called *mulboos khas* and the building housing the workshops was known as *mulboos khas-kotee*.[13]

According to J. Taylor, these workshops were superintended by an official, the *darogha*, who 'exercised uncontrolled authority over all persons employed in them' the most expert weavers in the province were selected to work here. The names of these artisans were registered and they were compelled to attend daily at the appointed hours, until the different tasks assigned to them were finished. Inspectors carefully examined the thread that was brought to the looms and hence was permitted to be used until it was compared with the standard mustors and approved of.

The English commercial resident in Dacca (such residents appeared there in 1787) wrote, 'The incessant inspector of the *daroghas* and their people and the fear of incurring punishments for any deviation of the duty expected of them must have effectively deferred the weavers, while manufacturing the cloths, from attempting any improper practices'.[14]

Karkhanas of the European Companies

Sometimes the European companies, too, felt need for centralized production and control and tried to organize karkhanas of their own to fulfil their own needs, namely, to guarantee regular supply of standard goods and to exclude or limit the competition of others. The early attempts of the English in this direction in silk at Patna (1618-21) were not very profitable. However, it was a reasonable procedure and the European companies followed the usual method to have the goods produced for the market with hired artisans working on raw materials under proper control. The largest known factory was the silk factory of the Dutch at Kasim Bazar with 700-800 weavers. The saltpetre refineries of the Dutch (at Hughli and Pipli) and of the English (at Ahmedabad) substituted the inferior local pans by copper kettles and pans. Similarly experts were imported to train local artisans in different processes in textiles like silk.[15]

In the first half of the seventeenth century, Patna was famous not only for the production of raw cotton and manufacture and supply of cotton clothes of various kinds but also for being an important centre of silk trade. In 1620-21, under orders from the English East India Company's authorities at Surat, the first commercial mission to Patna was organized under Messrs Hughes and Parker to procure Ambati calicoes and other cotton goods. Hughes purchased 6 maunds of Serbandy and started a karkhana (filature, winding house) with 30 silk winders as an experiment. Encouraged by its results he increased the number to 100 and intended to employ 200 or 300, working for the whole year if the scheme and the price would be approved of by the Surat authorities. The fact that Hughes gave advance money to silk winders to work in the Company's karkhanas throw some light on their economic position.[16]

It does not appear that artisans, especially those engaged in textile production, came into direct contact with Europeans on a regular basis. European business intercourse with them was largely through brokers or middlemen who arranged it through the 'putting out' system or ad hoc purchase of goods from artisans.[17] Direct contacts were established in cases where the artisans appeared personally with their articles to sell them in the market[18] or when instances of broker's frauds were brought to light.[19] Direct contacts could also occur when artisans were employed in karkhanas sporadically erected by European companies, the earliest example of which comes from Patna wherein the English Company had employed a number of artisans for producing silk fabrics.[20] About Bengal there is the information, 'The Dutch have sometimes seven or eight hundred natives employed in English and other merchants employ a proportionate number.[21] At Palakollu on the Coromandel coast the Dutch built in 1652 a 'factory of a large compound, where they dye much Blew cloth, having about 300 jars set in the ground for the work'.[22] There is no record of the number of Indian workers employed, but that it must have been quite large is clear from the extensive amount of the work described. There was also the erection of 'dyeing workhouses' by English factors at Surat where once again the number of Indian artisans went unrecorded.[23]

Furthermore during the second of the seventeenth century, the English company sent a few English dyers, weavers, throwsters, etc. to Kasim Bazar in Bengal, who are reported to have trained craftsmen in the European technique of dyeing some special colours (black, blue etc.) which the latter were unfamiliar with.[24]

Direct contacts could also be shown in the saltpetre industry.[25] But there is very little evidence of any meaningful relationship between Europeans and the peasantry, at the most an occasion for getting together might have occurred in the course of the purchase of indigo, sugar, tobacco etc. though it is doubtful whether transactions in all these articles were carried out directly with the producers. Most probably brokers and merchants were the dominant link in these transactions. Another channel of close contact was the practice of Indians employing

Europeans in several capacities. The former sought the services of Europeans as artillery men, gunfounders, ship-building and navigational experts, jewellers and physicians. Bernier and Manucci served as physicians under Indian nobles and sovereigns.[26]

This process occurred in reverse form too. Europeans started employing Indians. Thus there was seen the employment of Indian artisans in the karkhanas maintained by Europeans. Further there was a category of consumers who were probably interested in some European manufacturers. The upper class in India comprising sovereign princes, and nobles was in a position to foster the production of European articles in these karkhanas. Was it because they could afford to pay for these costly articles, or did the procurement of European expertise in this sector pose a problem? Take clocks and watches. It is clear that the principal source for members of this class of these goods was by way of gift. A.J. Qaisar rightly questions the judgement of Ovington for denigrating Indian artisans with the jibe that the Chinese were able to understand the mechanism of the clock while Indians never attempted to.[27] Indian artisans never attempted it because they were not asked by their patrons and clients to do so. Jahangir asked carpenters to prepare European coaches after a model, or artists to copy European paintings, but why could he not have asked the artisans to copy the basic mechanism of clocks? A matter of taste perhaps, or whim.[28]

Establishment of European Factories

With the influx of Europeans and their establishment of the seventeenth century, the date regarding the day-to-day life of the people is multiplied and thus glimpse of economic set-up is available much more than what contained in the Persian chronicles which are mainly a record of events at royal courts and the lives of the noblemen of the kingdom and they throw very little light on the economic structure of the country.

So far as the kingdom of Tilang is concerned European trade and commerce centered round the port of Masulipatam. This port existed long before the advent of Qutb-Shahi dynasty but its 'meteoric rise' came with the establishment of that dynasty and its position as the chief port of the kingdom. But prior to the establishment of the English and the Dutch factories there is little data to rely upon. The Dutch were the first to explore the potentialities of trade through Masulipatam. They had the advantage of the possession of the larger islands of the East Indies. The first trading contacts of the Dutch with the Indonesians date as back as 1596. This was followed by the establishment of Dutch United East India Company in 1602 and when a few years later a Dutch merchant opened his firm in Masulipatam a new vista was opened for the Dutch trade. In 1606 an agreement was signed between the officers of Sultan Mohammad Qutb Shah and the Dutch factors, under which they established factories at Masulipatam and the neighbouring Nizampatam (former Petapoli) followed by the Pulicat factory in 1610.

It is interesting to note the conditions under which a license was given for the establishment of the factory. The royal officers at the port demanded 16 per cent of the value of the exported goods and the usual *chappadallala* or stamp for brokerage which was paid by both the foreigners and the citizens on all sales. The Dutch appealed to the king and orders came from Hyderabad that the tax on exports which the Dutch may have to pay should not exceed 4 per cent while their factories were totally exempted from the stamp on brokerage. On the other hand the English factors were exempted from *jankens* (tamil *chungum*) which was a toll levied within the kingdom on goods transported from place to place.[29]

The English East India Company was formed on the last day of the year 1600. They established their Masulipatam and Nagapatam factories in 1611 but could not establish a factory at Pulicat till 1621. The English did not have the advantage of an outlet for their commerce in the east such as the Dutch had in the East Indies with their centre at Jkarta renamed Batavia after the Roman home for Holland. The conditions under which these two sets of factories worked were also different. While the English had to pay custom duties on the goods handled, the Dutch later, contracted to pay the royal officials a lump sum of 3,000 pagodas or 12,150 Mughal rupees annually for the clearing of goods carried by them.[30]

The volume of trade increased as time passed. In the beginning it was mainly good cotton yarn, indigo, and coarse cloth which were the objects of overseas trade, but later spices, silk, porcelain, lead, quick silver, alum, brass, broad cloth and many other commodities were handled.[31] Diamond trade seems to have slackened a little with the discovery of a diamond mine near Elluru. Previous to that the mines were leased to the Dutch and they carried the profits home, but it appears that in 1623 the king made up his mind not to lease these mines but to have them worked as a royal monopoly by state officials.[32]

There was a kind of race between the Dutch and the English, and the English were on the look out for new articles which could be sold in Europe with advantage. Early in Sultan Muhammad's reign one Giles James was commissioned to make enquiries about 'broad linen cloth from Golconda made in the fashion sheets 'etans' (*than*) 4½ cavits long and 2½ cavits broad, also a kind of stuff called *tessa* (*tassar*). Both are likely to be suitable in England, also to inquire about gum lac, pepper, copper and dry ginger'.[33]

There was obviously no love lost between the Dutch and the English factors and when the Dutch governor Van Uffelen was beaten 'by the natives' the president of the Dutch factory at Batavia wrote to the Dutch factors at Masulipatam that 'this should be a warning to the English that they should be treated in a like manner'.[34]

It was during the reign of Qutb Shah that Tavernier and Bernier came to the Deccan and wrote their *Memoirs* regarding the condition of life in the Qutb-shahi dominions. Tavernier was in Deccan during 1638-39, again in 1651 and lastly in 1657 while Bernier was at Hyderabad in 1666 and Thevenot was in Deccan about the same time.[35]

Fort St. David was already the site of an English factory, Nagapatam was of Portuguese while the Dutch had their factory at Pulicat. Perhaps the most profitable industry of the region was mining, refining and cutting of diamonds, a process which made Golconda famous the world over.

Various Other Industries

The subcontinent had achieved great expertise in metallurgy. The high quality of the native made iron and production in copper and brass gave her a prominent position in ancient metallurgical world.[36] The Indian sword and dagger became byword in Persian and Arabic literature. Many articles of utility were made of iron for domestic use and export. Ma Huan noticed 'basins, cups, guns, knives and scissors and some cooking utensils large and small as well as locks, nails, needles and tools and implements of various kinds made of iron.[37] There was a good deal of fine work in silver and gold. A land where there was such a craze for jewellery, silver and goldsmiths were found in every small towns. Inlay work, damascened articles encrusted with precious stones and 'sword hilts of exquisite workmanship were in good demand by the richer classes. The melting and mixing of metals for different alloys was fully understood.

Banaras was famous throughout the country for brass, copper and bell metal wares. Other important centres for this industry were Mathura, Nasik, Poona, Hardwar, Delhi, Lahore, Agra, Oudh, Ahmedabad and Dacca. Many other metal crafts such as enamelling, damascening work were chiefly used in ornamenting arms like shields etc. It was practised in Kutch, Punjab and Sindh towns like Sialkot, Kotli, Lahore etc. The towns of Rajputana also excelled in all kinds of artistic work specially in enamelled jewellery. Stone carving was also carried on in Rajputana cities. There was a little division of labour existing in some industries, for example, wire manufacturing etc. In order to attain a particular fineness the wire had to pass through different sets of workers and labour was specialised though of course imperfectly.[38] There were other industries which cannot be classed under any division. There was smelting of ores, like copper, iron, gold and silver, bangle making, saltpetre industries etc. Inayat Khan makes mention of a costly lamp called *Gul Muhammadi* purchased at Rs 10,000 which was decked with rubies and jewels and costly jades and diamonds valued at Rs 250,000 and the cost of the entire lamp was Rs 3,50,000. This meant that the labour charge must have been nearly a lakh of rupees before being sent to Medina. Great and elaborate was its artistic efficiency.[39] The Peacock Throne of Shahjahan was constructed at a huge cost of crores of rupees in seven years (in AD 1634). It was by itself a great wonder of the world and spoke highly of the artistic talents bestowed by the craftsmen of the country.[40] This meant a great patronage to fine arts.

Besides these the inlay work in marble and filigree work were highly encouraged and developed. From Akbar to Shahjahan there was a golden period for the development of every type of Indian art.

Leather Goods

No mention of this industry occurs in the contemporary accounts, however, as hides were not exported and leather manufactures not imported, it is easy to conclude that in the agriculturally developed regions, there must have been no dearth of hides. The manufactures of boots and shoes, saddlery and buckets for irrigation must have been practised locally. The *Ain* gives details of harness used in Akbar's time but it is noteworthy that leather rarely finds a mention in the large list of articles used. Saddles were chiefly made of cloth and halters of rope. The industry as a whole was less extensive than what is at present. The urban areas employed a large number of leather workers for saddlery in addition to shoes. Book covers, scabbards of swords and bags were also made of leather.[41]

Perfumes

Flower beds occurred in some of the gardens primarily for their beauty and fragrance. For example, the gardens laid out by the aristocracy adjoining their mansions used to be so planned to consist of fruit bearing trees and sweet scented attractive blossoms. The immigrant Muslims had introduced some flowers of the Islamic countries, for example, roses and their cultivation by about the sixteenth century had become quite common. Odoriferous plants of both foreign and Indian origin were used for extracting scented oil[42] required generally for anointing the skin and hair,[43] so that its industry gained considerable importance. Agra,[44] Jaunpur[45] and Ghazipur[46] were then noted centres for the manufacture of scented and sweet smelling oils. But the more sophisticated perfumes too were extracted from flowers, having stronger and more refined scents such as that of roses gul-i-henna, jasmine, saffron and so on. According to Abul Fazl on perfumes, 'His Majesty is very fond of perfumes and encourages this department from religious motives. The court hall is continually scented with ambergris, aloewood, and compositions according to ancient recipes or mixtures invented by His Majesty, and incense is daily burnt in gold and silver censers of various shapes, whilst sweet smelling flowers are used in large quantities. Oils are also extracted from flowers and used for skin and hair'.[47] Out of 34 varieties of perfumes enumerated by Abul Fazl, *duwelak* was the cheapest from 3 to 4 *dams* per seer which could not have been difficult for the common man to acquire. The most expensive one was *ambar-i-ashhab* whose price ranged from one to three mohurs per tola or eighty to two hundred and forty mohurs per seer.[48] The use of perfume has a religious sanctity for Muslims and continued to command a certain domestic market. Large tracts of land were brought under these odoriferous plants around Champaner,[49] Ahmedabad, Surat and Sironji and perfume making industry developed in these towns as also at Nausari.[50] The indigenous perfume was evidently not as yet comparable to the Persian perfumes, but the fact that during this period the art had been introduced and was making headway is the most significant aspect. At times the flower plants also yielded dyeing content such as the henna or saffron. Those dyeing agents were used for dyeing cloth, paper, utensils,[51] hands, feet and hair.[52] Some flowers possessed medicinal values and as such were largely in demand by the chemist, roses, saffron and henna being important ones. Local dyers worked for the English and were paid wages. The point to remember is that these craftsmen did not take up the job under compulsion as they used to do in the karkhanas established by the royalty or the nobles. Thus there is found the birth of an important element of system of production, the presence of workmen willing to exchange their skill for wages.[53]

Textile Industry

Out of all valuable crops cotton and relatively to a lesser degree silk occupied a singular position in medieval economy. The weaving of cotton fabrics became as universal as the cultivation of cotton because the textile industry was the dominant industry of medieval times in much the same manner in which at present the metal working industries dominate in the economy. And it was mainly through this industry that Mughal India was able to acquire an eminently advanced position in the market of contemporary world with an ample and running supply of raw cotton from the adjoining villages, the urban weavers added, expanded and raised urban output of cotton textiles. Towns were then the principal seats of this industry.[54] By virtue of his life in town the urban weaver was able to avail of the facilities not known to the rural craftsmen. The urban weaver could devote maximum working hours just to weaving, passing over other processes necessary to make the piece marketable to those who were engaged in those particular processes. Thus stimulated, cotton textile industry made rapid progress which in turn exercised deep impact on the general pattern of economy.

The most important new factor which gave impetus to the textile manufacture in India in the seventeenth century[55] was the enormous foreign demand for Indian commodities. Raw silk being an expensive item the weavers could not have taken up weaving of silk fabrics on their own.

Masalik-al-Absar, a fourteenth century source informs us of the silk weavers employed in royal karkhanas of Firuz Shah Tughluq. Abul Fazl refers to silk weaving karkhanas of Akbar where under the guidance of master craftsmen its weaving was carried on.[56]

A silk fabric woven in karkhanas by a famous craftsman (Ghiyas-i-Naqshabad) was sold for 50 mohars. Apart from the karkhanas of the emperor or nobles the silk weavers found employment with the Europeans also.

Sugar making enterprises owned by local capitalists who employed hired labour were set up in the late eighteenth century and early nineteenth century also in Maharashtra. Sugar manufacture reached the highest degree of development in Bengal. Features of developing capitalist manufacture in India at the close of the eighteenth century stand out clearly also in the manufacture of indigo dyestuffs, which was likewise based on the processing of agricultural produce.

The prosperity of the cities was sustained by trade and industry. In those textiles had the place of pre-eminence though, of course, other articles were also manufactured and exported. The textiles embraced practically every kind of material, cotton, silk and woollens. Some writers have doubted the existence of silk worm in the subcontinent but the evidence of Ma Huan should prove conclusive because he came from China, the home of sericulture.[57] Silk garments were used so extensively within the subcontinent itself that the supply could be sustained only by local production or large scale imports, but no authority mentions the import of silk yarn. The best woollen materials were manufactured from the wool of the mountain goat which is soft and shining like silk, of course the rough wool of sheep and camel was also used a great deal. So large was the textile industry in volume that Cambay and Bengal supplied cloth to Persia, Tartary, Turkey, Syria, Barbary (that is Africa, Arabia, Fleix, Ethiopia, India (Portuguese possessions) and a multitude of inhabited islands,[58] and Gujarat alone sent fine and coarse cloth to 'Arabia, Persia, India (that is Portuguese India), Malacca, Sumatra (Melynde), Malaya, Magadozo and Mambosa'.[59] All this cloth was manufactured on handlooms and thus provided employment to a large number of weavers.

The textile industry had certain allied crafts. For instance the production of carpets, darries, prayer carpets, niwar was fairly common in the cities where these articles were mostly in demand. The most important subsidiary industry, however, was that of dyeing and printing. The subcontinent was rich in the production of indigo, a good deal of which was used locally as the basic and cheapest dye. Other dyes were also made from local earths, flowered leaves. Barbosa mentions 'quilts and testers of beds finely worked and painted.[60] Saris with coloured borders were common and men used coloured scarfs and articles of dress. Similarly brocades were used by the rich and exported abroad. Even common people used gold and silver brocades for caps.

Silk Manufactures in Gujarat

The extent to which the manufacture of silk goods of the most beautiful expensive and variagated type had become at this period localized in Gujarat and especially in the two principal cities of Ahmedabad and Surat is not generally known, though it is one of the most prominent facts in the economic history of the province. Sericulture of the breeding of the silk worm on the mulbery tree has not indeed been practised in Gujarat at any time, as neither the soil nor the climate are favourable for the purpose. That industry was, however, very flourishing in Bengal at this period and it is learnt that the 'village' of Kasim Bazar was able to furnish no less than 22,000 bales of silk every year. Of this amount, the Dutch generally purchased from six to seven thousand bales for export to Holland and to Japan, the merchants of Tartary and of the Mughal empire bought a similar number of bales for export purposes; and the balance viz. from eight to ten thousand bales, remained with the people of the country for the manufacture of silk fabrics, and practically the whole of this stock was forwarded to the province of Gujarat, specially to Ahmedabad and Surat for being woven into beautiful cloths.[61]

Wood work and work in ivory was common. Carved doors, pillars and beams were in demand. Ivory was used for bed sheets, chess boards, chessmen and dice. Ivory sword hilt and bracelets were fairly common. Both the Chinese and Arab varieties of paper were manufactured, the former from the bark of the tree and the latter from rags. The former was made in Bengal and the latter mostly in Gujarat.[62] Paper was originally manufactured in China and it was in use as early as AD 105. Several centuries later in AD 751 some Chinese paper makers taken prisoners by Muslims were sent to fabricate paper in Samarqand. That the state karkhanas of Agra and Lahore were producing paper may be inferred from the *Ain* 34 of Abul Fazl. The known existence of a Kaghazai Bazar at Farrukhabad would point in same direction.

Mining was well understood and there were mines for extracting precious stones and some metals. Apart from catches for local consumption, there were fisheries in Sind for catching sea fish and drying it mainly for export.[63] There was a specialized industry manufacturing artificial diamonds, rubies, topazes and white sapphires, which were in demand for 'the genteel poor' and export. Indigo was widely manufactured for domestic use as well as export.

Decline of Imperial Karkhanas by the Eighteenth Century

The imperial karkhanas numbered 69 in the *Zawabit-i-Alamgiri* (f. 132b) towards the end of the seventeenth century, indicating the decline in production under the Later Mughals.[64] These lasted till the eighties of the eighteenth century.

However, the imperial tradition survived in the eighteenth century among some local rulers. Jai Singh II of Jaipur not only settled weavers there who were expected to outdo the Ahmadnagar textiles but also provided tools of special varieties of wood in his workshops.[65] Again the Nawabs of Bengal and 'special establishments (*mulboos Khas Kootee*) in Dacca, Sonargaon, Jangalbaree and Basetpoore for production of first grade muslins (*mulboos khas*) as yearly *peshkash*' to the Mughal Emperor. The workshops were supervised by the *darogha*, having uncontrolled authority over all employees the most expert weavers in the province selected. They were registered and had to attend daily for scheduled hours till the completion of the tasks. The thread used was carefully examined by inspectors and had to conform to the standard masters approved. In the time of Siraj ud daula half of the wages of the weavers was deducted as perquisites of the officers and servants. The Nawab of Oudh and Nizam of Hyderabad also had similar karkhanas for supplying their own needs.[66]

The eighteenth century witnessed certain interesting trends in industrial organization thanks to the expansion of the market by the middle of the century. While the artisan system continued as before, the practice of paying wages to artisans became widely prevalent. If the sixteenth and seventeenth centuries were marked by absence of private workshops owned by private artisans, the eighteenth century was characterized by the advent of artisans as capitalist entrepreneurs. Traders, including Armenians in Bengal employed winders (*nakads*) as wage earners in silk reeleries. Rich weavers began to emerge in Bengal with their own capital who sold their goods freely. A few carpenters in Bengal and Bihar hired others for working in their workshops. Wealthy artisans, master craftsmen or textile printers themselves, of Lucknow having their own equipment engaged poorer artisans or apprentices numbering as large as 500. In Kashmir shawl craftsmen engaged poorer workmen for their looms numbering up to 300. Economically the best instance of advanced or large scale industrial organization now was shipbuilding. The Parsee master carpenter or shipwright engaged hired labourers to meet orders for ships for European companies on contract. Thus arose the graded artisans.[67] The karkhanas exercised considerable influence on urban life and relations between the village and the town. These helped mobility of labour from village to town. Country artisans of proved technical ability were drawn, either voluntarily to the karkhanas or forcibly (as during Aurangzeb's Deccan vice-royalty, from Masulipatam, famous for Calico printing).[68] Thus occupational specialization helped the artisan to acquire status. Further, the karkhanas reinforced the organization of exclusive castes and guilds. As Bernier notes: 'The embroiderer brings up his son. . . . No one marries but in his own trade or profession and this custom is observed almost as rigidly by the Muhammadans as by the Hindus'.[69] The construction of architectural edifices naturally encouraged stone workers, sculptors, carpenters etc. At the same time this led to the growth of a nascent middle class, consisting of such classes as shopkeepers, traders, bankers, brokers, shipbuilders etc. Pelsaert observes that the shopkeeper was held in greater respect than the workman and some of them are well to do but they must not let the fact be seen.[70] Again, the example of the crown infiltrated downwards and tended to diffuse talent. The provincial governors and nobles also encouraged local artisans and workmen, either for their own needs or for offering presents to the great.[71] Thus it is not surprising that cotton and silk weaving became widespread in every household and was pursued during the vacation from agriculture.[72] With the lapse of time changes took place in the industrial organization. But these were too slow and limited to cause any break with the past or usher into industrial revolution. Increase in production to meet the exigencies of a growing market was effected not so much by centralized production and application of superior technology as by the older processes of localization and advances (*dadan*). The artisan system was still pre-eminent. An industrial society was yet to come.

Notwithstanding the qualitative output and the qualitative excellence of India's staple industries, her industrial organization was limited. The workers used cheap instruments. Their fixed and working capital was small. Their technology was elementary. The traditional social system with its hereditary classes generally resulted in a somewhat uniform family centered production under the head who was also the master craftsman, though exigencies of demand and nature of goods (e.g. monuments, sea going ships) occasionally modified it. The social system regulated the impact of market forces. The difference between skilled and unskilled labour was so small that a superior artisan class could grow. Increasing specialization in production led to proliferation of castes. Again, social or caste traditions (and the ruling class) prevented diversity in organization by tying the artisan to a lower social and economic status. Conversely higher caste men could hardly ever hope to own or even control work units. Thus unlike Europe neither the artisan could be an entrepreneur nor did the high caste men take to manufacturing activity.[73]

Role of Karkhanas

The government required diverse products for the satisfaction of its civil and military needs. For this purpose it set up karkhanas or *buyutat*. They played an important role in developing techniques and providing employment to master craftsmen and training to their apprentices. The high quality of the articles used locally and exported abroad has been noticed by travellers.

Price System and Expenditure on the Imperial Household

From Abul Fazl's account it seems that the valuation of goods in the imperial store houses was made on the basis of prevailing market prices. Only this can explain the appointment of experienced men to inquire into previous and current prices.[74] This implies that the 'value' did not represent the actual cost of manufacture, whenever these were products of the imperial karkhanas. Abul Fazl gives an example of such a departure from cost. Carpet woven at a cost of Rs 1802 (*ba kharch raft*) in the imperial karkhanas was valued at Rs 2715 (*arj per nihad*).[75] In other words the price was fixed here at 5 per cent above the cost. Such high valuation might be an exception, but generally speaking the values assigned to goods in imperial store houses were probably higher than the actual cost incurred on acquiring them. The scale over estimation might reasonably be fixed at 25 per cent; that is the actual amount spent on these goods was 20 per cent less than their recorded value. The values given by Pelsaert could be scaled down by 20 per cent to get the actual expenditure.[76]

The annual cost of acquisitions worked out in this way would include the wages of workmen and other employees as well as other expenses on the imperial workshops (karkhanas) where perhaps most of the articles stored in the imperial store houses were made. Thus no separate calculation for expenses in workshops were made.

According to Pelsaert the value of the cloth in the imperial stores was Rs 1,60,13,231 (woollen articles valued at Rs 5,03,252. Other kinds at Rs 1,55,09,279). Reducing the amount by 20 per cent to get the cost price, and, after conversion into *dams* proceeding by the method of calculation already described, the figure of 1,67,32,193 *dams* for the expenditure on cloth for (1595-96) is obtained.

This amount is by no means excessive since from the account given in the *Ain*, one would certainly expect a large amount of expenditure on the wardrobe (*tosha khana*). 'Every season, there were made one thousand complete suits for the imperial wardrobe, and one hundred and twenty, made up in twelve bundles, were always kept in readiness.[77]

Such a large number of garments were perhaps needed because of the practice of conferring robes of honour (*khilat*) on favoured persons. That the robes were given out of the *khasa* dresses is evident from Abul Fazl's statement that Akbar's clothes were found to fit everybody whether tall or short,[78] a fact which has hitherto puzzled many.

There is little specific information in Abul Fazl's description to build up any kind of estimate of annual costs in this department. He says that in Lahore alone there were 1,000 karkhanas making shawls.[79] But since the figure probably included the karkhanas of nobles and even of merchants, it does not help in estimating the imperial expenditure on shawls. Abul Fazl does provide with the prices for a variety of golden (*zarrin*), silken (*abreshmi*) and cotton (*resmani*) cloth.[80] He mentions woollen cloth too as being manufactured at the imperial karkhanas but does not give prices.[81]

The tailoring costs of some dresses are given, but since the number of these is not recorded, one cannot estimate the expenses on the *tosha-khana*. It may, however, be supported that the actual expenditure was even higher than that arrived at from the value given by Pelsaert, since perhaps in the case of robes received in offerings or presents. Pelsaert gives the value of gold pots, dishes, cutlery, figurines, silver utensils as well as chandeliers, bed steads etc., copper ware and porcelain crockery, as Rs 1,42,92,802, this should be scaled down by 20 per cent to give approximate cost prices following the method of calculation the figure of 1,49,34,520 *dams* for expenses is derived during the year

(1595-96). It is assumed that the value of gifts received was offset by the loss through wear and tear which ought to have been high in the case of porcelain. There is little reason to believe that the emperor gave away articles of this kind in gift to his nobles.

Abul Fazl mentions rich trappings and pieces of harness that were used to decorate the *khasa* animals (elephants, horses, camels etc.) for ceremonial occasions these were in addition to the usual harness which was changed periodically.[82] From Pelsaert's statistics the amount spent in (1595-96) on pieces of expensive harness can be calculated at 26,39,043 *dams*.

Akbar had a remarkably rich library, Pelsaert says that there were 24,000 volumes, originals (authors autographs) as well as copies, the estimated value being Rs 6,46,373. The high cost (more than Rs 259 per volume) seems justified because it is not only the high quality of hand made paper and splendid calligraphy that made the books precious, but they were often illustrated profusely by Akbar's painters. This can be seen from such MSS, as have survived. One book, the *Qissa-i-Hamza* contained no less than 1,400 illustrations.[83] The costs might well have included payments made to calligraphers as well as painters and even perhaps to translators of Sanskrit texts which Akbar patronized.[84] A number of calligraphers and painters were on the imperial pay rolls.[85]

Following the method which has been adopted so far the expenses on the library can be estimated at 67,53,940 *dams* in (1595-96). This estimate is possibly on the lower side since it does not include the amount spent on the library staff (the salary of *piyadas* appointed in the department ranged from 600 to 1200 *dams* a month[86] and the payment made to readers who read books aloud to the emperor.[87] It is of interest that the books were not only given away as presents but were given in armas (payment in kind to the army).[88] On the other hand books were also acquired as war booty, as well as in offerings and presents, and possibly as part of property acquired in escheat. These acquisitions probably balanced the losses through imperial presents.

According to Pelsaert the value of tents and other articles used in camps, as entered in the account books was Rs 99,25,545. This in turn gives an expenditure of 1,03,71,182 *dams* for (1595-96). Abul Fazl's detailed description of the layout and organization of the camp in his chapter on the *farrash khana* accords with the high value assigned in Pelsaert's record to tents and furniture. The *Ain* says that one tent designated the *bargah* cost Rs 1000 and there were eleven other kinds of tents, some double storeyed, as well as folding.[89] The *sayabans* (hanging shades) of the tents were made of brocade and velvet and embroidered with gold.[90]

Pelsaert valued the precious stones in the royal treasury at Akbar's death at Rs 6,05,20,521 and the gold ornaments at Rs 190,06,745. These are very high values, yet the fact that they are not round, but detailed, suggests their being totals of actual or detailed valuations of individual pieces. The valuation of the stones must have been a difficult task, and somewhat arbitrary.[91]

But that the total value offered by Pelsaert is not excessive is supported by Abul Fazl's statements in respect of individual stones and gems. He mentions rubies worth Rs 52,000 each and strings of pearls in which each pearl was valued at 30 muhrs (Rs 270).[92]

In trying to estimate the annual expenditure based on the total value of precious stones and ornaments in 1605, one has to remember that several of them were seized as booty from defeated chiefs and rulers.[93] Since precious stones and gold ornaments do not wear out items reposing in the Mughal treasury in 1605 might have been in the possession of the Mughal imperial house for more than a generation and there must have been a recognizable portion inherited from Humayun. It may therefore perhaps be reasonable to assume that about one-third of the total jewels in the imperial treasure at the close of Akbar's reign, were those acquired in booty or as heirlooms. An allowance for presents has to be made (or rather the balance of presents being the value of presents received less than that of gifts awarded) which should have been considerable, since precious stones were the most acceptable items of gifts (*nazr/paishkash*) made to the emperor by the high nobles.[94]

There were in addition jewels acquired through escheat. At least 20 per cent of the gems and ornaments in Akbar's vaults in 1605 had been acquired through gifts and confiscations. The total expenditure on precious stones and ornaments in the 40th regnal year (1595-96) was 4,43,18,868 *dams*. According to Abul Fazl large sums were spent on the construction of forts, serais, schools, houses of worship (*riyaz kada*), tanks, wells etc.[95] He also recorded the wages of labourers and craftsmen and the prices of building materials. The average annual expenditure on buildings was at about one and a half crore *dams*. The emperor granted cash allowances paid out periodically (daily, monthly, yearly) from the imperial treasury. These were called *wazaif* (plural of *wazifa*) and considered part of the *suyurghal*.[96]

There were other departments belonging to the household establishment, viz. illumination (*chirag afrozi*) and the drum house (*naqqar khana*). The drums were used not only during the military marches but they were also used as time announcing device. Though the *Ain* describes these departments,[97] it is not possible to work out annual expenditure on the basis of the data provided for them.

Another head on which the expenditure would not have been inconsequential was the preparation of wines. Although Abul Fazl describes the process of liquor distillation in detail[98] he is silent about the provision of wine in the imperial household. In the seventeenth century, nobles as a matter of course maintained their own *suchi khanas* or wine provisioning establishments.[99]

The imperial household must have had a much larger establishment of this kind than the one maintained by any noble. There were other items too of expenditure such as perfumes and incense[100] and occasionally construction of boats.[101]

In the imperial karkhanas Abul Fazl has included animals and the arsenal within it, while he has placed hunting animals and cash grants and 'alms' under 'Army'. According to him the total expenditure on the household (*buyutat*) in the 19th regnal year amounted to 30,91,86,795 *dams*.[102] Taking all these items of expenditure that Abul Fazl counts under the household or *buyutat* the estimate is of 37,66,86,570 *dams*[103] for the 40th regnal year Abul Fazl does not count under *buyutat* who were put on the rolls of the army.[104] The pay of such officials as held *mansabs* or were *ahadis* is also included under mansabdars and the army establishments. But the large number of clerks, artisans and labourers who were as Abul Fazl explicitly tells elsewhere the rolls of the army appear under household establishment in the estimate.[105]

It is not unlikely that 'civil' or non military lower staff (formally on 'army' rolls) of the imperial establishments received an equal amount in wages and salaries, and that this is spread over in concealed form in the estimates of the expenses on various departments of the *buyutat*. The imperial expenditure on the three main heads viz. the salary bill of the nobles, imperial military establishment, and the imperial household were main.

The *Ahadis*, seemed to have formed the lower ranks[106] of the imperial service. They were also employed in imperial *karkhanas*.

References

1. *Maasir-i-Rahimi*, Persian Text, Vol. 3, pp. 1683-84.
1a. *Maasir-i-Rahimi*, Persian Text, Vol. 2, p. 577.
1b. *Adab-i-Alamgiri*, MS (Abdus Samad Collection, 326/96, Azad Library, Aligarh), f. 25a.
2. Ibid., f. 196a.
3. William Foster, ed., *The English Factories, 1618-21*, Vol. II, p. 198.
4. For a reference to Bakhtawar Khan's karkhanas established with his houses and palaces in Delhi, Agra, Lahore and Burhanpur, see Shaikh Muhammad Baqa, *Mirat-i-Alam*, MS (Abdul Salam Collection 84/314), f. 253b.
5. Shaikh Muhammad Baqa, op. cit., f. 253.
6. Saqi Mustaid Khan, *Maasir-i-Alamgiri*, Bib. Ind., Calcutta, 1871, pp. 405-06.
7. Moreland, *India at the Death of Akbar*, p. 174.
8. Bernier, op. cit., p. 258.
9. Mohammad Waris, op. cit., p. 373.
10. Shaikh Farid Bukhari, *Zakhirat-ul-Khawanin*, Vol. II, p. 88.
11. Sumbul Halim Khan, 'Mughal Court and the Nobility (1707-1715) as seen from the reports of Amber', *PIHC*, 1986.
12. William Foster, ed., op. cit., pp. 149-52.
13. J.A. Taylor, *A Descriptive and Historical Account of the Cotton Manufactures of Dacca in Bengal*, London, 1851, pp. 82, 84.
14. Ibid., p. 82.
15. Streynsham Master, *The Diaries of Streynsham Master, 1675-80 and other contemporary papers relating thereto* (ed. R.C. Temple), Vol. II, pp. 173-74.
16. Jagdish Narayan Sarkar, 'Cotton Trade of Patna in Early Seventeenth Century', *IHQ*, No. 4, 1936, Chapter I, Sec. A; Peter Mundy, *The Travels*, Vol. II, pp. 142, 145, 150-51, 369.
17. Cf. A.J. Qaisar, 'The Role of Brokers in Medieval India', *IHR*, Vol. I, No. 2, 1974, pp. 220-46.
18. Ibid., pp. 245-46.
19. Ibid., p. 236.
20. William Foster, ed., op. cit., p. 198; M. Ahtar Ali, *The Mughal Nobility under Aurangzeb*, p. 157.
21. Bernier, op. cit., p. 44.
22. Thomas Bowrey, op. cit., p. 105.
23. *English Factory (1646-50)*, pp. 59, 64-65.
24. Cf. Bowrey, op. cit., pp. 214-15. Also Vilhelm Slomann, *Bizarre designs in silks*, pp. 110-11. For details see A.J. Qaisar, *The Indian Response to European Technology and Culture (1498-1707)*, p. 12.
25. Tavernier, op. cit., Vol. II, p. 12; S.A. Khan, ed., *Johan Marshal in India–Notes and Observations*, pp. 23-24; F. Pelsaert, *Remonstrantie*, tr. W.H. Moreland and P. Geyl as (*Jahangir's India*), p. 46; Jagdish Narayan Sarkar,

'Transport of Saltpetre in India in the Seventeenth Century', in *JBORS*, XXX, pt 1, 1939, pp. 34-51.

26. Tavernier, op. cit., Vol. I, p. 116.
27. A.J. Qaisar, *The Indian Response to European Technology and Culture*, p. 132.
28. Cf. Otto Kurz, *European Clocks and Watches in the Near East*, London, 1975, pp. 62-63.
29. Moreland, *From Akbar to Aurangzeb*, pp. 223, 283. Nizampatam was the first port in the Eastern Coast of India where the English landed.
30. William Foster, ed., op. cit., p. 141.
31. Ibid., p. 327.
32. Ibid., p. 229.
33. Ibid., p. 99.
34. Ibid., p. 5.
35. Tavernier, op. cit., Vol. I, pp. 121-28; Bernier, op. cit., pp. 18-20; S.N. Sen, ed., *Indian Travels of Thevenot and Careri*, p. 138.
36. *Imperial Gazetteer of India*, Vol. IV, p. 128.
37. Ma Huan, op. cit., p. 405.
38. *Ain*, Vol. I, pp. 143-47.
39. Inayat Khan, *Shahjahan Namah*, p. 206.
40. Abdul Hamid Lahori, op. cit., E&D, Vol. VII, p. 46.
41. Macro Polo, *Travels*, Vol. II, pp. 383, 394.
42. Abul Fazl has listed a dozen varieties of perfumed oils, briefly describing the ingredients used and the method employed. See *Ain*, Vol. I, pp. 79-80. Likewise, *Majma-us-Sana* on p. 25 (Raza Library, Rampur, MS) also describes some perfumed oil making processes.
43. Barbosa, op. cit., Vol. I, p. 112; *Ain*, Vol. I, p. 79. Also Yusuf Hussain, *Medieval Indian Culture*, pp. 133-34.
44. *Ain.*, Vol. II, p. 190; *Tuzuk-i-Jahangiri*, pp. 3-5.
45. W. Finch in Foster, *English Factories*, p. 177; Shah Nawaz Khan, *Mirat-i-Aftab-nama*, MS, Asiatic Society, Calcutta, 244a.
46. Murtaza Hussain, *Hadiqatul Iqalim* (Nawal Kishore Press, Lucknow, 1879), p. 125a.
47. *Ain*, Vol. I, pp. 78-79.
48. Ibid., pp. 80-81.
49. Ibid., Vol. II, p. 122. Here it was extracted from aloe wood and was called *mandali* the best variety of wood.
50. Ibid., Vol. II, p. 123.
51. *Majma-us-Sana*, pp. 17, 21. For the dyeing of paper also see *Bayaz-i-Khushbie*, iiia, 121b, 123b (I.O.L., Ethe 2784).
52. *Majma-us-Sana*, p. 39.
53. Surendra Gopal, 'Forms of Textile Production in Gujarat in 17th Century', in *PIHC*, 1965.
54. H.K. Naqvi, *Urban Centres and Industries in upper India (1556-1803)*, pp. 137-42.

55. Pelsaert, op. cit., pp. 2, 9; Bernier, op. cit., pp. 202, 439, 441.
56. *Ain*, Vol. I, p. 94; Vol. II, pp. 170-353.
57. Ma Huan quoted in H.L. Chablani, *Economic Condition of India during the 16th Century*, p. 37.
58. Varthema, Ludovic di Varthema of Bologina, *Travels in Egypt, Syria, Persia, India, Ethiopia*, pp. 107, 111-12.
59. Barbosa, op. cit., Vol. I, p. 154.
60. *Imperial Gazetteer of India*, Vol. IV, Calcutta, 1930, p. 128.
61. Tavernier, op. cit., tr. V. Ball, Vol. II, pp. 2-3.
62. Ma Huan, op. cit., p. 532 for Bengal; for Gujarat *Amir Khusrau, Qiran-us-Sadain*, p. 228.
63. Barbosa, op. cit., Vol. I, pp. 189, 223; Varthema, op. cit., p. 107.
64. Jadunath Sarkar, *Mughal Administration*, p. 125, till the eighties of the eighteenth century.
65. Ali Muhammad Khan, *Mirat-i-Ahmadi, Supplement*, p. 11.
66. J.A. Taylor, op. cit., pp. 82-84. According to Chicherov certain features of the Mughal workshops were similar to those of the state manufactories in France at the close of the seventeenth century and beginning of eighteenth century as well as with the imperial manufactories in Czarist Russia in the seventeenth century, employing mainly serfs as handicraftsmen. Chicherov, op. cit., p. 184n; Irfan Habib and Tapan Ray Chaudhuri, ed., *Cambridge Economic History of India* (hereafter *CEHI*), Vol. I, p. 287.
67. Bernier, op. cit., p. 254; *CEHI*, Vol. I, p. 284; Vol. II, p. 24; K.K. Dutta, *Survey of India's Social Life and Economic Conditions in 18th Century*, Calcutta, 1961, pp. 109-10.
68. Jadunath Sarkar, *Mughal Administration*, p. 128.
69. Bernier, op. cit., p. 259.
70. Pelsaert, op. cit., p. 61.
71. Manucci, op. cit., Vol. II, p. 431.
72. Robert Orme, *Historical Fragments of the Mogul Empire*, London, 1805, p. 409; William Foster, *Early Travels in India* (Delhi Reprint), Vol. I, pp. 1-4.
73. *CEHI*, Vol. I, pp. 277-78, 287.
74. *Ain*, Vol. I, p. 101.
75. Ibid., p. 51.
76. Moreover if the valuation kept on being revised, it might have been influenced by a rise in price levels which, though restrained in Akbar's time must have resulted in inflating valuation of earlier purchases to some extent. This would have the result of increasing the annual expenditure calculated for the 40th R.Y. well above the real figure.
77. *Ain*, Vol. I, p. 96.
78. Ibid.
79. Ibid.
80. Ibid., pp. 98-101.

81. Ibid., pp. 101-02. (The prices are not given in the text).
82. Ibid., pp. 134-38, 143.
83. Ibid., pp. 107-13. Arif Qandhari says each volume of *Qissa-i-Hamza* prepared in two years cost 20,000 *dams* (pp. 45-46).
84. Ibid., pp. 111-13; Badauni, *Muntakhab-ut-Tawarikh*, Vol. II, pp. 336-66.
85. Ibid., pp. 113-15.
86. Ibid.
87. Ibid., p. 110.
88. Badauni, op. cit., Vol. II, p. 202.
89. *Ain* (tr.), Vol. I, pp. 55-57.
90. Ibid., p. 55.
91. Tavernier, op. cit., Vol. I, pp. 112-13; Vol. II, pp. 72-73. It is related that only the deposed Emperor Shahjahan was able to estimate the value of a particular diamond correctly.
92. *Ain*, Vol. I, pp. 15-16, compares Tavernier's prices for a ruby (Rs 95,000) and a large topaz (Rs 181,000) in the Mughal treasury (Vol. II, pp. 100-102).
93. *Akbar Nama*, Vol. II, p. 214; Vol. III, p. 836.
94. John Mildenhall, *Early Travels (1599-1606)*, p. 55; Abul Fazl, *Akbar Nama*, Vol. II, p. 149; Nizamuddin Ahmad, *Tabaqat-i-Akbari*, Vol. II, p. 155. Cf. Tavernier, op. cit., Vol. II, pp. 100-01.
95. *Ain*, Vol. I, pp. 232-37.
96. Ibid.
97. Ibid. (tr.), Vol. I, p. 50.
98. Ibid.
99. Munshi Nand Ram Kastha Srivastya, *Siyaqnama A.D. 1694-6*, lithographed (Nawal Kishore, Lucknow, 1879), p. 184.
100. *Ain*, Vol. I, pp. 78-81.
101. *Akbar Nama*, Vol. III, p. 716. In the 41st Regnal Year Rs 16,338 were spent on building a boat of a tonnage or more than 15,000 men.
102. *Ain* (tr.), Vol. I, p. 9.
103. This covers expenditure incurred on animals, arsenal and the entire expenditure on the household calculated.
104. *Ain* (tr.), Vol. I, pp. 259-60.
105. The estimate for the pay of foot retainers on the army rolls amounts to 6 crore *dams*.
106. See Shireen Moosvi, *The Economy of the Mughal Empire*, pp. 224-25. It is however doubtful if the *ahadis* constituted the lower rank in the imperial service.

6

Labour during the Mughal Period

The most useful purpose served by the state karkhanas was that the system provided greatest encouragement to the workers to improve their skills. The refined taste of the emperors determining the quality of the goods set the standard and provided models for the craftsmen of the country to emulate them and lead to widespread diffusion of the skill throughout the country, a skill that passed on from generation to generation and when the state karkhanas were gone the skill still continued in the country.

The emperor also required that the valuable and artistic articles produced either in the karkhanas of the capital or the provinces be placed before him in the *Diwan-i-Am* and that the artisan who was the maker of the piece be also presented along with the exhibit. This process gave an opportunity to the emperor to know personally the skilled workmen[1] and at the same time inspired the craftsmen to perfect their skill and get into the employment of the state karkhanas so that they could get the opportunity of being presented before the emperor which they considered as the highest honour.

The major factor that induced the artisans to secure employment in the state karkhanas was the deplorable condition of the artisans who worked independently of their own. The lot of the labourers was not happy nor conducive to the true economic development of the country. At the capital which was the largest and richest city in the land, there were no private factories, no workshops owned and managed by skilful artisans on their own behalf. As Bernier rightly observes, 'If the artists and manufacturers were encouraged, the useful and fine arts would flourish, but these unhappy men are condemned, treated with harshness, and inadequately remunerated for their labour. The rich will have every article at cheap rate. When an Omrah or mansabdar requires the services of an artisan, he sends to the bazar for him, employing force, if necessary, to make the poor man work, and after the task is finished, the unfeeling lord pays, not according to the value of the labour, but agreeably to his own standard of fair remuneration, the artisan having reason to congratulate himself if the *korrah* has not been given in part payment. How then can it be expected that any spirit of emulation should animate the artist or manufacturer? Instead of contending for a superiority of reputation, his only anxiety is to finish his work, and to earn the pittance that shall supply him with a piece of bread. The artists, therefore, who arrive at any eminence in their art are those only who are in the service of the king or of some powerful Omrah, and who work exclusively for their patron'.[2] The artisan, therefore, always considered it safe to get into the employment of a state karkhana where he was sure of a fair remuneration either in monthly salary or daily wages according to the nature of the work.

The life style of the ladies of the royalty and nobility was exceedingly magnificent requiring the services of a large number of people of every vocation. This provided employment to the artisans and service class in and outside the palace in the royal karkhanas and to private artists. The superiority of Indian muslins, brocades, jewellery, decorated utensils, tapestry and carpets in India and abroad owes much to the dwellers. Their clothes, ornaments, cosmetics and make up articles, pandan and caskets provided sustenance to art and artists, 'The arts in the Indies would long ago have lost their beauty and delicacy' writes Bernier, 'if the monarch and principal Omrahs did not keep in their pay a number of artists who work in their houses . . . and stimulated to exertion by the hope of reward and the fear of *korrah*. The protection afforded by powerful patrons to rich merchants and tradesmen who pay the workmen higher wages tended also to preserve the arts. Rather higher wages, for it should not be inferred from the goodness of the manufacturers, that the workman is held in esteem, or arrives at a state of independence. Nothing but sheer necessity or blows from a cudgel keep him employed, he never can become rich and he feels it no trifling matter, if he has the means of satisfying the cravings of hunger, and of covering his body with the coarsest raiment. If money be gained, it does not in any measure go into his pocket, but only serves to increase the wealth of the merchant who, in his turn, is not a little perplexed how to guard against some act of outrage and extortion on the part of his superiors'.[3] The karkhana was the proprietor of the weaving shop. The weavers were mostly poor because of the exploitation of the karkhanadars. They were meagrely paid. The karkhanadars employed the artisans and paid them in cash. The artisans trained their children and the art went down from father to son.

Abul Fazl had given sufficient attention to Akbar's effort to recruit new artisans from far off places and settle them in the cities of north India. Father Monserrate also recorded of such attempts. Jahangir and Shahjahan continued this tradition and carpet or shawl industry of Kashmir and Lahore owed their fame to their patronage which gave impetus to the different industries within the country that created some of the world's best artisan work of the contemporary period. However, excepting a few, most of the artisans had remained anonymous and if we believe Bernier and other foreign travellers, their life was neither attractive nor rosy. The huge demand of the state must have needed hundreds of artisans throughout the empire.

Since Muaiwiyah (661-80) Muslims established and adopted the Persian custom of awarding robes of honour which were manufactured locally. Mughals followed this customs and bestowed *khilats* twice a year, besides the robes of condolences to the bereaved heir. Robes (*khilat-i-haft parcha*) consisted of seven articles. They were distributed on two birthdays of the emperor, according to Lunar and Solar year, then on the occasion of lunar anniversary of coronation, two Ids, Nauroz when the sun enters the Aries as well as to new entrants to nobility and on other occasions like the success in the field of battle and so on. Therefore there were karkhanas all over the country, some with specialization and some owned by the princes. Taken all together the number of artisans would constitute sizeable work force which increased as the number of nobility increased. Of course, the emperors wanted the artisans to be treated well and often instructed *Mir Saman* to do so. How far it was done is a different matter.

The craftsmen were not free agents. The services of only those men who had attained a high degree of skill in the manufacture of particular commodities were requisitioned. Such craftsmen were transported from different parts of the empire to the capital where they worked in the state factories (karkhanas) under expert guidance. Subedars and eminent nobles vied with each other in securing the services of best craftsmen by offering liberal rewards. Speaking of prince Khurram (afterwards Shahjahan), Pelsaert says, 'He was a patron of all craftsmen to whom he paid such high wages that he attracted all the splendour of his father's court'.[4]

The knowledge of manufacturing classes is much fuller. The workmen at Agra, as Pelsaert informs, followed hereditary occupations. Among the manufacturing classes the weavers and the workers in metal, for example, the blacksmith, the goldsmith (who were also dealers in gold), and the manufacturer of bell metal utensils (*kansari*) were the more important ones. Certain classes of artisans appear to have been either directly depending on or closely associated with the provincial government and its officers. There are repeated references in the *Baharistan*[5] to the workmen and labourers of the navy. Elsewhere the same work refers to the government karkhanas and their workers.

There was a different pattern like the migration of weavers from Sindh to Bombay or the practice of placing surplus trainees from the imperial karkhanas with the nobles and rajas all over the country. Urban industries in western Deccan seem to have further developed having few industries by the middle of the century except for the karkhanas established by the government. There were several large scale industries which were distinct from the ordinary urban industries.

Many artisans were engaged in royal karkhanas. Others worked to private orders with raw materials handed in.

As far as the impact of these karkhanas on urban life and the relation between the village and the town is concerned it requires a detailed study but certain features deserve special mention.

First of all these helped the mobility of labour from village to town. Country artisans of proved technical ability were drawn, either voluntarily to the karkhanas or forcibly (as during Aurangzeb's Deccan viceroyalty), from Masulipatam, a place famous for calico printing. Thus occupational specialization helped the artisan to acquire status. Secondly they helped organization of exclusive castes and guilds as Bernier notes, 'The embroiderer brings up his son as an embroiderer, the son of a goldsmith becomes goldsmith and a physician of the city educates his son for a physician. No one marries but in his own trade or profession, and this custom is observed almost as rigidly by the Mahometans as by the Gentiles, to whom it is expressly enjoined by their law'.[6] The construction of architectural edifices naturally encouraged stone workers, sculptors, carpenters etc. At the same time this led to a nascent middle class consisting of such classes as shopkeepers, traders, bankers, brokers, shipbuilders, etc. Pelsaert observes that 'the shopkeeper was held in greater respect than the workman and some of them were well to do but they must not let the fact be seen.[7] Thirdly, the example of the crown infiltrated downward and tended to diffuse talent. The provincial governors and nobles also encouraged local artisan and workman, either for their own needs or for offering presents to the great. Thus it is not surprising that cotton and silk weaving became widespread in every household and was pursued during the vacation from agriculture.

With regard to urban labour in Mughal India, it appears that there was prevalence of *begar* or forced labour or ill paid labour.

Possibly they were unwilling and had to be given some material inducements to work there. But there is no hint to their unwillingness in the records. For it may be said that the winders insisted on prior payment in order to save their position by taking advance wages. The Dutch factor at Agra (1620-26), Pelsaert observes that, 'there are three classes of people who are indeed nominally free but whose status differs little from voluntary slavery; workmen, peons or servants and shop-keepers. For the workman again there were two scourages—low wages and oppression by the governors, nobles, the diwans, the kotwals, the bakshis and other royal officers. If any of these wants a workman, the man is not asked if he is willing to come, but is seized in the home or in the street, well beaten if he should raise an objection and in the evening paid half his wages or nothing at all.'[8]

Bernier's observation has been quoted earlier regarding the treatment given to artisans.[9] Bernier's assertion that agricultural oppression led the peasants to migrate to the town and to the camps indicates that absconding or displaced peasants became wage labourers and leaving the villages to migrate towns. In Aurangzeb's revenue regulation of the first decade of his reign also the flight of peasants loomed large. Was this increasing flow of peasants responsible for the worsening position of the workers and artisans and growth of servile classes? 'The amount of labour expanded in the performance of personal services', was, according to Moreland, 'one of the outstanding economic facts of the age of Akbar'.[10] Babur found the craftsmen of Hindustan organized in rigid and exclusive castes.

Babur's praise for India as containing unnumbered and endless workmen of every kind probably suggests that the scarcity of artisans in the new techniques was long over. 'Another good thing in Hindustan is that it had unnumbered and endless workmen of every kind. There is a fixed caste (*jami*) for every sort of work and for everything, which has done that work or that thing from father to son till now. Mulla Sharf, writing in the *Zafar Nama* about the building of the Timur Beg's stone mosque lays stress on the fact that on it 200 stone-cutters worked, from Azarbaijan, Fars, Hindustan and other countries. But 680 men worked daily on my buildings in Agra, Sikri, Biana, Dulpur, Gwalior and Koil. In the same way there are numberless artisans and workmen of every sort in Hindustan'.[11]

The specialization in different handicrafts and resultant proficiency of the respective craftsmen according to Bernier's observations regarding rigid adherence to one's hereditary profession are echoed by Stavorinus, 'Artificers confine themselves to one single work . . . a goldsmith will not work in silver nor a silversmith in gold. In the *aurungs* or looms, a weaver will only weave one single sort of stuff during the whole life unless he be compelled to take another in hand'.[12]

European travellers, by and large, have expressed their higher appreciation of the skills of Indian metal workers. An important factor characterizing the socio-economic position of the small scale commodity producing artisan was his allegiance to a definite caste connected with a definite kind of production activity. Caste membership was determined first and foremost by the hereditary occupation that was passed on from father to son, and also by the tradition of marrying within one's own caste. The caste organization served to perpetuate the traditional methods of cloth manufacture while definite castes and subdivisions of caste specialized in the production of definite sorts.

According to E. Ives, an English traveller, who visited India in the mid-eighteenth century, the artisans 'will never be put out of their old way of working and should you be ever so desirous of instructing them, or showing them a more expeditious method, they will plead the custom of their forefathers, for which they have so great a veneration that they were never known even in a single detail to depart from it'.[13] However, the development of the productive forces in the crafts, the depending of the social division of labour, market demands and other factors undermined and destroyed these caste limitations.

The caste organizations of the artisans waged a resolute battle for privileges in the feudal system of social relations. The caste organization was often used by the artisans to struggle against the exploitation by the nobles and merchants. Feudal exploitation exerted an enormous influence on the condition of the small scale commodity producing artisans. The nobles who directly or indirectly appropriated an enormous share of the trading profits throve also on the commercial exploitation of the artisans. The class of the nobles which was controlling the state machine, could use so powerful an instrument of exploitation as the taxation system. Thus high taxes on Hindus (the introduction of *jazija*, a special tax on non-Muslims) under Aurangzeb at the end of the seventeenth century, and the persecution of 'infidels' in general became the state policy during that period and inflicted a heavy blow on the crafts and commerce in the country.

The system of state monopolies on the production or purchase of certain goods (saltpetre, dyes, salt, diamond, etc.) enabled the officials of the state and some nobles and also the tax farmers (for these monopolies were often sold to private persons), merchants or nobles to oppress the artisans in many ways. Similar 'monopolies' could be introduced by will of the ruler on any item. Thus in the early seventeenth century 'the Great Mogul and the Persian Shah took great affection into fine paintings' manufactured near Masulipatam, which were famed for their quality. The nobles, using their right of monopoly purchase were among the main consumers of the artisan made articles, particularly the high quality ones. Special decrees fixed the prices for various goods and the labour of the artisans. The arbitrary rule of the nobles, extended to many spheres of the artisan's economic and political life. The rulers could resettle large group of artisans to newly built towns, suburbs, etc. Sometimes the nobles opposed the introduction of progressive technological innovations by Europeans which tended to change the traditional techniques.

The authorities strove to control the relations between the artisans and the market. Abul Fazl tells us that the town head, the kotwal 'of every guild of artificers . . . should name one as guild master and another as a broker by whose intelligence the business of purchase and sale should be conducted'.[14]

The nobles often strove to use the caste organization of the artisans for their ends. The artisans were subjected to all sorts of plunder and violence on the part of various representatives of nobles elite–from the Shah or rajah and their satraps down to the lowest functionary of the state apparatus and the small zamindar land owner. Information on such plunder is contained in numerous source materials of the sixteenth and eighteenth centuries. Thus Ferishta gives a vivid picture of the arbitrary acts committed by the jagirdars in Bijapur in the late sixteenth century to squeeze money from peasants and artisans.[15]

At the beginning of the seventeenth century in Golconda the artisans were compelled to 'pay somewhat to the governor where they live, or do his work gratis . . .'. Bernier wrote, 'that the jagirdars, governors and contractors have an authority almost absolute over the peasantry, and nearly as much over the artisans and merchants of the towns and villages within their district and nothing can be imagined more cruel and oppressive than the manner in which it is exercised'.[16] He wrote that this was one of the main reasons responsible for the decline of commerce and the crafts in Mughal empire in the second half of the seventeenth century. Describing the violence exercised by Aurangzeb's soldiers, Manucci, an Italian, wrote that they seized everything they could lay their hands on.

The grim life of the Indian artisans was described also by Pelsaert in 1620s. He wrote, 'for the work there are two scourages, the first of which is low wages. . . . The second is oppression of the governor, the nobles, the diwan, the kotwal, the bakshi and other royal officers'.[17]

During this period Indian artisans were passive objects of exploitation by land owners and moneylenders. They conducted a stubborn and at times successful struggle to preserve and improve their position in Indian society. A passive form of that struggle was the departure of the artisans notably the weavers from places where they were subjected to oppression. The artisans often used their caste organizations in the struggle for their rights. The Indian artisans were waging continuous struggle against the exploitation of nobles, merchants, moneylenders and the new colonial exploitation. The artisans also participated widely in the popular movements of the Sikhs, Marathas and others which in the seventeenth and eighteenth centuries threw Mughal India into a deep political crisis.

Training to Artisans

The caste organization was itself a training ground for the artisans. Various occupations were hereditary as castes were the representatives of the various crafts. From father to son by heredity and family training, the skill in the artist was handed down. In the days of Mughals there is no mention of existence of schools and colleges for the training of arts and crafts. Babur writes, '. . . another advantage of Hindustan is the infinite number of craftsmen of all professions and industries which abound in it. This is not perhaps as astonishing when one considers that industries are practised in the family being handed in from father to son'.[18] Abul Fazl mentions, 'skilful masters and craftsmen have settled in the country to teach people an improved system of manufacture'.[19] Very ably Pelsaert sums up labour in Jahangir's India. He says '. . . workman's children can follow no occupation other than that of their father, nor can they intermarry with any other caste'.[20]

'The embroiderer brings up his son as an embroiderer', says Bernier, 'a goldsmith's son becomes a goldsmith and the physician of the city educates his son for a physician. No one marries but in his own caste and profession and this custom is observed almost rigidly by the Mahometans, by the Gentile to whom it is expressly enjoined by the law'.[21]

'Skilful artisans', says Jadunath Sarkar, 'trained in the imperial workshops, specially apprentices, after completing their technical education found employment with the nobles and the rajas, as all of them were not required by the Mughal government. . . . In this way their skill was transplanted all over the country. The most notable instance of the diffusion of their talent and elevation of the cultural level of the country by the action of the court is supplied by the school of careful painters and musicians'.[22]

During the hey days of the Mughals, however, private factories or workshops owned and managed by skilful independent artisans on their own behalf seemed to have been non-existent.

Economic Position of Artisans

The information on the economic position of artisans is extremely scanty. Very few incidental details are available from the *Memoirs* of Babur, *Ain-i-Akbari* and some observations of a few foreign travellers but no connected account in contemporary chronicles is available to us. Babur alludes in his *Memoirs* to the 'unnumbered and endless workmen of every kind', infinite number of artisans in different crafts and industries as one of the advantages of Hindustan.[23] Abul Fazl speaks of skilled masters and craftsmen having settled in the country. He also mentions the wages of skilled and unskilled labourers of different categories.[24] Except such isolated bits of information there is no sixteenth century account of the condition of industrial labour. But in the absence of any economic revolution, the condition in the seventeenth century might be considered to be equally applicable to the sixteenth century as well.

Broadly speaking the industrial workers or artisans may be divided into two categories corresponding to the forms of industrial organization; the free artisans working on their own under the artisan system, and the regimented workers working to order under the karkhana system. Under the artisan system the artisans, possessing little resources, worked at home on their own initiative, from the raw material to the marketing state. At times they worked to order of foreign merchants or the brokers with advances of money but could not always deliver finished goods. Even Delhi had no private workshops of skilled independent artisans. Most artisans sought to improve their lot by joining the state karkhanas.

Under the state karkhana system the artisan seemed to exchange freedom for security. They worked under strict regimentation and to dictation as day labourers from morning to evening as is described in the accounts of Pelsaert and Bernier. The latter writes, 'The artisans repair every morning to their respective karkhanas where they remained employed in the whole day and in the evening return to their homes.[25] The accounts of Howkins, Pelsaert and De Laet to the effect that a work done by a single European worker would be done by 3 or 4 Indian labourers might mean either that the efficiency of the latter compared unfavourably with the Europeans or that there was excessive specialization. The absence of private factories by artisans in the seventeenth century was not due to 'want of genius' among Indians as according to Bernier there were ingenious men in every part of the Indies.[26] In fact there were serious disadvantages operating against the artisans.

Notwithstanding the combination of such a dismal array of adverse conditions, the standard of excellence attained by individual artisans was very high. Bernier approvingly writes, 'Numerous are the instances of handsome pieces of workmanship made by persons, destitute of tools, and who can scarcely be said to have received instructions from a master. Sometimes they imitate so perfectly articles of European manufacturing that the difference between the original and copy can hardly be discerned. Among other things the Indians make excellent muskets, and fowling pieces and such beautiful gold ornaments that it may be doubted if the exquisite workmanship of those articles can be exceeded by any European goldsmith. I have often admired the beauty, softness and delicacy of their paintings and miniatures and was particularly struck with the exploits of Akbar painted on a shield by a celebrated artist, who is said to have been seven years in completing the picture. I thought it a wonderful performance. The Indian painters are chiefly deficient in just proportions and in the expression of the fact but these defects would soon be corrected if they possessed good masters and were instructed in the rules of art'.[27] It may reasonably be held that the standard would have been much higher under more encouraging circumstances or that the high standard would have been limited not to a few individuals but become general.

In fact there were some favourable conditions for the artisans. Of these the first was royal encouragement. Akbar directed some ranks of nobles to wear special kinds of local fabrics. He also persuaded the carpet weavers of Persia to settle in Agra, Fatehpur Sikri and Lahore. Such patronage helped the development of silk, carpet and shawl industries in the country and tended to improve the condition of workers in such crafts. Abul Fazl writes, 'Through the attention of His Majesty, a variety of new manufactures is established in the country and the clothes fabricated in Persia, Europe and China have become cheap and plenty. The skill of manufacturers has increased with their number. Again Kashmiri shawls, formerly costly and used by nobles, became cheaper and came to be worn by people of all degree. Lahore alone had more than 1000 manufacturers of shawls. Akbar had intelligent artisans deputed to Goa to 'examine and bring to the emperor's knowledge, the various productions of art and skill to be found at that time'. Such artisans after gaining knowledge there returned and were applauded for their skill.[28]

The second favourable factor was the encouragement of some powerful or influential nobles. But these were not such as to neutralize the bad effects of the adverse ones. Bernier remarks that the degradation of artistic handicrafts was retarded by (i) the influence of the imperial workshops and by (ii) the protection of a few powerful patrons which resulted in (iii) the payment of higher wages tends also to preserve the arts. Bernier continues, 'I say rather higher wages for it should not be inferred from the goodness of the manufacturers, that the workman is held in esteem or arrives at a state of independence. Nothing but sheer necessity or blows from a cudgel keeps him employed, he never can become rich and he feels it no trifling matter if he has the means of satisfying the cravings of hunger and covering his body with the coarsest garment. If money be gained it does not in any measure go into his pocket, but only serves to increase the wealth of the merchant, who in his turn, is not a little perplexed how to guard against some act of outrage and extortion on the part of his superiors'.[29]

The imperial workshops helped to diffuse talent and raise the cultural level of the country. All the skilled trained artisans or apprentices, finishing their technical education (e.g. painters and musicians) were not absorbed there. The surplus was employed by the nobles and the rajahs. Again in conformity to the accepted rules of court etiquette, the nobles had to present the rarest or best articles, natural or manufactured, to the king, princes and ministers. Hence the former had to get presentable and worthy goods manufactured by local craftsmen after supplying them with money and materials. This encouraged arts and crafts.

But by and large the condition of artisans, craftsmen and industrial workers as portrayed in contemporary sources was bad during the sixteenth and seventeenth centuries. Moreland has summed up the position, saying that the artisan in mid-seventeenth century was 'substantially in the same position (at least as bad) as about 1923. He worked mainly for the benefit of merchants, purchasers and middlemen, depended on them for current expenses and had no reserve left to face a period of stress or crisis. Judged by the familiar test or resistance to the stress of famine (e.g. the Gujarat famine of 1630-31) his economic position was unsatisfactory. The only prospect of improvement lay in the influence of a rich and powerful patron. But only a few individuals could expect such enlightened patronage. The vast majority of workers lived on the bare margin of subsistence.[30] So it may be concluded accordingly that the lot of the labourers was not happy, nor conducive to the true economic development of the country.

The karkhanas or manufactories maintained by the Great Mughals at important places for supplying their needs or those of official aristocracy seemed to have lingered up till the middle of the eighteenth century. What Abul Fazl and Bernier have said about these are faintly echoed by Foster, 'The native princes and chiefs of various description, the retainers of numerous dependents, afforded a constant employment to a vast number of indigenous manufactures, who supplied their masters with gold and silver stuffs, curiously flowered plain muslins and diversity of beautiful silks and other articles of Asiatic luxury.[31]

Weavers were not wholly concentrated in European settlements, though the Europeans were the chief buyers of cloths woven by them. The court of directors, as also its servants in Bengal tried to encourage weavers to reside under their protection within the bounds of Calcutta.[32]

Apart from the karkhanas of the emperor or nobles the silk weavers found employment with the Europeans. Many English factors in Bengal used to purchase raw silk and employed weavers for carrying on private trade.[33] The Dutch and the French had also many weavers in their employment.[34] Bernier reported that there were as many as 700 silk weavers in the service of Dutch and 300 to 400 each employed by the French and the English.[35] However, much of the raw silk was sent to Gujarat where the weaving was carried on.[36]

Though certain technological innovations seemed to have been incorporated, the looms of Indian weavers remained simple and could be manufactured locally.[37]

The process of separation of crafts from agriculture and the town from country was intensified particularly throughout the seventeenth and eighteenth centuries. This process led to the rapid growth of weaver settlements and also to the increase in the number of weavers among the urban population. There were weavers in practically all Indian towns, commercial and industrial centres–they comprised the numerous army of artisans–commodity producers. In the 1620s Masulipatam had 7000 weavers, Hariharpur (Orissa) had 3000 weavers, who were 'house keepers'. In Banaras and its suburbs there were about 7000 weavers in the 1640s.[38] In the 1630s there were about 3000 'families of weavers' in each of the two large towns of Sindh-Thatta and Nasarpur.[39] At the beginning of the seventeenth century weavers accounted for the greater part of the population in such towns as Hooghly, Kasim Bazar, Patna, Balasore, Surat, Ahmedabad, Baroach, Baroda, Burhanpur and others.[40] Dacca, one of the a largest centres of cotton cloth production had in the 1620s a population of about 150,000 to 200,000.[41] Weavers accounted for a large part of its population. In the town of Malda, another major weaving centre of Bengal, there were about 4000 looms in 1807. In the early seventeenth century many weaver settlements were located around large commercial and industrial centres in Gujarat. According to the testimony of Pelsaert, a Dutch traveller, in the 1620s the population of the Bengal towns of Chabaspur and in Sonargaon and also in the 'surrounding villages . . . all live by the weaving industry and the practice has the highest reputation and quality.[42] Weavers lived also in the settlements around Dacca.[43] In the seventeenth and the eighteenth centuries the weaver settlements around towns could be found also in Orissa, where weavers living in the skirts of Balasore produced special sort of cotton cloth (*sannol, sanu*) as well as in Malabar and other parts of the country.[44]

During the great famine in 1630 a large number of weavers who had settled around Surat literally starved to death and many thousands of weavers died in Pulicat, Sao Tome, Madras and other towns on the Coromandel Coast. Links with the market and the development of social division of labour increasingly converted the weavers' implements into commodities. Particularly important is the fact that in the sixteenth century in Bengal towns there were special artisans manufacturing reeds for looms. In this period many small scale commodity producer-weavers took their products to the market for sale.

In the second half of the eighteenth century the English East India Company punished weavers who failed to fulfil their obligations. For example, weavers who did not hire workers and could not return the advances they had received from the company were prohibited from weaving cloth 'for bazaar sales'.[45]

The weaver organizations were sometimes headed by merchants. At the end of the eighteenth century and the beginning of the nineteenth century in Maharashtra the urban weavers were divided into special schemes for the payment of taxes.

At Qasim Bazar in Bengal in the middle of the seventeenth century the Dutch employed 700 to 800 silk weavers and the English and the French probably 300 to 400 each but mostly in the cottages of these men the labourers seemed to have lacked foresight and even the integrity of the purpose so necessary for a better wage.

Tavernier refers to high efficiency of Brampour weavers in making clean and white fine muslins which were transported to Persia, Turkey, Muscovie, Poland, Arabia, Cairo and other places. Likewise the efficiency of Sironj chintz painters and manufacturers has been praised. He says . . . muslin at Sironj is so fine that one appears naked by putting it on. . . . The governor sends it to lords and the Mughal Seraglio. Women of harem make garments for hot weather and the kings are glad to see them dance in this cloth garments.[46] Likewise efficiency of silk stuffs of Ahmedabad manufacturers has been highly spoken of. Tavernier also praises muslin manufacturers of Malwa. *Mirat-i-Ahmadi* refers to the efficiency of weavers in the art of weaving golden and silken stuffs such as *kin khabs* velvet gauze and embroidery unequalled in India for colour and beauty.[47] Durate Barbosa speaking of the arts and crafts of Bombay pays high tribute to the genius of the skilled mechanics and craftsmen of all types 'no less experts than weavers and artisans of the flemish towns of this period'.[48] Among the many commodities produced by them are mentioned, cotton fabrics of many kinds, silk cloths, velvets, satins and thick carpets. Barbosa specially mentions the great quantity of ivory employed in the laid and cunningly turned articles such as bangles, sword hilts, dice, chessmen, chess-boards and bed stands. At Bassein Pyrard de Lavel found efficient ship and boat builders in 1609.[49]

Bernier and Thevenot have given vivid descriptions in support of the hardships in which the workmen were compelled to work by the gentry and the nobles. The burden of taxation was high though from Akbar to Aurangzeb the imperial farmans were being issued to remit the unauthorized taxes.

Nature of Employment

As regards the nature of employment, there was no state control over conditions of employment in any industry. Employees were free to do what they liked, with the result that Indian labour was exploited to the fullest extent possible. Hours of labour were inordinately long. There was no regulation for the age at which children could be employed; there were no periodical or weekly holidays and there was no legislation to safeguard Indian workers from injury through accident caused by entanglement with unfenced machinery. That there was no interest for the artist to willingly import his efficiency in the art is clear from the remarks of Bernier. Writing to Colbert he says, 'No artist could be expected to give his mind to his calling in the midst of a people who are either wretchedly poor, or who, if rich, assume an appearance of poverty, and who regard not the beauty and excellence, but the cheapness of an article, a people whose grandees pay for a work of art considerably under its value, and according to their own caprice, and who do not hesitate to punish an importunate artist, or tradesmen, with the *korrah*, that long and terrible whip hanging at every Omrah's gate'.[50]

In his letter to M.d la Mothe le Vayer, Bernier pointed out that there were no workshops of the artists in Delhi not because the people did not cultivate the art but because of the abominable treatment that these people received from them. The genius of the workmen was apparent from the instances of handsome pieces of workmanship made by persons destitute of tools and those who could scarcely be said to have received any training from any master in a regular way. If proper encouragement would have been afforded to fine arts, those would have flourished. The artists who arrived at any eminence in their art were only those Umaro and who worked exclusively for their patron.[51]

As regards the method of recruitment, the system of caste organization did exist and the professions had acquired hereditary character. In karkhanjats of the provinces or the capital, the sons and near relatives of the artisans could, it appears, bring their own men to take up the job when more labourers were needed. There is a description at length how in times of emergency the labourers could be made to work on meagre wages, and even on some occasions on the fear of *korrah*. Though the wages were not satisfactory considering high standard of work, the living conditions were not really bad. There was no unemployment amongst the labourers. As the means of communication were not developed, mobility of labour was rather too little though of course, towards the capital it was often apparent because demand for labour in the capital was too great. 'Not that labour was required for any productive purpose, it was simply needed to enhance the reputation of the employer. The greater the number of servants are kept in India the greater the prestige'.[52] Marshal rightly says, 'poverty is the cause of all degradation'. Tavernier has made reference to the deceits committed by the labourers in the manufacture of silk wares, fine muslin (Calicuts) embroidered cloth and indigo etc.[53] The brokers acted as middlemen who earned their own profit at the cost of labourers who could not even take their evening meals and contented themselves only with a little sweetmeat and the glass of water at the broker's house. Above all things they (labourers) caution him (broker) to look to his bits and to cheat than to be cheated.[54] During Aurangzeb's reign forced labour was a distinguishing characteristic of the emperor who made the policy worse by giving it a religious tinge. Aurangzeb being against art of any form the demand for labour was rather limited. He had no appreciation for beauty and workmanship. Pant rightly observes, 'appreciation of beauty was to him akin to idolatory. There was no demand for Hindu intellectuals, no demand for artisans whether Hindu or Mohammadan. Labour consequently became immobile. Only force could make it move. Labour reached its nadir in the reign of Aurangzeb'.[55]

During this period there was lack of growth of industrial organization and no state control over conditions of employment in any industry. Employers, the central and the provincial karkhanjats, the nobles, the Omrahs, the contractors and the like were free to do what they liked. With the result that the labour supply was exploited to the fullest extent possible. Long hours of work, low wages, bad conditions of employment, absence of state regulation for the welfare of the labouring classes, all combined to produce an adverse effect upon the efficiency of labourer.

Speaking of the efficiency of labour under state patronage Abul Fazl in his *Ain* has referred to the care and attention bestowed by the emperor upon the manufacture of various stuffs in state karkhanjats. The karkhanjats, the imperial workshops and the cities of Lahore, Agra, Fatehpur, Ahmedabad made skilful products of arts in a variety of fashions which astonished foreign travellers. His Majesty personally acquired all necessary theoretical and practical knowledge of the existing arts and the workman considerably improved and the imperial workshops finished articles manufactured in European, Iranian and Mangolian countries. 'A taste for fine material became general and the drapery used at feasts surpassed every description'.[56] Jadunath Sarkar rightly maintained that Masulipatam in the Golconda kingdom was the home of many artisans skilled in calico printing and many letters of Aurangzeb, then viceroy of the Deccan, exhibit his ardent desire to send some of the artists to the state factories of Agra and Delhi. This was practically forced labour.[57]

Besides, the articles of luxury consumption also occupied the attention of artisans, the emperors, the nobles, and the export traders. The articles produced after satisfying the pleasure of the emperor were presented to the nobles as a matter of administrative practice and the rest were sold to private persons. The nobles engaged small number of artisans for manufacture of rare presents to the king and this did mean encouragement to the art. For articles of day to day use, patronage was afforded by the foreign travellers. They followed the medieval custom of giving *dadan* or an advance to the workman and looking after them in their cottages, very few articles being produced in the *kothis* or factories.

Speaking of the efficiency of Kashmir labourers, Bernier speaks of the high workmanship displayed in the manufacture of *palkeys*, bed-sheets, boxes, spoons and various other things of domestic use including varnishing, imitating the beautiful veins of curtain wood, inlaying gold thread with elegance and perfection embroidered shawls. Thus shawls costing even Rs 150 and Masulipatam chintz exhibited the efficiency of labourers.[58]

Oppression of Officers and Forced Labour (Begar)

With regard to urban labour in Mughal India, European factory records and accounts of foreign travellers illustrate the extent of coercion, official or non-official on the artisans skilled or unskilled. After referring to the first scourage of low wages, Pelsaert writes, 'The second (scourage) is the oppression of the governor, the nobles, the diwan, the kotwal, the bakshi and other royal officers. If any of these wants a workman, the man is not asked if he is willing to come, but is seized in the house or in the street, well beaten if he should dare to raise any objection and in the evening paid half his wages or nothing at all.[59] Instances of forced labour were found when skilled calico printers and artisans were conscripted from Masulipatam to work in the state factories at Delhi or Agra. The great distress of the artisans in the city and villages of the province of Gujarat caused by the exaction of forced labour by the officials is testified to by Aurangzeb's farman of 1665, which abolished it.

Some of the European companies not only employed slave labour but also resorted to forced labour. A few examples of the latter may be noted. The Dutch and the English hired many Indian artisans in various capacities in different places, for example, weavers of cotton and silk, bleachers, printers, joiners, blacksmiths, etc. Early in the seventeenth century the Dutch resorted to forced labour by engaging 200-300 cloth printers and bleachers at Pulicat. In the seventies of the seventeenth century the Dutch engaged in their workshops at Hughli the Indian weavers manufacturing sail cloth or producing ropes who were paid 'small wages', from one to two annas daily. Early in the seventeenth century the Patna Factor Hughes (1620-21) had to give advance money to the silk winders to work in the Company's karkhanas.[60] Probably they were unwilling and had to be given some material inducements to work there. But there is no hint to their unwillingness in the records. So it may be that the winders insisted on prior payment, in order to save their position by taking advance wages. That this apprehension was not groundless is clear from the prevalence of forced labour or *begar*. During the sixties and seventies of the seventeenth century the English hired on a monthly wage basis. Indian yarn twisters, weavers, painters, dyers etc. besides brokers (*paikars*) and treasurers (*potdars*) through whom advance (*dadan*) was given to the artisans or local merchants. In 1679, the monthly wage system was replaced by remuneration per piece for greater effort, and the brokers were to get a commission of one fourth in a rupee of the Company's recouped investments in the particular articles.[61]

Another adverse factor was the middleman's share. Mandelslo found (1638) that the craftsman had to surrender to the middlemen a considerable portion of his profits as the same piece of work passed through several hands before reaching the consumer.[62] This seems to be corroborated by Bernier when he continues his observations on the artisan. 'He never can become rich. . . . If money be gained, it does not in any measure go into his pocket but only serves to increase the wealth of the merchant.[63]

All this created an un-economic outlook on the part of artisans. The masses could, because of poverty, exercise no effective demand on production of goods of superior workmanship. They wanted cheap necessities of life. Fear of oppression led to concealment of wealth and permanent inurement to a low standard. Bernier writes that 'no artist can be expected to give his mind to his calling in the midst of a people who are either wretchedly poor or who, if rich, assume an appearance of poverty and who regarded not the beauty and excellence but the cheapness of an article . . .'.[64] The reaction of this low standard (as testified by Pelsaert, De Laet and others) and uneconomic position of the artisans is mutual and the two were related as cause and effect. Hence there was no or little incentive or effort to endeavour to raise this economic standard by additional work besides their daily routine. As Bernier remarks, 'In this quiet and regular manner their time glides away, no one aspiring after any improvement in the conditions of life, wherein he happens to be born'.[65]

Division of Labour

Lack of aspiration was partly caused by the division of labour and rigid caste rules both among the Hindu and Muslim artisans. Pelsaert, De Laet and Bernier bear this out. Pelsaert writes: 'Scarcely anyone will make an effort, for a ladder by which to climb higher is hard to find, because a workman's children can follow no occupation other than that of their father, nor can they intermarry with any other caste'. In a similar strain De Laet remarks, 'The artisans can never rise to a higher station, for fathers generally teach their children the same handicrafts which they themselves practise'. In a classic passage Bernier observes: 'The embroiderer brings up his son as an embroiderer, the son of a goldsmith becomes a goldsmith and a physician of the city educates his son for a physician. No one marries but in his own trade or profession and the custom is observed almost as rigidly by the Mohammadans as by the Hindus.[66] Caste constituted a rigid economic steel frame which tended to discourage economic mobility of groups or individuals. Mobility of labour was strictly limited. Rural producers might go to the local production centres. Occupational mobility would take place when agriculturists took to weaving. Horizontal mobility would occur if artisans of the same caste group (e.g. carpenters, braziers, goldsmiths, blacksmiths, coppersmiths, masons, stone cutters, etc.) would change their crafts. But rare indeed was regional mobility as skills did not easily move regionally. The English faced difficulties in the mid-seventeenth century in bringing weavers from Kasim Bazar to Hughli and completely failed to induce them to go to Madras for fear of losing their caste in crossing the sea (*kalapani*). The Dutch failed to get Gujarati weavers to come to Bengal. Again as the corporate organization of the artisans had caste and no economic basis, all outsiders were debarred from there. Lastly there was no upward mobility of the artisans of

Mughal India as there was no encouragement of commercial profit as in Europe. India's impressive network was woven by men and women, pursuing, notwithstanding exploitation by rulers and merchants, hereditary vocation. There were, however, occasional protests. The weavers of Broach mutinied against the English buying cotton yarn in 1630 and left the city as a protest against governor's tyranny. In 1686 all the Indians of Madras went on strike to protest against a tax levied by the English under order of caste heads. But such rare protests did not imply any dynamic sustained move.

If the cost of materials was excessive (e.g. metals, raw cotton) the worker without sufficient capital would be at the mercy of the middlemen or financier or *mahajan*, providing these. This encouraged exploitation which, according to Bernier, was the rule.

There is little direct information regarding taxation on handicrafts. There are, however, references to occasional state remissions of taxes by Akbar, Jahangir and Aurangzeb which suggest that such remissions were not permanent and were counteracted by exactions of subordinate authorities. Akbar sought to relieve the workers by remitting several imports, cesses and taxes, e.g. tax on artificers on particular products (e.g. blankets) or occupations (e.g. tanning, manufacture of lime, etc.). But his good intentions were set at naught by local officials. From the *Mirat-i-Ahmadi* it is learnt that Aurangzeb abolished various forms of license tax on artificers. Every class of artificers throughout the Mughal empire was subject to exaction of a poll tax (*muhtarfa*) by officials, though it was repeatedly condemned by Aurangzeb. Again, cotton dressers and sugarcane pressers coming to a new place in Gujarat to start business had to pay Rs 1½ to the official for permission to start their trade. Further, an artisan, wishing to learn any branch of the weaver's or embroiderer's art, had to pay a 'craft learning' fee to the local officers on completing his training. Specific statements of official exactions have been made by Terry and Tavernier. According to the first, officers in different parts of the Mughal empire exacted money from those who made curious manufacturers. According to the latter the weavers of Benares had to get every piece of cloth stamped by the 'farmer' (tax-contractors) before sale. There are general statements by the foreign visitors that the people paid taxes according to their means. It may be inferred that the artisans were liable to miscellaneous cesses and taxes which affected their economic position. This threw them at the mercy of the middlemen and financiers. They could not overcome periodic crisis of scarcity and famine which made them destitute. Again the market of chief handicrafts and artistic handicrafts being confined to the limited class of Mughal aristocracy, there was little scope of expansion for this class of crafts.[67]

References

1. Jahangir, *Tuzuk*, II (R&B), pp. 20-21, 98-99.
2. Bernier, *Travels of the Mogul Empire*, pp. 255-56.
3. Ibid., pp. 228-29.
4. Pelsaert, *Jahangir's India*, p. 37.
5. Mirza Nathan, *Bahristan-i-Ghaybi*, Vol. I. For details see Tapan Ray Chaudhuri, *Bengal under Akbar and Jahangir*, p. 200.
6. Bernier, op. cit., p. 259.
7. Pelsaert, op. cit., p. 61.
8. Ibid., p. 60.
9. Supra, p. 121-22.
10. W.H. Moreland, *India at the Death of Akbar*, p. 87.
11. *Babur Nama*, Vol. II, p. 520.
12. Stavorinus, *Voyage to the East Indies*, Vol. I, pp. 411, 474.
13. E. Ives, *A Voyage from England to India in the Year 1754*, London, 1773, p. 52. For details see A.I. Chicherov, *India: Economic Development in the 16th-18th Centuries*, p. 83.
14. *Ain*, Vol. II, p. 42.
15. Muhammad Kasim Farishta, *The History of the Rise of the Mohamedan Power in India till the Year 1612*, Vol. 4, p. 107.
16. Bernier, op. cit., p. 225.
17. Pelsaert, op. cit., p. 60.
18. *Tuzuk-i-Babari* (text), p. 213 (trans.), p. 520.
19. *Ain*, Vol. I, p. 93.
20. Pelsaert, op. cit., p. 60.
21. Bernier, op. cit., p. 259.
22. *Ain*, Vol. I, pp. 93-94.
23. *Babur Nama* (trans.), p. 520.
24. *Ain*, Vol. I, pp. 93, 235-36.
25. Pelsaert, op. cit., pp. 60-61; Bernier, op. cit., pp. 238-39.
26. Bernier, op. cit., pp. 254-56.
27. Ibid., pp. 254-55.
28. *Ain* (tr.), Vol. I, pp. 97-98.
29. Bernier, op. cit., pp. 228-29.
30. Moreland, *India at the Death of Akbar*, p. 175.

31. *Ain*, Vol. I, p. 12; Bernier, op. cit., pp. 258-59; W. Foster, *Journey*, Vol. I, p. 4.
32. N.K. Sinha, *The Economic History of Bengal from Plassey to the Permanent Settlement*, Vol. I, p. 157.
33. S. Master, *The Diaries of S. Master*, Vol. I, p. 106. Master ordered that this practice be stopped as it was detrimental to Company's interests.
34. Master, op. cit., p. 46.
35. Bernier, op. cit., p. 439.
36. *English Factories (1618-1621)*, p. 111 (raw silk from Patna sent to Ahmedabad). Manucci, *Storia do Mogor*, Vol. I, p. 83. Spinning of silk yarn was done at Ahmedabad and Surat. See Tavernier, *Travels in India*, Vol. I, p. 72.
37. For textile technology, see Irfan Habib, 'Note on Indian Textile Industry in the 17th Century' in *S.C. Sarkar Felicitation Volume*, Delhi, 1976, pp. 181-92; Vijaya Ramaswamy, 'Notes on Textile Technology in Medieval India with special reference to the South', *IESHR*, 1980, pp. 229-32.
38. S. Manrique, *Travels of Fray Sabastian Manrique (1629-43)*, Vol. 2, p. 147.
39. W. Foster, ed., *The English Factories in India: A Calendar of Documents in the India Office (1634-36)*, pp. 128, 130.
40. Ibid. (1618-21), pp. 75, 128, 151, 171, 238; Pelsaert, op. cit., p. 43; W. Foster, ed., *Early Travels in India (1583-1619)*, London, 1921, p. 16.
41. Manrique, op. cit., Vol. I, p. 45.
42. Pelsaert, op. cit., p. 8.
43. S. Master, *The Diaries of Streynsham Master, 1675-80 and other contemporary papers relating thereto*, Vol. 2, p. 14.
44. Ibid., p. 86.
45. N.K. Sinha, op. cit., p. 165.
46. Tavernier, op. cit., pp. 42, 46.
47. Hussain Muhammad Khan, *Mirat-i-Ahmadi* (Per. MSS), p. 62; Eng. tr. of *Mirat* by Ali and Sadan, p. 7.
48. Durate Barbosa, *The Book of Durate Barbosa* (tr.), M.L. Dames, p. 114.
49. Pyrard, *The Voyage of Francois Pyrard de Lavel to the East Indies* (tr.) for the Hakluyt Society (1887-89), p. 188; Commissariat, *History of Gujarat*, p. 534.
50. Bernier, op. cit., p. 228.
51. Ibid., pp. 255-56.
52. D. Pant, *Commercial Policy of the Mughals*, p. 70.
53. Tavernier, op. cit., Vol. I, Chapter X, pp. 131-32.
54. Bernier, op. cit., p. 66.
55. Pant, op. cit., p. 226. Use of force has been labourer's last right from the early Sultanate period. Timur had forcibly sent the good masons of India to Samarqand for the construction of the Great Friday mosque which he designed to raise in his capital. *Cambridge History of India*, Vol. III, Chapter VII, p. 199.
56. *Ain*, Vol. I, pp. 93-94.
57. Jadunath Sarkar, *Mughal Administration*, p. 128.

58. Bernier, op. cit., pp. 402-04. The *Ain* contains some important information on the industry of Kashmir. *Ain*, Vol. I, p. 97.
59. Pelsaert, op. cit., p. 60.
60. *Slave Labour* by Portuguese Linschoten, i, pp. 187-88; by Dutch T.K. Raychaudhuri, Jan Co. in Coromandel, S.G. Ravenhag, Martimers Nijhoff (1962), p. 150. *Forced Labour*, Dutch, T.K. Raychaudhuri, p. 145. *EFI (1630-33)*, pp. 231-35, *IA (1914)*, p. 100.
61. C.R. Wilson, *The Early Annals of the English in Bengal*, Asiatic Society, Calcutta, Vol. I, p. 396. Chicherov, op. cit., pp. 227-29.
62. Mandelslo in Oaten, *European Travellers in India*, p. 187.
63. Bernier, op. cit., p. 229.
64. Ibid., p. 228.
65. Ibid.
66. Pelsaert, op. cit., p. 60; De Laet, *Empire of the Great Mogol*, pp. 88-89; Bernier, op. cit., p. 258.
67. Ali Muhammad Khan, *Mirat-i-Ahmadi*, i, p. 260. For details see Jadunath Sarkar, *Mughal Administration*, Chapter V; R.K. Mookerjee, *Economic History of India (1600-1800)*, Allahabad, 1967, pp. 73-74.

7

Wages

In the state karkhanas, the wages paid to the workers were very low. The skilled labourer received 3 to 4 *dams* a day as wages while the carpenters were paid from 3 to 7 *dams* daily.[1] As we do not get enough evidence of an organized labour in Mughal India, it is difficult to make any suggestion regarding the discontentment of the labour class. Since their requirements were very few and very cheap, it is unlikely that they would have resorted to any kind of organized unrest against the state.

The artisans were paid monthly cash salaries or daily wages according to the nature of the work. Skilled labour was mostly paid in regular salaries, and great favour was shown to good hands. They were all known personally to the emperor and were presented before him or summoned by him whenever they exhibited unusual skill or workmanship in their profession.

According to the author of the *Mirat-i-Ahmadi* in the 1660 'The administrators (*mutassadi*) of state construction projects, gardens and other karkhanas reported to *padishah* Aurangzeb that until recently the wages (*ujura*) of hired workmen (*mozduran*) were paid in *phalsa* (a small copper coin). However, since beginning with the year (1667-68), new *phalsa* were minted . . . the workmen refused to accept the new coins, because they said, their value was far below than that of the former *phalsa*. The *padishah* then ordered the Diwan of Subah (Finance department) to raise the daily wages (*youmie*) of workmen and to pay them 1.5 tanka for every tanka they had received before'.[2]

Muhammad Khan gives similar data also with regard to the remuneration of the labour of construction workers. In 1671-72, it became known that 'potters, diggers, carpenters and other hired workmen (*ujuradaran*) at the construction projects of Ahmedabad were complaining about the low daily wage (*ruzana*) they were receiving from the high sarkar. For this reason the Diwan of Subah was ordered to see to it that employers pay a higher wage (*ujara*) in keeping with the practice established in other (probably private) construction projects'.[3]

The remuneration of the wage workers differed from workshop to workshop. In some workshops wages were paid in cash; in others the labourers received a share of finished product for their work. Labourers in workshops were paid in accordance with their role in production. The payments in kind, when reduced to monetary terms generally coincided with cash wages. This demonstrates that the distribution of shares of the output did not essentially differ from remuneration in cash. In some workshops for example, in Velater, remuneration was mixed, in money and in grain.

According to modern economists remuneration of the labourer in wages might either be in terms of money in which case it is called 'money wage' or it might be in terms of necessaries, comforts and luxuries in which case it is called 'real wages'. As Pigou[4] holds, wages and standard of living are closely connected and act and react upon one another through the medium of the efficiency of the labourers. The same view is held by Pigou. 'The information necessary for a comprehensive study of the industrial wage system in India has not yet been collected.'[5]

It is not possible to form an accurate idea of the economic condition of the people without a knowledge of the income of wage earners and prices of necessaries of everyday life. There is a dearth of adequate material on wages and prices in this period and as such an approach for a correct estimate of the general standard of living of the labourers of the period is not feasible.

The *Ain*[6] gives a long list of wages paid to artisans engaged in different crafts and vocations in Akbar's time. Though exhaustive the list is silent about the source from which the data was collected or the area within which the rates of wages operated. The wages given in the *Ain* ranged from 2 *dams* to 7 *dams* per diem according to the standard of skill of the labourers, that is from the twentieth part of a rupee to 7/40th of a rupee as explained likewise:

1. *Gilkars* (workers in lime); first class workmen 7 *dams*; second class, 6 *dams*, and third class 5 *dams*.
2. *Sangtarsh*; first class 7 *dams*, second class 6 *dams* for each *gaz*; one who did plain work got 5 *dams* and a labourer employed in quarries got 22 *jitals* for breaking one maund.
3. *Carpenters*; first class 7 *dams*, second class 6 *dams*, third 4 *dams*, fourth 3 *dams* and fifth 2 *dams* for each plain job. A first class carpenter got 1 *dam* 17 jitals for one *gaz*, second class 1d 6 *jitals* and the third class 21 *jitals*.

4. *Pinjara-saz* (A lattice worker & wicker worker): first when the pieces were joined (fastened with strings) and the interstices to be dodecagenal, 24 *dams* for every square *gaz*, when haxagonal 18 *dams*, when *jaffari* (or rhombus-like one diagonal being vertical, the other horizontal), 16 *dams*, when *shatranji* or square fields (as on chess board) 12 *dams* for every square *gaz*. Secondly, when the work is *ghayrwasli* (the sticks not being fastened with strings, but skilfully and tightly inter-woven), for first class work, 48 *dam* per square *gaz*, for second class 40 *dams*.
5. *Arra-kash* (one who saws beams); for job work per square *gaz* 2½ *dams* if sisam wood; nazhu 2 *dams*. A labourer employed for the day 2 *dams*. There were three men for every saw, one above and two below.
6. *Beldars* (Brick layers); first class daily 3½ *dams*, second class 3 *dams*, if employed by the job for the fortress walls with battlements 4 *dams* per *gaz*, for laying foundations 2½ *dams*, for all other walls 2 *dams* and for digging a ditch ½ *dam* per *gaz*. The *gaz* of labourer contained 32 *tassuj*.
7. *Chah-kan* (Well diggers); first class 2 *dams* per *gaz*, second class 1½ *dams* and third class 1¼ *dams* per *gaz*.
8. *Ghotakhor* (divers who cleaned wells); in the cold season 4 *dams* per diem and in the hot season 3 *dams* if done by job for cleaning a depth of 1 *gaz*.
9. *Kisht-tarash* (Tile makers); for 100 moulds, smoothened 8 *dams*.
10. *Surkhi-kob* (Pounders of old bricks); 1½ *dams* for a heap of 8 *mans*.
11. *Glass cutters*; 100 *dams* per *gaz*.
12. *Chappar-band* (thatchers); 3 *dams* per diem, if done by job, 24 *dams* for 100 *gaz*.
13. *Bamboo-cutters*: 2 *dams* per diem.
14. *Patal-band*; 1 *dam* for 4 *gaz*.
15. *Lakhira*; they varnished reeds etc. with lac. Wages 2 *dams* per diem.
16. *Abkash* (water carriers); 2 to 3 *dams* per diem—first class 3 *dams* per diem; second class do, 2 *dams*. Such water carriers as are used for furnishing house builders with water for mortar and quick lime get 2 *dams* per diem. Moreland classified the labourers in Akbar's time on the basis of figures adduced in the *Ain*, and says that the value of the *dam* could be taken to be 2 annas

and 9 pies.[7] It is well to note that this value held good in 1920, the year of the publication of Moreland's book, *India at the Death of Akbar*. His classification is as follows:

Class	*Sanctioned Rate*	*Modern Equivalent Year 1920*
1. Ordinary labourers	2 *dams* daily	5½ annas
2. Superior labourers	3-4 *dams* daily	8 to 11 annas
3. Carpenters	3-7 *dams* daily	8½ annas to Rs 1-4-0
4. Builders	5-7 *dams* daily	14 annas to Rs 1-4-0

' "These rates", Moreland observes, "applied primarily to expenditure in the Imperial Camp, which by itself formed the largest city in the Empire; their purchasing power may therefore be calculated on the basis of the prices recorded by Abul Fazl".'[8] Though the wages paid in Akbar's times were small, their purchasing value was much greater than that of modern times. What was within the reach of an unskilled labourer of Akbar's time is as good as the payment of his successor of the twentieth century.

Before the evidence adduced by various European writers is discussed, it is important to bear in mind that wages in this period were not uniform throughout the Mughal domains but uniformity did prevail in some localities. Writing of Agra, Pelsaert quoted one set rates for all classes of artisans. A few years earlier Methwold had noted the same fact on the East Coast; and the existence of this uniformity would justify in drawing inferences regarding workers in general from the data available for particular classes, provided, they related to the area under consideration'.[9] For want of necessary data on the subject 'it is to be relied for comparative purposes on the monthly wages paid to the peons employed in European factories, that is to say, to servants with no exceptional qualifications'.[10] But even this method is not free from defects as it is not certain whether monthly payments were for 30, 31 or even 40 days. According to Pelsaert 40 days were often counted as one month in Agra and as such the salary of Rs 4 meant only a payment of Rs 3 for a month. Besides deductions were made for clothes and articles. 'Since Agra set the standard in such matters for a large part of India, in some other places also monthly rates may contain a similar over statement. A Dutch account tells that the governors (in Golconda) paid their staff in rice and salt valued at one third above cost'.[11]

'The agricultural labourer', writes Moreland, 'was ordinarily a serf, receiving in return for his work an amount of commodities determined by custom, and about sufficient to keep him and his family alive'.[12] Custom determined wages of village artisans. 'If Akbar's workmen received the full sanctioned rates they were rather better off than the modern workmen of the United Provinces, but not so well off as those of Punjab, it is more probable that they got something less than the sanctioned rates and that their actual position was little worse, but the general conclusion to which these figures point is that urban real wages in the north of India stood somewhere about the same level in Akbar's time as in 1911, and that there has been no pronounced change in the standard of remuneration of these classes of the population.[13]

The *Ain* gives a long list of the prices of various commodities and wages of artisans engaged in the manufacture of gold stuffs, cotton and woollen goods and silk pieces.[14] Speaking of the manufacture of carpets it adds: 'His Majesty has caused carpets to be made of wonderful varieties and charming textures; he has appointed experienced workmen, who have produced many masterpieces. The *qilims* of Iran and Turan are no more thought of, although merchants still import carpets from Gashkan, Khuzistan, Kirman and Sahswar. All kinds of carpet weavers have settled here and derived a flourishing trade. These are found in every town specially in Agra, Fatehpur and Lahore. In the imperial workshops *qilims* are made 20 *gaz* 20 *tassujes* long and 6 gaz 11½ *tassujes* broad at a cost of 1810 rupees, which those who are skilled in the business have valued at 2715 rupees'.[15]

This speaks of the efficiency of the craftsmen and the large difference between the cost and retail price must have been due to the profit and not higher wages.

At Jahangir's death a rupee meant 30 *dams* as compared to 40 during Akbar's reign. According to Careri in 1695 a rupee was valued at 54 paise (one paisa was equal to half a *dam*). The ordinary labourer in terms of paise received 3 or 4. Pelsaert writing at the end of Jahangir's reign (AD 1626) mentioned Rs 3 to 4 as wages of a servant for a month of 40 days.[16] Radha Kamal Mookerjee doubts that monthly wages were calculated at the rate of 40 days.[17] He places reliance upon Terry who mentions that wages were 5 shillings. The account book of Agra Dutch Factory (1637) shows that wages were monthly paid on the day of full moon and that the wages of servants were Rs 3½ monthly, porters and sais (horsemen) Rs 3, sweepers and washermen Rs 5. 'A simple servant between victuals and clothing spends not more than Rs 3 a month', observes Petro Valle from Surat in 1623. In AD 1634 wages at Surat were 3 to 7 *Mahmudis* per mensem (i.e. Rs 2½ to 3½) but by 1638 wages increased to 8 to 10 *Mahmudis*.[18] In 1637 the Dutch paid generally

Rs 3½ to Rs 5 per month or 6 to 8 pice per day to ordinary labourers in their factory and 7 pice to superior man. Hawkins also mentions that the usual wages paid in the Mughal camp and the court were Rs 3 to Rs 10 per month. These figures indicate that wages were practically doubled in Jahangir's times. 'In several instances the lowest grades of servants were entitled to less than 2 rupees monthly (65 *dams* for a sweeper, 60 for a camel driver, 70 for a wrestler and so on), while the bulk of the menials and ordinary foot soldiers began at less than Rs 3. The minimum for subsistence at the court is probably marked by the lowest grade of slaves, who were allowed one *dam* daily, equivalent to three quarters of a rupee monthly in the currency of the time.[19]

Wages Compared

In 1920 Moreland calculated 5½ annas as then money equivalent of two *dams* which was a low wage for an unskilled labourer in the time of Akbar, but which could purchase 9/1b 4/Oz of wheat or other articles of daily consumption, of course rice and salt being dearer.[20]

'In the modern times', although money wages have risen, real wages have practically remained unchanged. Some persons have gone so far as to suggest that the possibility of the real wages rising all round is always fairly narrowly limited by the fact that the available supply of primary food stuffs is for the time being fairly fixed and can only be increased after an interval of time. Prices rise and fall occasionally but wages (which usually contain a strong customary element) seldom fall as much as prices fall.

As for whether the present day labourer is economically better off than one under the Mughal times in general and in that of Akbar in particular one can only look towards the wage figures adduced in the *Ain* etc. It is true those few who were to get a job in the imperial or provincial *karkhanjats* were better off than many labourers of the present times. But as there was no security of employment, no fixed hours of work, no welfare and social service provisions, no trade unions and above all, the constant fear of forced labour and 'korrah' (lash) hanging at every Umrao's entrance gate, these produced an adverse effect upon the economic prosperity of the labouring class.

'The labourer does not need money for its own sake,' says Pigou, 'What is of real importance to him are the real necessaries, comforts and luxuries which he can purchase with the money wage he receives'.[21] On the application of this principal which is a universal truth for all times, the wages of labourers in the times of Akbar were not at least worse off than those of the present times. But the labourer of those times was too much dominated by the upper classes of society and even forced to work. The wages of artisans were stable and there is no evidence to prove that urban wages rose higher.[22]

The Mughal emperors displayed great taste in building operations, not in the works of public utility. Shahjahan was a great palace builder and donated huge sums to the members of his family and courtiers. There appears to be no evidence on the treatment of remuneration of the large number of labourers employed on royal building operations. 'The immediate effect of such undertakings was inevitably to hinder ordinary commercial activities. Thus all the carts at Agra were impressed for the works in progress at Delhi and on one occasion goods in transit for the coast had to lie on the way for some months, after 'they had been by the king's officers cast down in the fields, and the carts taken for his use'.[23]

There is no evidence of the wages earned by artisans. They are generally represented in contemporary records as having been badly circumstanced throughout the sixteenth and seventeenth centuries. The same may be told of the craftsmen and industrial workers who frequently had to pay fines and *dassuri* to the superiors and were often forced to work for nothing during the reign of Akbar's successors. The circumstances indeed seemed to have deteriorated under Jahangir and Shahjahan and resulted in the time of Aurangzeb in constant migration under stress of poverty from rural to urban areas.

'It is stability of earnings that enables a well devised standard of life to be built up and not stability of wages'.[24] The wages might have been stable in the period, but the earnings were not stable. The workman was the victim of low wages and oppression. This was the primary cause of people of the labouring classes to lead a shabby life. Besides being trifling wages were often in arrears.

Speaking of the seventeenth century De Laet writes in the same trend. The daily wage of the labourer was very small, merely 30 taccas (30 taccas equal to 24 stivers equal to one rupee) or four or five Dutch stuferi.[25] In 1624 Della Valle gave a glimpse of Surat. 'Wages were very low and slaves cost nothing to keep'.

There were serious disadvantages operating against the artisans. Pelsaert, chief of the Dutch factory at Agra observes on the basis of his seven years experience (1620-26) that 'there were three classes of people who were indeed nominally free but whose status differs little from voluntary slavery, workmen, peons or servants and small shopkeepers'. Again for the workmen there are two scourages, the first of which is low wages. Goldsmiths, painters, embroiderers, carpet makers, weavers, by working from morning to night can earn only 5 to 6 taccas, or about 1/5th of a rupee. This is also corroborated by De Laet and some other foreign travellers.[26] These conditions in the seventeenth century can be certified from the rates of the daily wages of workers in Akbar's time (1595) as given in the *Ain-i-Akbari*.[27]

References

1. *Ain*, I, pp. 235-36.
2. Ali Muhammad Khan, *Mirat-i-Ahmadi*, Vol. I, p. 267.
3. Ibid.
4. A.C. Pigou, *Economics of Welfare*. For details see S.S. Kulashreshtha, *The Development of Trade and Industry under the Mughals*, p. 64.
5. Veera Anstey, *Economic Development of India*, p. 117.
6. *Ain*, Vol. I, pp. 235-36.
7. W.H. Moreland has calculated the purchasing power prevailing in the year of publication of the book *India at the Death of Akbar* (1920).
8. Moreland, op. cit., p. 178.
9. W.H. Moreland, *From Akbar to Aurangzeb*, p. 194.
10. Ibid.
11. Ibid., pp. 194-95.
12. Moreland, *India at the Death of Akbar*, p. 177.
13. Ibid., p. 179.
14. *Ain* (tr.), Vol. I, pp. 98-102.
15. Ibid., p. 57.
16. Pelsaert, *Jahangir's India*, p. 62.
17. Radha Kamal Mookerjee, 'Economic History (1600-1800)' in *U.P. Journal of Historical Society*, December 1941, No. XIV, pt II, pp. 62-63.
18. De Laet borrows Pelsaert's figures in his description of India vide his *Empire of the Great Mogol*, pp. 89-90.
19. Moreland, *India at the Death of Akbar*, p. 179.
20. Ibid., p. 178.
21. Pigou, *Economics of Welfare*, pp. 467-68.
22. Moreland, *From Akbar to Aurangzeb*, p. 195.
23. Ibid., p. 196.
24. Pigou, op. cit., p. 582.
25. De Laet, op. cit., pp. 88-89.
26. Pelsaert, op. cit., pp. 60-61; De Laet, op. cit., pp. 88-89.
27. *Ain* (tr.), Vol. I, pp. 235-36.

Bibliography

Abul Fazl Allami, *The Akbar Nama*, Vols I and II (in one Vol.), edited by Agha Ahmed Ali and Maulvi Abdur Rahim, Vol. I, Calcutta, 1877; Vol. II, Calcutta, 1979, English translation by H. Beveridge, *The Akbar Nama*, Vol. I, Delhi, 1972; Vol. II, Delhi, 1972; Vol. III, Delhi, 1973.

——, *The Ain-i-Akbari*, Vol. I, edited by H. Blochmann, Calcutta, 1872; Vol. II, Calcutta, 1875; English translation Vol. I by H. Blochmann, Calcutta, 1873, second edn, revised and edited by E.C. Phillot, third edn, Delhi, 1977; Vol. II by H.S. Jarrett, second edn, corrected and further annotated by Jadunath Sarkar, Calcutta, 1949; Vol. III by H.S. Jarrett and Jadunath Sarkar, Calcutta, 1948.

Abdullah, *Tarikh-i-Daudi*, edited by Shaikh Abdur Rashid, Aligarh Muslim University, Aligarh, 1954; E&D, Vol. IV (extracts).

Abdul Hamid Lahori, *Padshahnama*, edited by Maulvi Kabiruddin and Maulvi Abdur Rahim, Bib. Indica, Calcutta, 1866-67. Extracts in E&D, Vol. VII.

Afif, Shams-i-Siraj, *Tarikh-i-Firozshahi*, edited by Maulvi Wilayat Hussain, Calcutta, 1890.

Ali Muhammad Khan, *Mirat-i-Ahmadi*, edited by Nawab Ali, 2 vols. and supplement, Baroda, 1927-28, 1930.

Amin Qazwini, *Padshahnama*, MS. Raza Library, Rampur.

Anand Ram Mukhlis, *Safarnama-i-Mukhlis*, edited by S. Azhar Ali, Rampur, 1946.

Anonymous, *Khulasatu-s-Siyaq* (*c.* 1700), Br. Mu. Add. 6588.

Anonymous, *Sirat-i-Firozeshahi*, Bankipur/vii/547.

Aufi, *Jawani-al-Hikayat*, extracts tr. in Elliot & Dowson, *History of India*, Vol. II.

Babur, Zahiruddin Muhammad, *Babur Nama*, translated from the original Turki text by A.S. Beveridge, New Delhi, 1970.

Badaoni, Abdul Qadir bin Mulukshah, *Muntakhabu-t-Tawarikh*, edited by Maulvi Kabiruddin Ahmad and Maulvi Ahmad Ali, 2 vols; Vol. I, Calcutta, 1868; Vol. II, Calcutta, 1869; English translation,

Vol. I by G.S.A. Ranking, Calcutta, 1898, Delhi, 1973; Vol. II by W.H. Lowe, Calcutta, 1925.

Barani, Ziauddin, *Tarikh-i-Firuz Shahi*, edited by Sir Sayyid Ahmad Khan, Calcutta, 1862.

Biruni, Abu Rayhan, *Kitab ul-Hind*, edited by E.C. Sachau, London, 1887; *Alberuni's India*, English translation with commentary by E.C. Sachau, 2 vols (in one format), New Delhi, 1984.

Firishta, Muhammad Qasim Hindu Shah (Astarabadi), *Tarikh-i-Firishta* or *Gulshan-i-Ibrahimi*, Lucknow, 1865, Vols 1 and 2 (in one format); English tr. by John Briggs entitled *History of the Rise of Mahomedan Power in India*, 4 vols, New Delhi, 1981.

Firuz Shah Tughluq, *Futuhat-i-Firuzshahi*, English translation by Shaikh Abdur Rashid, published in Muslim University Journal, Aligarh, 1943; also translated into English by N.B. Roy in *Islamic Culture*, October 1941.

Gulbadan Begam, *Humayun Nama*, translated into English as *The History of Humayun* by A.S. Beveridge, New Delhi, 1983.

Gulam Hussain Salim, *Riyaz-us-Salatin*, Bib. Ind., 1898. A History of Bengal in AD 1786-87. Eng. translation by Maulana Abdus Salam, Asiatic Society, 1902.

Hasan Nizami, *Tajul Maasir*, tr. S.H. Askari in *Patna University Journal*, 1963; E&D, Vol. II.

Haider Dughlat Mirza, *Tarikh-i-Rashidi*, tr. N. Elas and E. Denison Ross, Patna, 1973.

Isami, *Futuhus-Salatin* or *Shahnamah-i-Hind*, edited by Mahdi Husain, Agra, 1938; also A.S. Usha, University of Madras, 1948.

Inayutullah Khan, *Akham-i-Alamgiri*, 2 vols, MS. Jadunath Sarkar Collection, National Library, Calcutta. A collection of notes, orders and letters of Aurangzeb collated and edited by Inayatullah Khan.

Jauhar, *Tazkirat-al-Waqiat*, translated by Major Charles Stewart entitled *Private Memoirs of the Moghul Emperor Humayun*, New Delhi, 1972.

Jahangir, *Tuzuk-i-Jahangiri*, tr. A. Rogers, ed. by H. Beveridge, 2 vols, London, 1908, 1909, 1914.

Khafi Khan, *Muntakhab ut-Lubab*, extracts in Elliot and Dowson, *History of India*, Vol. II.

Khwandamair, *Qanun-i-Humayuni* or *Humayun Nama*, English tr. Baini Prashad, Bib. Ind., Calcutta, 1940.

Kamgar Hussaini, *Maasir-i-Jahangiri*, MS. Or. 171.

Minhaju-s-Siraj Jurjani, *Tabakat-i-Nasiri*, edited by Nassu Lees, Khadim Hussain and Abdul Hayy, Calcutta, 1864: translated by H.G. Roverty, 2 vols, Delhi, 1970; edited by Habibi, 2 vols, Kabul, 1963 and 1964.

Mir, Khvand, *Qanun-i-Humayuni*, Calcutta, 1940.

Muhammad Waris, *Badshah Nama*, MS. Add. 6556.

Muhammad Sadiq Khan, *Shahjahan Nama*, MS. Or. 174.

Muhammad Salih Kambu, *Amal-i-Salih*, edited by G. Yazdani, 4 vols, Bib. Ind. Calcutta, 1912-46.

Mulla Abdul Baqi Nihavandi, *Maasir-i-Rahimi*, edited by Shamsul-Ulama M. Hidayet Hussain, vols. II and III, Calcutta, 1925.

Mirza Nathan (Shitab Khan), *Bahaaristani-Ghaibi*, English translation by Mohammad Islam Borah, 2 vols, Gauhati, 1936.

Munshi Muhammad Qazim, *Alamgir Namah*, edited by Maulvi Khadim Hussain and Abdul Hai, Bib. Ind., Calcutta, 1868.

Munshi Nand Ram Kayastha Srivastava, *Siyaqnama* (1694-96), lithographed, Nawal Kishore, Lucknow, 1879.

Mutamad Khan, *Iqbalnama-i-Jahangiri*, Litho, edited by Nawal Kishore, Lucknow, 1870.

Nizamuddin Ahmad, *Tabqat-i-Akbari*, tr. B.De, 3 vols, Calcutta, 1927-39. (Published by the Asiatic Society of Bengal, Vol. I, 1927, Vol. II, 1936, Vol. III, 1939).

Rai Chaturman Saksena, *Chahar Gulshan*, MS. Bodleian Library, Oxford, portion translated by Jadunath Sarkar in his *India of Aurangzeb*, Calcutta, 1901.

Ruqqat-i-Alamgiri, Letters of Aurangzeb, translated by Joseph Eales. Asiatic Annual Register III, pp. 92-100.

Saqi Mustaid Khan, *Maasir-i-Alamgiri*, Bib. Ind., Calcutta (1870-73).

Shah Nawaz Khan, *Maasir-ul-Umara*, tr. H. Beveridge, 3 vols, Calcutta, 1911.

Shaikh Farid Bhakkari, *Zakhirat-ul-Khwanin*, edited by Syed Moin ul Haq, 3 vols, Pakistan Historical Society, Karachi, 1961.

Shaikh Muhammad Baqa, *Mirat-al-Alam*, MS. Abdus Salam, 84/314, Aligarh.

Sirhindi, Yahya bin Ahmad bin Abdullah, *Tarikh-i-Mubarakshahi*, edited by M. Hidayat Hussain, Calcutta, 1931, English tr. by K.K. Basu, Baroda, 1932.

Sujan Rai Bhandari, *Khulasat-ut-Tawarikh*, edited by Zafar Hasan, Delhi, 1918.

Wali, Abu Turab, *Tarikh-i-Gujarat*, edited by Sir Denison Ross, Calcutta, 1909.

TRAVELS

Barbosa, Durate, *The Book of Durate Barbosa* (L.M. Dames), 2 vols, London, 1918, 1921, also known as *An Account of the Countries Bordering on the Indian Ocean and their Inhabitants*, 2 vols, London, 1918.

Bernier, Francois, *Travels in Mogul Empire, A.D. 1656-1668*, edited by A. Constable, Oxford, 1934.

Bowrey, Thomas, *A Geographical Account of Countries Round the Bay of Bengal, 1669 to 1679*, edited by Richard Temple, Cambridge, 1905.

——, *The papers of Thomas Bowrey 1669-1713*, edited by Richard Temple, London, 1927.

Commissariat, M.S., *Mandelslo's Travels in Western India (A.D. 1638-39)*, Oxford University Press, 1931.

Conti, Nicolo, *Travels of Nicolo Conti in the early part of the fifteenth century*, English translation by J. Winter Jones, edited by R.H. Major, *India in the fifteenth century*, London, Hakluyt Society, 1858 (tr. of the narratives of Conti, Nikitin and Abdur Razak).

De Laet, Joannes, *The Empire of the Great Mogol*, tr. J.S. Hoyland and S.N. Banerjee, Bombay, 1928.

Della Valle, Pietro, *The Travels of Pietro Della Valle in India*, translated by Edward Grey, Hakluyt Society, 2 vols, London, 1892.

Fryer, John, *A New Account of East India and Persia, Being Nine Years' Travels 1672-1681*. Edited by W. Crooke, 3 vols, London, 1909-15.

Foster, William, ed., *The English Factories in India, 1618-1669*, 13 vols, Oxford, 1906-27. *Early Travels in India (1583-1619)* being a collection of the narratives of Fitch (1583-91), Milden Hall (1599-1606), Hawkins (1608-13), Finch (1608-11), Wilhington (1612-16), Coryat (1612-17) and Terry (1616-19), London, 1927.

Hamilton, Alexander, *A New Account of the East Indies*, edited by William Foster, 2 vols, London, 1930.

Ibn Batuta, *The Travels*, tr. with revision and notes from the Arabic text, edited by Defremery and B.R. Sanguinetti, by H.A.R. Gibb, Vol. I, Cambridge, 1858; Vol. II, Cambridge, 1962, Vol. III, Cambridge, 1971.

——, *The Rehla of Ibn Batuta* (India, Maldive Islands and Ceylon), tr. with commentary by Mahdi Hussain, Baroda, 1953. Second edition Baroda, 1976; *Travels in Asia and Africa*, abridged edition by H.A.R. Gibbs, London, 1929, reprinted, New Delhi, 1986.

Ludovic di Varthema of Bologina, *Travels in Egypt, Syria, Persia, India, Ethiopia (1502-8)*, edited by G.P. Badger, London, 1863; tr. by John Winter Jones, London, 1928.

Manrique, Sebastien, *Travels of Fray Sebastien Mantrique 1629-1643*, edited by C.E. Luard, 2 vols, Oxford, 1927.

Manucci, Niccolao, *Storia do Mogor*, 1653-1708, tr. William Irvine, 4 vols, London, 1930.

Macro Polo, *The Book of Sir Marcopolo*, 2 vols, translated and edited with notes by Colonel Sir Henry Yule and Henry Cordier, London, 1975.

Master Streynsham, *The Diaries of Streynsham Master 1675-1680*, edited by Richard Carnac Temple, 2 vols, Indian Records Series, London, 1931.

Monserrate, Antony Father, *Commentary on His Journey to the Court of Akbar*, tr. J.S. Hoyland, London, 1922, annotated by S.N. Banerjee, Cuttack, 1922.

Mundy, Peter, *The Travels of Peter Mundy in Europe and Asia*, edited by R.C. Temple, London (1907-1936).

Nikitin, Athanasius (d. 1475), *Voyage to India* (original Russian), trans. (1) Wielhorsky, in R.H. Major, ed, *India in the 15th Century*, London, 1857.

Ovington, J., *A Voyage to Surat in the year 1689*, edited by H.G. Rawlinson, London, 1929.

Pelsaert, Francisco, *Jahangir's India: The Remonstratie of Francisco Pelsaert*, edited by W.H. Moreland and P. Geyl, Cambridge, 1925.

Purchas, Samuel, *Purchas, His Pilgrims* (1) London, 1625 (2) edited by Maclehose, 20 vols, Glasgow, 1905.

Roe, Thomas, *The Embassy of Sir Thomas Roe to India 1615-1619*, edited by W. Foster, London, 1926.

Sen, S.N. ed., *Indian Travels of Thevenot and Careri*, New Delhi, 1949.

Shihaba-l-Dinal Umari (d. 1348), *Masalik-al-Absarfi Mamalik al-Ansar*, translated by I.H. Siddiqui and Q.M. Ahmad, *A 14th Century Arab Account of India*, Aligarh, 1979.

Tavernier, Jean Baptiste, *Travels in India*, translated by V. Ball and edited by W. Crooke, 2 vols, London, 1925.

MODERN WORKS

Ahmad, Muhammad Bashir, *The Administration of Justice in Medieval India*, Aligarh, 1941.

Akbar, Muhammad, *The Punjab under the Mughals*, Lahore, 1948.

Al Hasan, Ahmad Y., and Hill, Donald R., *Islamic Technology*, Cambridge, 1986.

Alam, Muzaffar, *Crisis of the Empire in Mughal North India, Awadh and the Punjab (1707-1748)*, New Delhi, 1986.

Ali, M. Athar, *The Mughal Nobility under Aurangzeb*, Bombay, 1966.

——, *The Apparatus of Empire (Awards of Ranks, Offices and Titles to the Mughal Nobility (1574-1658)*, Delhi, 1985.

Alvi, M.A. and Rahman, A. *Fatullah Shiraji: A Sixteenth Century Indian Scientist*, New Delhi, 1968.

——, *Jahangir–The Naturalist*, New Delhi, 1968.

Anne K.S. Lambton, *State and Government in Medieval Islam*, London, 1981.

——, *An Introduction to the Study of Islamic Political Theory*.

Ansari, M.A., *Social Life of the Mughal Emperors* (1526-1707), Allahabad, 1974.

——, *European Travellers under the Mughals*, Delhi, 1975.

——, *Administrative Documents of Mughal India*, 1984.

Ashraf, Javed and Ahmad, Tasneem, *Geographical Glimpses of Medieval India*, Vols I-III (Introduction with English Abstracts), Delhi, 1989.

Ashraf, K.M., *Life and Conditions of People of Hindustan*, Delhi, 1959.

Aziz, Abdul, *Arms and Jewellery of Indian Mughals*, Lahore, 1947.

——, *Thrones, Tents and Their Furnitures used by Indian Mughals*, Lahore, n.d.

——, *The Mansabdari System and the Mughal Army*, Lahore, 1945.

——, *The Imperial Treasury of Indian Mughals*, Delhi, 1972.

——, *The Imperial Library of the Mughals*, Lahore, 1967.

Banerjee, Jamini Mohan, *History of Firuz Tughlaq*, Allahabad, 1967.

Bayley, E.C., *Local Muhammadan Dynasties of Gujarat*, edited by Nagendra Singh, 1970.

Begley, W.E., and Desai Z.A. (edited and compiled), *The Shahjahan Nama of Inayat Khan*, Delhi, 1990.

Bilmoria, Jamshed, H., *Rukatt-i-Alamgiri* or *Letters of Aurangzeb*, Delhi, 1972.

Bird, J.S., *History of Gujarat*, 2 vols.

——, (tr.) *Medieval Gujarat, Its Political and Statistical History* based on Muhammad Ali Khan's *Mirat-i-Ahmadi*, Delhi, 1985.

Binyon, L. and T.W. Arnold, *Akbar*.

Blake, Stephen P., Shajanabad: The Sovereign City in Mughal India, 1639-1739, Delhi, First 2nd Edn., 1993.

Boswarth, C.E., *The Ghaznavids, Their Empire in Afghanistan and Eastern India, 994-1040*, Delhi 1992.

——, *The Later Ghaznavids: Splendour and Decay. The Dynasty in Afghanistan and Northern India, 1040-1186*, Delhi, 1992.

Boyle, J.A., ed., *The Cambridge History of Iran, The Saljuk and the Mongol Periods*, Vol. 5, Cambridge, 1968.

Briggs, H.G., *Cities of Gujararashtra*, Bombay, 1849.

Brown, Percy, Indian Paintings under the Mughals, Oxford, 1924.

Brown, Percy, *Indian Paintings, The Heritage of India*, Calcutta, 1953.

——, *Indian Architecture* (Islamic Period), Bombay, n.d.

Buchanan, D.H., *The Development of Capitalist Enterprise in India*, New York, 1937.

Burn, Sir Richard, ed., *The Cambridge History of India*, Vol. IV, Cambridge, 1937.

Cambridge Economic History of India, Vol. 1, (1200-1750), ed., Tapan Ray Chaudhuri and Irfan Habib, Indian edn, Delhi, 1984, Vol. II, 1757-1970, ed., Dharma Kumar, Delhi, 1984.

Cambridge History of India, Vol. 4, the Mughal Period, Cambridge, 1922.

Cambridge History of Iran, Vol. 6, Cambridge, 1986.

Cambridge History of Islam, Vol. 2A, Cambridge, 1970.

Chand, Tara, *Influence of Islam on Indian Culture*, Allahabad, 1946.

Chaudhuri, S., *Trade and Commercial Organization in Bengal, 1650-1720*, Calcutta, 1975.

Chatterjee, Anjali, *Bengal in the Reign of Aurangzeb, (1658-1700)*, Calcutta, 1967.

Chandra, Moti, *Costumes, Textiles, Cosmetics and Coiffure in Ancient and Medieval India*, 1973.

——, *The Technique of Mughal Pain*, Lucknow, 1946.

Chandra, Satish, *The Parties and Politics at the Mughal Court (1707-1740)*, Aligarh, 1959.

Chicherov, A.I., *India, Economic Development in 16th to 18th Centuries, Outline History of Crafts and Trade*, Moscow, 1971.

Chopra, P.N. *Some Aspects of Society and Culture during the Mughal Age (1526-1707)*, Agra, 1963.

——, *Life & Letters under the Mughals*, Delhi, 1976.

Commissariat, M.S., *A History of Gujarat (1573-1758)*, Vol. II, Bombay, 1957.

Das, A.K., *Mughal Painting during Jahangir's Time*, Calcutta, 1978.

Dhamija, Ram, ed., *Sixty Years of Writing on Arts and Crafts in India* (Roop Lekha, 1928-88), Delhi, 1988.

Dosabhai, Edalji, *A History of Gujarat from the Earliest Period to the Present Time*, Delhi, 1986.

Egerton, W., *An Illustrated Handbook of Indian Arms*, London, 1880.

Elliot, H.M. and Dowson, J., *History of India as told by its own Historians*, 8 vols, London, 1867, and C. Reprinted, Kitab Mahal, Allahabad.

Elliot, Henry, *Bibliographical Index to Historians of Mohammadan India*, London, 1849.

Elphinstone, Mounstuart, *The Rise of British Power in the East*, edited by Edward Colebrooke, London, 1887.

——, *History of India*, London, 1841, 1889.

Erskine, W.A., *A History of India under the First two Sovereigns of the House of Taimur*, London, 1854.

Ettinghausen Richard and Grabar Oleg, *The Art and Architecture of Islam (650-1250)*, London, 1987.

Farooque, R.W., *Roads and Communications in Mughal India*, New Delhi, 1977.

Faruki, M., *Aurangzeb and His Times*, Bombay, 1935.

Fergusson, J., *History of India and Eastern Architecture*, 2 vols, Delhi, 1971.

Frykenberg, R.E. ed., *Delhi Through the Ages: Essays in Urban History, Culture and Society*, Delhi, 1986.

Ganguli, B.N., ed., *Readings in Economic History*, Delhi, 1964.

George Watts and Percy Brown, *Arts and Crafts of India*, Delhi, 1979.

Ghoshal, U.N., *A History of Indian Political Ideas*, Bombay, 1966.

Gopal, L., *Economic Life of Northern India, c. AD 700-1200*, Delhi, 1965.

Gopal, Surendra, *Commerce and Crafts in Gujarat 16th and 17th Centuries*, Delhi, 1975.

Grant Duff, J., *History of Marathas*, 3 vols, 1826.

Gribble, J.D.B., *History of the Deccan*, Vol. III, London, 1896.

Grewal, J.S. and Banga, Indu, ed., *Studies in Urban History*, Amritsar, 1981.

Gupta, I.P., *Urban Glimpses of Mughal India, Agra, The Imperial Capital 16th and 17th Centuries*, Delhi, 1986.

Gupta, O.P., *Trade of Surat under the Mughals*.

Habib, Irfan, *Agrarian System of Mughal India*, Bombay, 1963.

——, *An Atlas of the Mughal Empire, Political and Economic Maps*, Delhi, 1982.

——, 'The Technology and Economy of Mughal India', Dev Raj Chanana Lectures (memeographed, Delhi, 1970).

——, 'Potentialities of Capitalist Development in the Economy of Mughal India', *Enquiry*, N.A. III(3), (O.S. No. 15), Delhi, 1971.

——, 'Notes on Indian Textile Industry in 17th Century', *S.C. Sarkar Felicitation Volume*, New Delhi, 1976.

——, 'The Currency System of Mughal Empire (1556-1707)', *MIQ, IV*, Nos 1-12, Aligarh, 1960.

——, 'Banking in Mughal India', in contribution to *Indian Economic History* (F.K.L. Mukhopadhyay and Company), Calcutta, 1960.

——, 'Usury in Medieval India', *Comparative Studies in Society & History*, 1963-64.

——, 'Technological Changes and Society, 13th and 14th Centuries', Presidential Address, Section II, *PIHC*, Varanasi session, 1969.

Habib, M., *Politics and Society During the Early Medieval Period*, collected works edited by K.A. Nizami, Vol. I, Delhi, 1974; Vol. II, Delhi, 1981.

Habib, M. and Nizami, K.A. ed., *A Comprehensive History of India*, Vol. V, *The Delhi Sultanate*, Delhi, 1970.

Habibullah, A.B.M., *The Foundation of Muslim Rule in India*, second edn, Allahabad, 1961.

Hambly Gravin, *Cities of Mughal India*, New York, 1968.

Hasan, Ibn, *The Central Structure of the Mughal Empire*, reprint, Delhi, 1970 (Oxford, 1936).

Hasan, Mohibul, *Kashmir under the Sultans*, Calcutta, 1959.

Huart, Clement, *Ancient Persia and Iranian Civilization*, tr. by R. Dobie, London, 1927.

Hussain, Agha Mahdi, *The Rehla of Ibn Batuta* (India and Maldive Islands & Ceylon), tr. and commentary, Hussain, Agha Mahdi, Baroda, 1953.

——, *The Rise and Fall of Muhammad bin Tughluq*, Delhi, 1972.

——, *Tughluq Dynasty*.

Hussain, M.K. *Catalogue of Coins of the Mughal Emperors*, Bombay, 1968.

Hussaini, S.A.Q., *Administration under the Mughals*, Dacca, 1952.

——, *Arab Administration*, Madras, 1949.

——, *Constitutions of the Arab Empire*, Lahore, 1954.
Hughes, T.P., *Dictionary of Islam*, New Delhi, 1976.
Irvine, William, *The Army of the Indian Mughals: Its Organization and Administration*, London, 1903.
Irving, B.A., *The Commerce of India*, London, 1858.
Irwin, J., *Golconda Cotton Printing of Early 17th Century*, Lalit Kala, New Delhi, 1958.
Jain, V.K., *Trade and Traders in Western India (AD 1000-1300)*, Delhi, 1990.
Jain, L.C., *Indigenous Banking in India*, 2 vols, London, 1929.
Jafar, S.M., *Some Cultural Aspects of Muslim Rule in India*, Delhi, 1972.
——, *Education in Muslim India (AD 1000-1800)*, Reprint, Delhi, 1973.
Jauhari, R.C., *Firuz Shah Tughluq*, New Delhi, 1968.
Joshi, Rita, *The Afghan Nobility and the Mughals, 1526-1707*, Delhi, 1985.
Khan, Ashan Raza, *Chieftains in the Mughal Empire during the Reign of Akbar*, Simla, 1977.
Khan, S.A., *The East India Trade in the Seventeenth Century in Political and Economic Aspects*, London, 1923.
Khosla, R.K., *The Mughal Kingship and the Nobility*, Allahabad, 1934.
Kulshreshtha, S.S., *Development of Trade and Industry under the Mughals (1526-1707)*, Allahabad, 1964.
——, *Indian Economy under the Mughals*, Modinagar, 1968.
Kulkarni, A.R., *Maharashtra in the Age of Shivaji*, 1969.
Kurz, Otto, *European Clocks and Watches in the Near East*, London, 1975.
Lal, K.S., *The Mughal Harem*, New Delhi, 1988.
Lapidus, Ira M., *A History of Islamic Societies*, Cambridge, 1988.
——, *Muslim Cities in the Later Middle Ages*, Cambridge, 1967.
Law, N.N., *Promotion of Learning in India*.
Levy, *Social Structure of Islam*, Cambridge, 1957.
Lugs, J., *Fire Arms Past and Present*, London, 1975.
Maclagen, E.D., *The Jesuits and the Great Mogul*, London, 1932.
Mahmud, Syed Jafar, *Metal Technology in Medieval India*, Delhi, 1988.
Major, R.H., *India in the Fifteenth Century*, London, 1858 (for narratives of Conti, Niketan and Abdur Razzak).
Misra, Rekha, *Women in Mughal India*, Delhi, 1967.

Misra, S.C., *The Rise of Muslim Power in Gujarat*, Delhi, 1963.

Mookerjee, Radha Kamal, *Economic History of India (1600-1800)* published originally in *JUPHS*. XIV (i) and (ii) and later as a book, Allahabad, 1967.

Mookerjee, T.N., *Handbook of Indian Products*, Calcutta, 1883.

——, *Art Manufactures of India*, reprint, New Delhi, 1974.

Moosvi, Shireen, *The Economy of the Mughal Empire*, Delhi, 1987.

Moreland, W.H., *India at the Death of Akbar*, London, 1920.

——, *Agrarian System of Moslem India*, Cambridge, 1929.

——, *From Akbar to Aurangzeb*, London, 1923.

——, *Relations of Golconda in the Early 17th Century*, London, 1931 (a collection of the relations of Methwold, scholars and anonymous Dutch Factor.

Momin, Mohiuddin, *The Chancellery and Persian Spistolograph under the Mughals*, Calcutta, 1971.

Narain, Brij, *Indian Economic Life, Past and Present*, Lahore, 1929.

Naqvi, H.K., *Urban Centres and Industries in Upper India (1556-1803), Bombay, 1968.*

——, *Urbanization and Urban Centres under the Great Mughals*, Simla, 1972.

——, *Agricultural, Industrial and Urban Dynamism under the Sultans of Delhi (1206-1555)*, Delhi, 1986.

Nigam, S.B.P., *Nobility under the Sultans of Delhi*, Delhi, 1968.

Niyogi, P., *Contributions to the Economic History of Northern India*, Calcutta, 1962.

Nizami, K.A., *Some Aspects of Religion and Politics in India during the Thirteenth Century*, Aligarh, 1961.

——, *State and Culture in Medieval India*, Delhi, 1985.

Om Prakash, *The Dutch East India Company and the Economy of Bengal*, Delhi, 1988.

Orme, Robert, *Historical Fragments of the Mogul Empire*, London, 1805.

Pant, D., *Commercial Policy of the Mughals*, Bombay, 1930.

Pant, G.N., *Studies in Indian Weapons and Warfare*, Delhi, 1970.

Pearson, M.N., *Merchants and Rulers in Gujarat: The Response to the Portuguese in the Sixteenth Century*, California, 1976.

Prasad, Beni, *History of Jahangir*, Allahabad, 1962.

Prasad, Ishwari, *A History of Qaraunah Turks*, Allahabad, 1936.

Puri, B.N., *History of Indian Administration*, Vol. II, Medieval Period, Bombay, 1975.

Qaisar, A.J., *The Indian Response to European Technology and Culture (1498-1707)*, Delhi, 1982.

——, *Building Construction in Mughal India*, Delhi, 1988.

Qanungo, K.R., *Sher Shah and His Times*, Calcutta, 1921, second edn, Delhi, 1965.

Qureshi, I.H., *The Administration of the Sultanate of Delhi*, Lahore, 1942.

——, *The Administration of the Mughal Empire*, Karachi, 1966.

——, *Akbar The Architect of the Mughal Empire.*

Radhey Shyam, *Kingdom of Ahmednagar*, Delhi, 1966.

——, *Life and Times of Malik Ambar*, Delhi, 1968.

Rahman, M.L., *Persian Literature in India during the time of Jahangir and Shahjahan*, Lahore, 1967.

Ray, Niharranjan, *An Approach to Indian Art*, Chandigarh, 1974.

——, *Mughal Court Painting: A Study in Social and Formal Analysis*, Calcutta, Indian Museum, 1975.

Raychaudhuri, T., *Bengal under Akbar and Jahangir*, Calcutta, 1953.

Richards, J.F., *Mughal Administration in Golconda*, Oxford, 1975.

——, *Document forms for official orders of Appointment in the Mughal Empire*, London, 1986.

——, ed., *The Imperial Monetary System of Mughal India*, Delhi, 1987.

Sandarson, M.G., *A Guide to the Buildings and Gardens: Delhi Forts*, Delhi, 1937.

Saran, Parmatma, *The Provincial Government of the Mughals (1526-1658)*, Allahabad, 1941.

——, *Islamic Polity*, Allahabad (n.d.).

——, *Descriptive Catalogue of Non-Persian Sources of Medieval Indian History*, Bombay, 1965.

Sardesai, G.S., *New History of Marathas*, 3 vols, Bombay, 1946 and 1948.

Sarkar, B., *Inland Transport and Communications in Medieval India*, Calcutta, 1925.

Sarkar, Jadunath, *Studies in Mughal India*, Calcutta, 1919.

——, *Mughal Administration*, Calcutta, 1952.

——, *Shivaji and His Times*, 5th edn, Calcutta, 1955.

——, *History of Aurangzeb–Mainly based on Persian Sources*, 5 vols, Calcutta, 1912-30.

——, *The India of Aurangzeb (Topography, Statics and Roads) Compared with the India of Akbar with Extracts from Khulasatut-Tawarikh and the Chahar Gulshan*, Calcutta, 1901.

——, *Anecdotes of Aurangzeb*, Calcutta, 1949.
——, *Military History of India*, Calcutta, 1960.
——, *House of Shivaji*, Calcutta, 1960.
——, *History of Bengal, Muslim Period (1200-1757)*, Patna, 1973.
——, *Fall of the Mughal Empire*, 3 vols.
Sarkar, Jagdish Narayan, *Life of Mir Jumla, The General of Aurangzeb*, Calcutta, 1951, Delhi, 1979.
——, *The Art of War in Medieval India*, Delhi, 1984.
Saxena, B.P., *History of Shahjahan of Delhi*, reprint, Allahabad, 1958.
Sen, S.N., *The Military System of the Marathas*, Bombay, 1958.
——, *Administrative System of the Marathas.*
Sharma, G.N., *Mewar and the Mughal Emperors (1526-1707).*
Sharma, R.S., *Social Changes in Early Medieval India, AD 500-1200*, Delhi, 1969.
——, *Perspectives in Social and Economic History of Early India*, Delhi, 1983.
Sharma, Sri Ram, *Mughal Government and Administration*, Bombay, 1951.
——, *A Bibliography of Mughal India (1526-1707)*, n.d.
——, *The Religious Policy of the Mughal Emperors*, Oxford, 1940, 2nd edn, Bombay, 1962.
Sherwani, H.K., *History of the Qutbshahi Dynasty*, Delhi, 1974.
Siddiqui, I.H., *Mughal Relations with Indian Ruling Elite*, Delhi, 1983.
Siddiqui, N.A., *Land Revenue Administration under the Mughals*, Bombay, 1970.
Singer, Hollymard and Hall, *History of Technology (1500-1750)*, Oxford, 1970.
Singhal, C.R., *Mint Towns of Mogul Emperors of India*, Bombay, 1953.
——, *Bibliography of Indian Coins*, Bombay, 1950.
Singh, M.P., *Town, Market, Mint and Port in the Mughal Empire (1556-1707)*, New Delhi, 1985.
Sinha, J.C., *Economic Annals of Bengal*, London, 1927.
Sinha, N.K., *Economic History of Bengal from Plassey to the Permanent Settlement*, 3 vols, Calcutta, 1956, 1962.
Srivastava, M.P., *Policies of the Great Mughals*, Allahabad, 1978.
Smith, V.A., *Akbar the Great Mughal (1542-1605)*, Oxford, 1919, Delhi, n.d.
Spear, P., *Twilight of the Mughals*, Cambridge, 1951.
Tamaskar, B.G., *The Life and Works of Malik Ambar*, Delhi, 1978.

Tawney, R.H., *Studies in Economic History* (collected papers of George Unwin), London, 1958.
Thomas, Edward, *The Chronicles of the Pathan Kings of Delhi*, reprint, Delhi, 1967.
——, *Revenue Resources of the Mughal Empire in India (1593-1707)*, London, 1871.
Tirmizi, S.A.I., *Some Aspects of Medieval Gujarat*, New Delhi, 1968.
——, ed., *Calendar of Acquired Documents (1402-1719)*, Vols I & II, National Archives of India, Delhi, 1982.
——, *Miscellany of Medieval India*, Delhi, 1986.
Tod, J., *Travels in Western India*, Calcutta, 1939.
——, *Annals and Antiquities of Rajasthan*, 2 vols, New Delhi, 1983.
Tripathi, R.P., *Some Aspects of Muslim Administration*, Allahabad, 1936.
——, *Rise and Fall of Mughal Empire*, Allahabad, 1956.
Verma, D.C., *History of Bijapur*, New Delhi, 1974. (Indian Institute of Islamic Studies).
Verma, H.C., *Dynamics of Urban Life in Pre-Mughal India*, New Delhi, 1986.
——, *Medieval Routes to India: Baghdad to Delhi*, Calcutta, 1978.
Verma, S.P., *Art and Material Culture in the Paintings of Akbar's Court*, New Delhi, 1978.
Watson, J.F., *Textile Manufacturers and the Costumes of the People of India*, London, 1860.
Watt, G., *Indian Art at Delhi*, London, 1904.
——, *Commercial Products of India*, London, 1908.
Welch, S.C., *The Art of Mughal India*, New Delhi, 1963.
——, et al., *The Emperor's Album, Images of Mughal India*, New York, 1987.
White, Lynn Tr., *Medieval Technology and Social Change*, New York, 1964.
Wilkinson, J.V.S., *Mughal Painting*, London, 1948.
Wolf, A., *A History of Science, Technology and Philosophy in the 16th and 17th Centuries*, London, 1950.
Wright, H.N., *The Coinage and Metrology of the Sultans of Delhi*, New Delhi, 1974.
——, *Catalogue of Coins in the Indian Museum*, Vol. II, Oxford, 1907.
Wulf, Hans E., *The Traditional Crafts of Persia*, M.I.T. Press, Mass., 1966.

ARTICLES IN JOURNALS

Indian Economic and Social History Review

Gopal, Surendra, 'Gujarati Shipping in the 17th Century', March, 1971.

Moosvi, Shireen, 'Production, Consumption and Population in Akbar's Time', 1973.

Qaisar, A.J., 'Shipbuilding in the Mughal Empire during the 17th Century', Vol. V, No. 2, June, 1968, pp. 149-70.

Indian Historical Quarterly

Sarkar, Jagdish Narain, (i) 'Cotton trade of Patna in Early 17th Century', No. 4, 1936; (ii) 'Silk Trade of Patna in Early 17th Century', 1939; (iii) 'Organization of Saltpetre Industry (17th Century)', 1938.

Indian Historical Review

Habib, Irfan, 'Currency System of the Mughal Empire (1556-1707), 1960.

Khan, Iqtidar Alam, 'Origin and Development of Gun Powder Technology in India AD 1200-1500', *IHR*, Vol. IV, No. 1, July 1977, pp. 20-29.

Qaisar, A.J., 'The Role of Brokers in Medieval India', 1974.

Indian Journal of Economics

Moreland, W.H., 'The Ain-i-Akbari' a possible base line for the Economic History of Modern India, I, 1961.

Journal of Bihar and Orissa Research Society

Sarkar, Jagdish Narayan, (i) 'Saltpetre Manufacture in India with Special Reference to Bihar', 1937; (ii) 'Transport of Saltpetre in India in 17th Century', 1939.

Journal of Bihar Research Society

Sarkar, Jagdish Narayan, (i) 'Private Trade in 17th Century India', Vol. 49, 1963; (ii) 'Imperial Monopoly in Indigo (1633-35)', 1964.

Journal of Economic and Social History of the Orient (JESHO)

Gokhale, B.G., 'Ahmedabad in 17th Century', 1969.
Naqvi, H.K., 'Progress of Urbanization in the United Provinces (1500-1800)', 10(1), 1967.

Journal of Indian History

Makhdoome, M. Akram, 'Gun Power Artillery in the Reign of Sultan Iltutmash of Delhi', *JIH*, Vol. XV, pp. 185-88.
Moreland, W.H., 'From Gujarat to Golconda in the Reign of Jahangir', 1938.
Wellbrand Geleynssem de Jongh, Extracts from tr. by W.H. Moreland as 'A Dutch Account of Mogul Administrative Methods', *JIH*, Vol. IV, 1925-26.

Journal of Royal Asiatic Society

Moreland, W.H., 'Prices and Wages under Akbar': Communication, 1917. 'The Value of Money at the Court of Akbar', 1918.

Medieval India, A Miscellany

Habib, Irfan, 'The Currency System of the Mughal Empire', Vol. IV, 1960 (1556-1707).
Qaisar, A.J., 'Merchants Shipping in India during the 17th Century', Vol. II, pp. 195-220.

Proceedings of Indian History Congress

Ahmad, Tasneem, 'Akbar's Love of Painting' (Punjab History Conferences), 20th Session, 1986.
Alvi, Rafi Ahmad, 'Aspects of the Political Career of a Notable Afghan Noble of Jahangir and Shahjahan', 47th Session, 1986.
Aziza, Hasan, 'Mints of the Mughal Empire: a study in Comparative Output', Patiala Session, 1967, part 1, Patna, 1968.
Chandra, Satish, 'Commercial Activities of Mughal Emperors during 17th Century', 1959.
Gopal, Surendra, 'Form of Textile Production in Gujarat in 17th Century', *PIHC*, Section 27, 1965.
Habib, Irfan, 'Technological Changes and Society, 13th and 14th Centuries', Presidential Address, Section II, 1969, Varanasi Ses-

sion. 'The System of Bills of Exchange (Hundis) in the Mughal Empire', 1972.

Jauhari, R.C., 'Royal Karkhanas of the Tughlaq Sultans', Section 27, 1965, Allahabad.

Khan, Iqtidar Alam, 'The Middle Classes in the Mughal Empire', Presidential Address, Section II, 1975, Aligarh Session.

——, 'Early Use of Cannon and Musket in India (1444-1526), Hyderabad Session, 1978.

——, 'The Nature of Handguns in Mughal India: 16th and 17th Centuries', 1991-92, Delhi Session.

Khan, Muhammad Afzal, 'Ali Mardan Khan the Great Iranian Noble of Shahjahan', 44th Session, 1983 (Burdwan).

Khan, Sumbul Halim, 'Karkhanas of a Mughal noble—Evidence from the Amber/Jaipur Records', Delhi, 1991-92.

Mattoo, Abdul Majid, 'Shawl Industry in Kashmir in the Mughal Period', 36th Session, 1975.

Moosvi, Shireen, 'Expenditure on buildings under Shahjahan: A Chapter of Imperial Finance History', 1985.

Prasad, Pushpa, 'Craftsmen in Delhi Sultanate: A Study of the Epigraphic Evidence', Kurukshetra, 1982.

Sharma, Rajiv, 'Weavers, Their Role and Economic Conditions during the 17th Century', 47th Session, 1986, Aligarh.

Siddiqui, Yasin Mazhar, 'Pattern of Expenditure of the Medieval Indian Aristocracy', 13th and 14th Centuries', Kurukshetra, 1982.

Srivastava, S.P., 'A Peep into the Economic History of Mughal India', 1943.

Verma, S.P., 'Mughal Atelier', 1986, Srinagar.

Zaman, M.K., 'Gun Manufacturing Techniques in Mughal India', 1981.

——, 'Organization of Commissariat in the Mughal Army', 1986, Aligarh papers.

Proceedings, Indian Historical Records Commission

Commissarat, M.S., 'Political and Economic Condition of Gujarat during the 17th Century', 1921.

Islamic Culture

Nadvi, Abu Zafar, 'The Use of Cannon in Muslim India', Vol. XII, No. 4, October 1938, pp. 405-18.

Bengal Past & Present

Sarkar, Jadunath, 'A Description of North Bengal in AD 1609', Vol. XXXV, pt II, April-June 1928, pp. 143-46.

Miscellaneous

Encyclopaedia of Islam, Vols I and II.
Steingass, F., *A Comprehensive Persian English Dictionary*, first Indian edition, 1973, New Delhi.
Collection of Letters, Administrative Literature, Accountancy Manuals, Biographies, etc.
Dastur-ul-Amal-i-Shahjahani wa Shuqqajat-i-Alamgiri, MS. Br.Mu. Add. 6588.
Dastur-ul-Amal-i-Alamgiri, MS. Br.Mu. Add. 6599.
Dastur-al-Amal-i-Ilm-i-Navisindgi, MS. Br.Mu. Add. 6599, ff. 134-85.
Adab-i-Alamgiri, MS., Abdus Salem Collection 326/96, Azad Library, Aligarh. (A Collection of letters written by Qabil Khan on behalf of Aurangzeb before his accession. The letters are addressed to Shahjahan, Prince Muhammad Sultan, Muazzam Khan, Mir Jumla, Najabat Khan, Khan-i-Dauran Nasiri Khan and others. This Collection also includes letter written by Muhammad Sadiq on behalf of Prince Akbar in 1680 during the Rathor rebellion.)
Khulasat-us-Siyaq, Ms Sir Sulaiman Collection, 410/143, Maulana Azad Library, Aligarh.
Zawabit-i-Alamgiri, MS. Br.Mu.Or. 1641.
Kewal Ram, *Tazkirat-al-Umara*, MS. Br.Mu. Add. 16,703.

PERSIAN MANUSCRIPTS

Adab-i-Alamgiri, Br. Mu. Or. 177.
Anand Ram Mukhlis, *Mirat-ul-istilah*, Br.Mu. Or. 1813.
Dastur-ul-Amal-i-Agahi, Br.Mu. Add. 1881.
Dastur-ul-Amal-i-Alamgiri, MS. Br.Mu. Add. 6599.
Dastur-ul-Amal-i-Aurangzebe, Br.Mu. Add. 6598.
Dastur-ul-Amal-i-Shahjahani, Br.Mur. Or. 1690.
Dastur-ul-Amal-i-Shahjahani wa Shuqqajat-i-Alamgiri, MS. Br.Mu. Add. 6588.
Khulasat-us-Siyaq, MS. Sir Sulaiman Collection 410/143, Maulana Azad Library, Aligarh.
Tarikh-i-Shakir Khani, Br.Mu. Add. 6585.
Zawabit-i-Alamgiri, MS. Br.Mu. Or. 1641.

Index